S0-AHR-475

Anthropology of Contemporary Issues

A SERIES EDITED BY

ROGER SANJEK

Chinese Working-Class Lives

GETTING BY IN TAIWAN

Hill Gates

Cornell University Press

Ithaca and London

First published 1987 by Cornell University Press.

International Standard Book Number (cloth) 0-8014-2056-3
International Standard Book Number (paper) 0-8014-9461-3
Library of Congress Catalog Card Number 87-47597

Printed in the United States of America

*Librarians: Library of Congress cataloging information
appears on the last page of the book.*

*The paper in this book is acid-free and meets the guidelines for
permanence and durability of the Committee on Production Guidelines
for Book Longevity of the Council on Library Resources.*

Contents

Contents

Preface

I wrote this book to help students and others with a new interest in things Chinese to encounter the culture of Taiwan's ordinary working people whose livelihood depends on their hands, backs, and wits. Too little of Chinese life is accessible to most of us in the West: Taiwan and the People's Republic of China are distant and expensive for travelers, though Americans who have been in those places are no longer rarities. Even for those who make the trip, however, Chinese societies turn a neutral-to-friendly mask toward most stranger guests. Getting behind it, in any part of China, is difficult but worthwhile, for only through knowing another society can we experience both the power of culture to shape our lives and the recognition of a common humanity that transcends cultural differences. Studying Taiwan's working class offers these experiences in full measure. The inevitable conflicts and misunderstandings between our two old, proud, and widely different civilizations must be balanced by mutual efforts at compromise and comprehension. This book is one such effort.

Much anthropology fieldwork begins with direct, personal encounters, as the anthropologist comes to know the women and men who will provide most of the material from which to fashion an image of their culture. Often that image is conveyed through carefully constructed abstractions and generalizations that all but obscure individual variation and sense of person. Here I decided to include instead not only a summary of my own understanding of Taiwan's working-class people but also life histories of nine of those people, in their own words. Thus the reader may juxtapose, and sometimes contrast, my observations about this small island's political economy, religious traditions, and status of women with the concrete particularities of real and singular lives. Readers, I hope, will appreciate the

inherent slipperiness of moving from such direct, personal, and idio-
syncratic data to conclusions about a time period, a family, a community of
believers, or a class. Moreover, I hope that they will make such connections
themselves, remembering the individuality that lies behind a display of
Taiwan-made shirts or a magazine story on Chinese elections.

It is the personal directness of fieldwork, I think, that makes anthropology so involving and anthropologists so partisan. In the context of
these nine voices, I have felt free to speak in my own voice about Taiwan,
rather than assume the impossible pose of a neutral, objective observer.
Naturally, my views are constrained within the limits of what other writers,
with different analyses, have published. To have an occasion to speak
frankly and even critically about a political system I have studied for twenty
years evolved, in the course of the work, as another reason for writing this
book.

It is for working-class Taiwan people themselves, however, to have the
final say about what has happened to them. No one can fully comprehend
the society in which she is immersed, for intimate knowledge complicates
and may cancel critical perspective. But views from outside the Chinese
world, or from "above" the working class in social prestige, are as partial
and partisan as those from inside, and often a good deal less well informed.
I would like others—Chinese as well as Americans—to listen carefully, as I
learned to do, to what these insider voices reveal about how their social
system serves these people.

I wrote the book as well, then, to preserve some common voices not
usually recorded. The people who speak in these pages wanted to tell
things about themselves to a wider world, once they found in my research
an avenue to do so. They expect me to get their viewpoints across, to
preserve the evidence of their searches for family stability, or loyalty unto
death, or perfect filiality, or big bucks. As much as any politician or scholar,
they want to be part of history, to leave a memorial to their existence in the
libraries that are a changing society's most persisting reminders of the past.
Some have complaints to register with history, or with fate, or with their
own or the American government; others would like posterity to be reminded mainly of their successes.

It is especially notable that none of these people speaks directly to the
political project of changing the present, however. If there is to be a
reckoning, their omissions imply, it will be made by academics and other
"great folk," not by people like themselves.

In the years since I collected these life histories, friends and kin of my
subjects have offered me *their* stories to add to my files. I wish they could
all be published—a great archive of events and adventures, each telling the

story of twentieth-century Taiwan as a different truth. With such a mountain of evidence, official history might be forced to drop its alliance with those who read and rule, and find a way to include everyone. With democratic histories to learn from, succeeding generations might prepare themselves by study not to justify retrospectively the current social inequalities but to speak for their present needs in a complex and insistent chorus.

Of all disciplines, anthropology may best reveal the collective origins of knowledge, for a work in this field is never constructed by one person. This book owes much to the nine people around whose life histories it is built, who cooperated with sincerity and style in what was to them an unusual venture. They have my thanks and, I hope, the thanks of readers who will also learn from them. Many other Taiwan people whose lives and names are not included here also contributed their time, patience, and insights to my study of Taiwan's working class; all taught me something I needed to know.

Thanks, too, are due to the women who assisted me in the field, as described in Chapter 2. Although they helped in many ways to collect and translate material, like the tellers of the life histories themselves, none had a hand in its arrangement or interpretation; for that the responsibility is mine alone.

Central Michigan University, with several small grants, a sabbatical leave, and a University Research Professorship, provided the time and funds without which this study could not have been completed. I very much appreciate this institutional support. Seeing the manuscript through typing and correction fell to the lot of Denise Jones and Michele St. Pierre, for whose precision and persistence I am grateful.

I am grateful, too, to colleagues who read the manuscript and criticized it: Alice Littlefield, Eugene Anderson, Wolfram Eberhard, Bernard Gallin, Rita Schlesinger Gallin, Roger Sanjek, George Spindler, and Margery Wolf. Stevan Harrell was especially diligent in removing inaccuracies and awkwardnesses. Edwin Chávez-Farfan prepared the map, for which I am most grateful. John Rohsenow, whose comradeship in Taiwan helped me enjoy my early fieldwork, offered support and suggestions on this as on other projects, along with his personal clipping service on the Chinese world.

Finally, I thank my mother, Vera Gates Humphreys, for her sustaining friendship over the years; and Norman Rasulis, for much editorial help.

HILL GATES

Mount Pleasant, Michigan

A Note on Chinese Romanizations

English speakers traditionally transcribe Chinese characters with letters of the alphabet representing various Chinese sounds, some of which are not found in English. This process is known as "romanization." The choice of letters to represent Chinese sounds depends on the connection the original romanizer made between her own variant of English and the variant of Chinese she was attempting to transcribe. While many systems of romanization are in use, only two are employed here. Words and names in Mandarin, China's "national language" (as the Nationalist government calls it) or "common speech" (as the Communist government calls it), are rendered in a system known as pinyin. Pinyin, the official romanization for the People's Republic of China, is growing in international popularity, although it is not used in Taiwan or in most pre-1970s sources on China.

The majority mother tongue in Taiwan is a south China language known as Minnanhua, or Taiwanese. Not a dialect, it is a separate language, not comprehensible to Chinese from outside of Taiwan and southern Fukien province. In this book, the few names and words given in Minnanhua are romanized according to the system of Nicholas Bodman (1955).

In pinyin, vowels are pronounced roughly as in Spanish and most consonants roughly as in English. Exceptions are *x*, pronounced *sy; q*, pronounced very far forward in the mouth as *ch; c*, pronounced *ts; zh*, pronounced *dj; si*, pronounced *sz; zhi, chi, zi, ci*, pronounced as if the *i* were an *r*; and *r*, pronounced like an English *r* with tongue flattened and teeth together.

In Bodmanized Taiwanese, vowels are also roughly like Spanish ones;

final *q* is omitted; final *p, t,* and *k* are unreleased; *c* is pronounced *ts;* and other consonants are roughly as in English.

In this book, the names of Miss Guo, Miss Ong, Mr. Kho, Mr. Go, and Mrs. Lim are given in their Taiwanese form, except for Mrs. Lim's given name, which is a Japanese one. Most other Chinese names and words appear in their Mandarin pronunciation; the few exceptions are marked with "(T)."

Chinese Working-Class Lives

[1]

Introduction

American production workers are increasingly being replaced in the world division of labor by workers from countries with lower wages, fewer freedoms, and different cultural assumptions. As any shopper knows, Taiwan is one of the most successful of these countries. Taiwan's textiles, finished garments, shoes, electronics, toys, and other products fill the shelves of our stores; much U.S. military equipment is also made in Taiwan. Typically, the factory workers who manufacture or assemble these goods are young people who are not yet supporting children and come from families with varied occupations that can partially protect them from the booms and busts of a capitalist labor market; therefore, they can work for the low wages that have drawn American and Japanese capital to Taiwan. For the most part, factory workers belong to households that prepare their daughters and sons to be obedient, hard-working, and frugal and to communities in which many will later build various careers. Taiwan's industrial labor force is socialized by and contributes to a working-class culture that still draws heavily on Chinese tradition and on the historical experiences of the past eighty years of outside domination.

Taiwan's working-class culture, the subject of this book, sharply differentiates the island from the many Third World countries whose economies remain trapped by the heritages both of imperialism and of aspects of their indigenous cultural patterns which render them vulnerable to capitalist exploitation. Taiwan's place in the international division of labor depends heavily on the historically specific cultural, social, economic, and political patterns that have shaped its working class. This book is an attempt to define that working class, explore its history, and introduce some of the

[1]

men and women who have carried on its traditions and given it an ever-changing shape.

The nine Chinese people who illustrate working-class culture in this book have lived their lives in a rapidly industrializing complex society with a developed market economy, good communications networks, public schooling, and many other "modern" institutions. The people of Taiwan, like those of the United States, are organized into a nation-state with a powerful government that shapes their economy, their educational system, and their social relations. Although they often identify closely with a "home town," whether a remote mountainside village or a crowded city neighborhood, they are also affected by and conscious of the country as a whole, the China mainland, and Taiwan's international position. The parochialism and autonomy of life lived outside the control of the state vanished from Taiwan almost a century ago. In this sense, too, Americans have much in common with the people of Taiwan.

Taiwan's society encompasses a great range of social positions, from the extreme wealth and power of the ruling Jiang family to the marginal existences of beggars and petty thieves. Most people, of course, exist somewhere in between, as white-collar workers, professionals, technicians, shopkeepers, factory hands, farmers, and the like. About three-quarters of the population can be considered working class, a category made up of people who work with their hands, earn relatively little, and have little education or social prestige. Some own small family businesses; others work for wages; most will have done both over a lifetime.

The nine women and men whose lives will be explored here have led typical working-class lives, centering on work and family. As nearly all of them are elderly, we may observe a long stretch of varied experiences over the same period of time. They are direct, hard-working, unpretentious people, more like most Americans—although they are also very different from us—than are the more highly educated Chinese elite. Taken together, accounts of workers' lives reveal much of the world in which ordinary Chinese have lived in this century.

That world has changed rapidly. The expansion of Japan's colonial empire to include Taiwan, the fall of the last Chinese imperial dynasty, the Communist revolution, and the emergence of Taiwan as a separate and economically thriving country have all been felt directly by these people, as has the greatly increased power of the United States in the Pacific basin. For them, the United States not long ago was only a distant market for local teas; now they are one of its most vigorous competitors on the Pacific rim.

Since the early 1960s the island has enjoyed an economic boom that has given its people the second-highest standard of living in Asia, after that of Japan. Taiwan's working class helped build this new economy with their exertions in the rice fields, the factories, the food-processing shops, and the export-import companies. As entrepreneurs, as patient assemblers of electronic gadgets, as sheer muscle, they created wealth and kept it in Taiwan for reinvestment and further growth. The island's "economic miracle" has attracted much attention and admiration and is therefore a hopeful and positive example of economic betterment in a world with all too few similar cases. Taiwan owes its success in part to the energy and resourcefulness of its people and to the complex cultural patterns that can be glimpsed through our sample of working-class lives.

The "economic miracle" should not be overstated, however. As the reader will learn, the second-highest standard of living in Asia is not, by middle-class American standards, very high. Taiwan's people must still work hard and step lively to earn their daily rice and to put a little by for their old age. For the working class, the family is the only social safety net; so families remain central to people's lives. Old customs, such as the lavish funerals and folk celebrations that link households into communities and supportive networks, still make practical sense. Although social movement "upward," into the world of mental rather than manual labor, is possible through education, the competition for more prestigious and secure jobs is extremely stiff. Most young people must therefore continue to rely on relatives, friends, and neighbors for future jobs and job training and for credit and guidance, as did the nine people discussed here. Social and cultural change has occurred as Taiwan's economy altered, but the more obvious changes—events that might be described as "Westernization"—do not much affect the working class. Extreme individualist and consumerist values are ones they cannot yet afford and do not much admire.

Economies do not "act" or "change" by themselves, although it must often seem that way to people who have little voice in major public decisions. In Taiwan, a powerful government, often strongly supported by U.S. military and economic might, has played an important role in the direction the island's economy has taken. In particular, the government has employed political power to limit working-class opportunities for expressing different views and opposing the official strategy. In the perhaps inevitable struggle between those who own or manage significant resources and those who only labor on them, Taiwan's governments have always stood with the former. Since the Nationalist regime came to power there in 1945, both obvious and subtle instances of state violence against the populace have made working-class people cautious about political participation and

[3]

expression. Rumors and memories of this violence deeply affect working-class culture in ways that almost all my subjects touched on while recounting their life experiences.

Chapter 2 presents a necessarily rather personal account of how I collected my data. The intimacy and trust necessary for the collection of life histories is not easily achieved, particularly because I was especially interested in learning about a politically sensitive period in Taiwan's history—the transition from the Japanese to Nationalist control. The discussion of my field method allows the reader to evaluate the circumstances within which these materials were gathered. An ancient Chinese wisely told us that "a gentleman is not an instrument," not simply a tool to be used, but a whole person. Neither is an anthropologist.

Chapter 3 examines the four historical migrations that have populated the island of Taiwan and given form to its present society. Austronesian-speaking Aborigines, south China peasants, Japanese colonialists, and the refugees of the Communist revolution on the Chinese mainland have all contributed to working-class culture in Taiwan. In Chapter 4 we see the changing economy of the Nationalist period shaping both ethnic and class relations and responding to the socially repressive political imperatives on which the power of the rulers rests.

Thereafter, following brief discussions of work (Chapter 5), kinship (Chapter 6), the roles of women and men (Chapter 7), folk religion (Chapter 8), and education (Chapter 9), I introduce the real subjects of this study: nine working-class women and men whose lives have told me more about the realities of Taiwan than all the documents of progress their government so enthusiastically publishes. The thematic introductions that begin these later chapters outline only some of the issues that Taiwan scholars have investigated. A great deal has been written, for example, on both Chinese kinship and folk religion in Taiwan, which must in turn be viewed in the context of the enormous literature on these subjects drawn from ancient and modern Chinese society in China proper and from the experiences of the multitudes of overseas Chinese who have migrated to every continent. A sketch of some of those resources will be found in Source Materials on Taiwan, following the conclusions drawn in Chapter 10.

As I listened to the telling of these lives, my inner responses to them wavered between "Yes, that seems perfectly natural" and "My, how strange!" Perhaps the reader will feel the same way. If the task of anthropology is to uncover and explain what we humans share and why we differ, such responses make a good beginning to the understanding of Chinese culture and to what it contributes to the way our world works.

[2]

Fieldwork in Taiwan:
Becoming a Little Chinese

The Chinese live in many climates, speak many languages, and follow widely differing customs. But they all share at least one thing: a strong and sophisticated belief that human relationships are more important than anything else. They are, indeed, so important that they cannot be left to the chance of individual idiosyncrasy but are governed by clear-cut and well-known rules to which everyone must conform. Those who do not—foreigners and rare Chinese eccentrics—are excluded from the inner circles of friendship and trust where all of life's real business is transacted. To learn as an anthropologist from Taiwan's people about their lives, I had to learn those rules and how to put them into practice in our relationships. I had to become a little bit Chinese.

To do so I had to change, at least temporarily, many ways of behaving, such as basic body language, that had always seemed perfectly natural to me. Chinese women, I came to understand, seem to tuck their head, limbs, and torso into a tighter, neater package than I was accustomed to doing; my relative looseness of posture appeared disrespectful or at least slovenly. Belching was socially acceptable, while blowing one's nose was not.

The Chinese language I had learned in the United States, which was supposed to be my main channel of communication, was full of traps and confusions, for I knew only how to say in Chinese what an American would say. A Chinese, in similar circumstances, often comes out with something quite different. Where we make small talk about the weather or current events, for example, they inquire if a new acquaintance has brothers and

[5]

sisters, or ask the amount of her salary. Where we are taught to accept a compliment with quiet thanks, a Chinese cannot comfortably do so, being obliged modestly to deny having any positive qualities.

Chinese etiquette presented me with many challenges. Seeing guests spit chicken bones and melon seeds onto the table or the floor at a formal dinner startled me, but I must have seemed equally rude to my fellow diners for following my hard-to-break habit of drinking when I felt thirsty, rather than politely toasting someone before sipping. Dinner guests are insistently helped to portions throughout a meal by the host or hostess, who is mortified at the sight of an empty bowl. I finally learned not to finish everything on my plate, thereby allowing my host to stop feeding me. This kind of hovering solicitude is one of the essentials of Chinese etiquette, one I found hard to like and harder yet to remember to copy. Small exchanges of courtesy—a friend offering to hold one's handbag on a crowded bus or taking her hand to cross a street, one person necessarily treating rather than each person paying her own way at restaurants, and the like—are constant, and are paralleled by the frequent exchanges of gifts that cement friendships.

Chinese behavior differs from American, too, in its emphasis on preserving people's "face," or dignity, in ways that sometimes lead to indirection and apparent evasiveness. When asked, for example, to do something she does not really feel able to do—although Chinese are very willing, by American standards, to help their friends—a Chinese rarely refuses directly. One must learn to detect more subtle signs of unwillingness, and must learn as well that to give a flat refusal to a request is dismaying, and even offensive.

Etiquette exists in part to smooth and order human relations, to create a framework within which friendship is possible. The meaning of friendship itself differs from the American version, however. Chinese make few casual, short-term acquaintanceships as Americans learn to do so readily in school, at work, or while out amusing themselves. Once made, however, Chinese friendships are expected to last and to give each party very strong claims on the other's resources, time, and loyalty. By learning these and a multitude of other cultural differences, I tried slowly to behave more like the people I wished to study.

First Encounters

I collected these life histories during a brief span of time, in the autumn of 1980. I could not have done this work on my first field trip to Taiwan, from 1968 to 1971, or, probably, during my second, one-year trip in 1974–75. These years of study and direct experience with Chinese people were necessary for me to learn how to be trustworthy and sincere in a Chinese way. With that knowledge, I felt ready to begin the highly personal field-work in which the anthropologist creates a picture of a culture and its changes by digging deeply into people's memories of their lives. I will examine here some of the complex prerequisites to what may appear to be the simple task of writing the life stories of nine ordinary people.

On my first field trip to Taiwan, I attained a modest fluency in Mandarin Chinese and a smattering of the Taiwanese language, collected enough information about work, worship, and politics to write a doctoral dissertation on the organization of an urban neighborhood, and began to come to grips with the multitudinous differences that separate American and Chinese culture. When I left Taiwan after that first field trip, my head held far more difficult questions about the nature of Chinese society than I had come with. One that especially puzzled me then was why some Chinese seemed so exceptionally friendly, helpful, and hospitable, while so many others were startlingly rude, cold, and "slippery." If ever a culture seemed riddled with contradictions, it was this one.

Part of the bafflement I felt at the apparent unpredictability of Taiwan's complex society was the result of a simple accident of my personal circumstances during those years. I was dividing my time among three groups of people who represented very different social categories of Chinese and who had different versions of "Chinese culture" to teach me.

I met the first as I studied language from teachers chosen for the standard purity of their Mandarin accents. My first Chinese associates, then, were well-educated women and men from the cultural centers of northern China, such as Beijing. Though few were rich, their prestige was substantial, and some were linked to wealthy and powerful families. All were post–World War II immigrants to Taiwan, "Mainlanders," and self-consciously proud of it. They taught me, along with language, as much formal politeness and customary behavior as they thought I needed, and they answered my questions about Chinese culture out of their own experience and sense of what was proper to reveal. To them I was a hard-working graduate student undertaking the clear-cut task of language learning, which many of them had also undertaken as they studied English. Soon I would be a university teacher. What I was and what I was to become were clear to them, and so was our honorable relationship as student and teacher.

My encounter with the second "group" began with just one person: Mrs. Zhang, the lively, cheerful woman engaged as housekeeper for my small household. She was also a Mainlander—the clear Shandong accents of her

[7]

native province still fall most naturally on my ears—but not a member of the immigrant elite. She and her husband had arrived after the 1949 retreat of the Nationalists to Taiwan, along with the more than a million other common soldiers and their households that make up most of Taiwan's Mainlander population. Through her I met her family, her friends, and their families—an ever-widening circle of military men and domestic servants to whom I was a recognizable and prestigious person—a university professor-in-training and a reasonably fair and generous employer, to be treated with a pleasing mixture of intimacy and respect.

The third category of Chinese with whom I spent much time consisted of the inhabitants of my chosen field neighborhood, Prosperity Settlement. These involuntary recruits to anthropology were the families of shop-keepers, construction workers, low-level clerks, laborers, and small-scale manufacturers who occupied a cluster of old residences in the recently expanded suburb of Taibei where I was living. Commercial astuteness and a wide network of social ties—not education—were the foundations of their occupational success, and all were deeply rooted in their native Taiwan.

Prosperity Settlement people were for the most part not impoverished, but most were not rich either, and their occupations were not prestigious. To put it bluntly, as a friend from the neighborhood did years later, "it was a very below-average place to live." They knew this. In consequence, my appearance among them made no sense, for they could see nothing about themselves or their community that merited research by a foreign graduate student. As I persisted in trying to learn about their lives, some lost their suspicions (that I was a Christian missionary or was trying to find out the community's secrets for the government), but most politely ignored my presence. In a community where lifelong ties of reciprocity are everything, I did not appear to have much to offer them in return for whatever it was that I wanted. I was young, I was a woman; perhaps, in their opinions, I too must have been "below average" to be doing my research there instead of in Taiwan's important universities and museums.

I had not expected to be so unimportant and uninteresting to my field informants; I was dismayed. After several nearly fruitless months of full-time attempts to gain rapport, I had a stroke of luck that brought me the help of Chen Fumei, a college graduate from the neighborhood. She was planning to go to the United States at about the time I was scheduled to leave Taiwan. She became my field assistant for the last six months of my stay, introduced me to people, and informally stood guarantor to her neighbors for my good faith. I gave her a salary, helped her prepare for an English-speaking future, and escorted her, when my work was completed, to her new married life in Madison, Wisconsin. It was a very happy arrangement and, I am sure, saved my fieldwork.

Through Chen Fumei, I was able to learn some of the things I needed to know to write about Prosperity Settlement as an organized community. But the frustrating effort of studying the neighborhood alone made me aware of other, and interesting, things about Chinese culture and my insertion into it. I experienced the relentless impersonality with which Chinese treat strangers and outsiders, the hermetically closed nature of Chinese primary groups, the practicality on which social relationships are founded, the constant fear of political action or discussion, and the lack of curiosity—and even condescension—expressed toward non-Chinese, whose ways, by definition, are inferior. For a mobile, rapidly urbanizing society heavily dependent on foreign trade and tourism, these were problematical attitudes, worth trying to understand.

I also learned from the contrasts between the behavior of my language teachers and that of Prosperity Settlement people. While my graduate training in anthropology had prepared me for variations within a culture as old, as large, and as internally complex as China's, the difference between Beijing teachers and Taiwanese construction workers seemed great enough to put the whole notion of *one* Chinese culture into question. Obviously some of that difference stemmed from the fact that with the first group I was known and respected, while with the second I was merely a nuisance. But there was more: subcultural differences great enough to be called "ethnic," differences of occupation, social class, and education, and differences in the fundamental attitude toward Americans as a group, separated them. None of this was clear enough, when I left Taiwan, to be very satisfactory. I would have to return to unravel the complexities.

In the summer of 1974 I returned to study the connections between Taiwanese-Mainlander ethnicity and social class. Living in a tiny apartment in Prosperity Settlement, I caught up with my friends among the neighborhood people but spent most of my time surveying sections of the city for background on studies of Taiwanese-Mainlander intermarriage, funeral practices, and religious activities. Accompanied and assisted by the most adventurous of my Chinese friends, Wang Chunhua, I collected data from government offices, temples, and people in many neighborhoods as we tried to factor out how class and ethnicity interacted in Taiwan's complex social structure.

Though the work was going well, my health was not, in part because of the discomfort of my living conditions. My apartment—two small rooms, and the shared use of a kitchen, bathing room, and toilet—had been partitioned off in a building that had once housed one large family but now crammed in six families, or about forty-eight people. The building was alive with vermin—large mice on the rafters, the occasional rat under the bed platforms, and swarms of two-inch cockroaches everywhere. In hot climates, cockroaches not only slither into dark crevices, including one's clothes, dishes, and the toilet bowl, but they also fly. I am not squeamish, but a *large* cockroach in one's bed at night encourages insomnia. The house, like nearly all houses in Taiwan, was unheated, though the temperature was in the forties, and the days were raw and rainy for weeks in midwinter. Bathing in a kettle of heated water in a drafty concrete bathing room was an ordeal.

My bedroom was enclosed with glass windows that I covered with whitewash so I could sleep and dress without being observed, although children regularly scratched it off to peek in. My living room was also the passageway through which the neighbors reached our common kitchen and bathrooms. Since those neighbors had four small children, it was not possible to leave anything of importance outside the bedroom, as the younger ones could not resist novelty. Nor could they resist watching me at mealtimes, hoping for a treat. My neighbors slept in a single adjoining bedroom on the same raised platform covered with Japanese matting where I spread my quilts each night. When anyone rolled over in bed, the rest of us felt it; when the newborn baby cried, I heard her mother's murmured, affectionate "Eat, little slave" as the infant slurpily took her breast.

Unlike that comfortable little family, however, I had learned to expect a good deal of quiet and darkness for sleeping, as well as privacy and quiet for eating and working. After six months of poor sleep in these extremely crowded living conditions that most Chinese take for granted, I found myself too ill to continue. While Wang Chunhua carried on several of my projects, I retreated to a friendly haven in the south of Taiwan for a few weeks' rest and recovery. Returning to tie up loose ends in early summer, I had gained a new respect for and curiosity about the personal side of life in a society that offers the individual so little physical and psychic space.

Collecting Life Histories

My decision to plan a brief field trip in 1980 around the gathering of life histories stemmed partly from this curiosity, but also from other sources. By the summer of 1975 I had met many Chinese people in the course of my work, and a few had shown me glimpses of their personal histories. Each revelation had been given in a moment of stress, as if she—they were all women—had lost control of a proper reserve, and let something very private spill over. On one occasion, I met my landlady from Prosperity Settlement by chance at the hairdresser's. As we walked home together, protecting our hairdos under the same umbrella, she poured out a torrent of grievances against her ungenerous old mother-in-law, her feeble husband, and the lifelong, unhappy relationship among the three of them. I was astonished at her candor and at how little of this I had seen or suspected, though I had known her for years and had lived in her house for months. Later I realized that there had been hardly a moment in her crowded, busy life when she might have spoken feelingly with another, in private. How much of the reserve I had felt so strongly from my Chinese friends was due simply to lack of opportunity and hence of the habit of expressing personal feelings? Collecting life histories in a comfortable, private setting might prove a valuable format for learning about Chinese life. And, I hoped, telling about long-suppressed feelings and experiences might, in some way, be helpful and positive for the tellers.

Life histories appealed to me as well, because by 1980 history itself was assuming greater importance in anthropology; researchers now took seriously the idea that we can understand social change and social reproduction only through diachronic perspectives. In addition, in analyzing the emergence of social class and ethnic patterns in Taiwan, I had become increasingly conscious of the absence of historical materials about an extremely significant period—the years of World War II, of the Japanese loss and Nationalist seizure of Taiwan, and of the decade or more of Nationalist misgovernment and economic chaos through the 1950s. Most people flatly refused to discuss those times, while those who would spoke of them guardedly, and only in places where they were certain not to be overheard. My researches into Prosperity Settlement's past and into the emergence of class and ethnic relations had repeatedly been frustrated by these responses. More indirect approaches were called for; perhaps the life histories of people who had lived through these events would give me the day-to-day texture of those times without my having to ask people to speak specifically about them. It was, I think, a Chinese solution. It saved my informants from being put on the political spot, and it worked.

Despite the way it is taught in universities, anthropological fieldwork is not an endeavor carried out by the anthropologist with the full cooperation of members of the society under study. It is often, quite simply, what our field informants allow it to be. I did not unilaterally choose the women and men who told me about their lives, though some of them chose me. I did,

[11]

however, have goals for the 1980 research which guided me in my final decisions about whom to search out and interview and about which interviews I would include in this study.

I wanted to talk with older people—in their sixties, at least—who had lived through the important events of Taiwan's recent past and who had been ordinary working people most of their lives. I wanted women and men, Taiwanese and Mainlanders, city-bred people, and those who had come as migrants to the city. Finally, of course, I wanted people whose lives have been eventful and who could tell of those events with some verve, some insight. Most of the life histories included here meet those criteria, though the group includes one remarkable younger woman whose life has been shaped more by her struggles with personal tragedy than by the results of social change.

I wanted to include people whose stories fill out the historical picture of the chaotic forties and fifties as well as the boom times of the sixties and seventies, in order to show something of the life of working-class people in a great and complex city, and to illustrate the range of contemporary Taiwan Chinese family types and the change in their kinship values. They were chosen, too, to exemplify some of the many variations on a well-lived life as each of these people struggled to attain the Chinese ideal of *zuo ren*—of "acting as a real human being"—within the limits that life imposed on them.

When I arrived in Taiwan, I contacted several people who I was sure would agree to tell me their stories. They were Mrs. Lim, a Prosperity Settlement neighbor five years ago; Mrs. Zhang, who had cooked for me on my first field trip and had remained a good friend since then; her husband, a retired air force man; and Miss Ong, an old Prosperity Settlement friend whose courage in adversity had kept mine up during my first fieldwork. I also hoped to get help from some of these people in persuading mutual friends whom I knew less well to talk to me; Mr. Kho's story is one result of these attempts.

A few other attempts failed. When the subject of an interview was broached, two or three acquaintances indirectly refused, saying that their lives were of no interest, that they were too busy, or simply giving the all-purpose Chinese excuse that such interviews were "not convenient." A few others gave me nothing but the barest chronology of their lives, and I found no questions that prompted them to become more expansive. One younger woman, a taxi driver, told me, "Most of life is very simple. We go through our days, getting by, and that's that. What is there to tell?" Not surprisingly, the shorter our acquaintance, the less likely people were to dig into their memories for my tape recorder.

[12]

Two of the people chronicled here essentially proposed themselves to me: Miss Guo and Mr. Kang both offered to tell me about themselves after watching me going about my work for some weeks, and Miss Guo invited Mrs. Lo to do the same.

Having found a woman willing to talk about her life, I invited her to my comfortable private room in the hostel where I was living. (No more sleepless nights in Prosperity Settlement this time, I vowed.) With men subjects, I made it clear that the interview would take place in the hostel's quiet public lounge, a respectable-enough location in which to meet a foreign woman. All, however, to my great pleasure, insisted that we conduct the interviews at their homes, giving me the opportunity to learn things about their lives that words do not easily convey. Most of them arranged for considerable privacy for our talks.

As we began, I explained my ground rules. I would like to tape our conversations, but in any case would put as much as I could of what they told me in writing. I would publish the material, in English, in the United States, but an English edition might possibly appear in Taiwan as well. I would not let anyone in Taiwan read or hear what they had told me in the original Chinese, except for my two field assistants. I would change family names to protect their privacy.

For some, these guarantees of anonymity seemed to be a relief, but a few were surprised by them. "My name is my name, and my life an honest one. There is no need to hide anything," said Mr. Zhang. To such responses, I replied that the book would contain not only their words but also my ideas and explanations, with which they might not completely agree: after all, they are Chinese and I am American, so our viewpoints might differ on some subjects. When the book was published, it would be best that I completely bear the responsibility for the contents. To this they all agreed.

In conducting the interviews I decided that, wherever possible, I would encourage people to tell their stories with little interruption or direction from me, although I asked them to speak especially about their work lives. At least initially, I wanted *their* version of their lives rather than a set of answers to questions I had framed. I did not want to press them unduly on matters that might embarrass or discomfit them, and I trusted most of them to speak frankly, if not with complete openness. Naturally, had I been more directive and pressed harder for certain details, I might have learned other interesting things. But at the same time, I might have gone too far, deflecting someone from the line of remembrance she thought most meaningful and rupturing the friendly confidence that made the interview possible. Ultimately, I think, I did not want to hurt or offend people who had generously agreed to share something of their inner lives with me and with an unseen reading public, and preferred to respect their choice of expression.

For the people whose stories are published here, this approach worked well. Here and there the reader will notice events, skimmed over vaguely at first mention, which the speaker later clarifies, as when Mr. Kang reveals his dramatic escape from the Communists which prevents his contacting his family. Mostly, however, people structured their descriptions of events around a dogged historical approach—my ancestors, my early childhood, my growing up, my marriage, and so forth—modeled after the many biographies of "virtuous people" to which most people have been exposed in school.

It is difficult to tell the story of one's life convincingly while leaving out significant events. The very telling calls up memories and feelings that carry the speaker along unself-consciously to reveal much, if not all, of what she has experienced. Not having worked much with a tape recorder before, I was surprised at how little attention informants paid to it, or to me, when they were deep into reviewing the memories that constituted their selves.

Occasionally, when I understood poorly the meaning of what was said or needed to ask a question, I stopped the flow of reminiscence for clarification. Sometimes the field assistant added a question or comment. Often we slacked off to eat, drink, or chat about peripheral matters, when the informant seemed to need a break. These were pleasant hours, though the memories I was hearing were often sorrowful ones. We usually worked about two hours at a time, and we returned four or five times to most of the informants.

How to make an appropriate return for an informant's time and trouble is a matter that often bedevils anthropologists. In Taiwan this matter was simplified by the fact that the Chinese follow an elaborate code that specifies what gifts to give and when to give them. To people I did not know well, I brought the kinds of presents given when one visits for the first time or asks a small favor—baskets of choice fruit and tins of cookies. For old friends with whom I was already linked by the gifts we exchanged on special occasions, the treats could be more closely matched to their tastes: the Zhangs like pig-ear shreds and sesame buns from a special shop; Miss Ong enjoys Tainan-style candied fruit. When I finished each interview, I brought a more substantial present: a dress length of fine mainland silk, well-made woolen sweaters, a small tape recorder, a bottle of unusual liquor. In a couple of cases I added gifts of money, properly concealed in the traditional red envelope, for a child or grandchild. I knew also that all these people would now feel free to ask favors of me: helping with a child's

English studies, or sending or receiving foreign currency, for example—knowing I would do my best to comply.

As is customary among Chinese people, I always gave copies of snapshots to people I had photographed. Such exchanges are important in Chinese society, where friendship is expected to express itself tangibly as well as symbolically. Many Chinese people are, by Western standards, quite sentimental about friendships, and love to have photos, souvenirs, and objects around them that remind them of happy occasions. I was glad I knew how to give appropriate gifts, and glad to give them. They helped knit me, a foreigner, into the fabric of a Chinese relationship by showing informants that I understood important Chinese cultural rules and standards, thus making me familiar and trustworthy despite my alien appearance and origin. Mutual usefulness framed by etiquette that demonstrates respect for each other's dignity comes close to being a definition of Chinese friendship. By 1980 I was comfortable with relationships that were so defined.

Two graduates of the anthropology department of National Taiwan University, Miss Zhang Xun and Miss Zhang Huiduan, contributed significantly to this project as field assistants, accompanying me on interviews, transcribing and translating, and carrying out a number of additional investigations. For some informants, the assistants' ties with the university gave my undertaking an additional air of dignity, for though two or three of the subjects had heard of such famous American universities as Hafo (Harvard) and Yelu (Yale), none of them was sophisticated enough to be familiar with Central Michigan University, my home base. It was reassuring for those who did not know me well that I had scholarly connections in Taiwan through the Miss Zhangs.

Both of these women possess unusual intelligence, charm, and tact. As Chinese people who have agreed to help one in a long-term way will nearly invariably do, they put their talents at my disposal, working enthusiastically and resourcefully at the tasks I set before them. Good interviewers themselves, they often found ways to pose clarifying questions to our subjects or to spot and resolve ambiguities that I might have overlooked. As they were reared in cultivated families, their polished etiquette and verbal mannerisms helped make up for the lapses of language and courtesy that I no doubt continued to make.

At the same time, they remained unobtrusive in interviews. There was little difference in the confidence shown me when I interviewed alone (as I did most times with Mandarin-speaking subjects) and when one of the Miss Zhangs accompanied me. The interview subjects treated them as my

[15]

lieutenants, apparently assuming that if I trusted their discretion, so could they.

When a life history was completed, I turned the tapes over to one of the field assistants for transcription into Chinese characters. This was not an entirely simple matter, for many informants spoke in the Taiwanese language commonly used by the native Chinese population of the island, rather than the "national language" (Mandarin) in which educated younger people are accustomed to write. While in theory any Chinese language can be written in the same ideographic characters used for Mandarin, in practice there are differences of grammar and of word usage in non-Mandarin languages such as Taiwanese which require special characters and conventions that have not been taught in Taiwan's schools for many decades. Taiwanese, which used to have a flourishing literature, has thus been reduced to a nonwritten language. The assistants' character transcriptions for Taiwanese-language tapes, therefore, contain some oddities. Tapes from one of the post-1949 Chinese immigrants to Taiwan, Mr. Zhang, presented similar problems, as he speaks in a Mandarin that is heavily influenced by the accent and speech forms of his native regional dialect. Just such variability in spoken Chinese in Taiwan—two major languages and many strong regional dialects—made the assistance of my field helpers a necessity and, through the companionship we shared, a pleasure as well.

From the Chinese-character transcription, the Miss Zhangs made rough English translations, which I later recast and edited. The final versions are considerably compressed from the elimination of repetition and extraneous conversation.

The major difficulty in final preparation was the problem of preserving, through translating and editing, a sense of the spoken style and personality of the informants, who range from well educated to illiterate, from earthy and direct to floridly euphemistic in their diction. Each also spoke in turns of phrase appropriate to her or his age and sex, using expressions drawn from many Chinese regional rhetorics. Though the English versions lose nearly all this verbal variety, I have attempted to retain some distinctions among the voices, sometimes by the substitution of English idioms for what was actually said in Chinese. Though these life histories are, I think, true to the spirit of the originals, they are not simply transcriptions from the tapes. If they could read them as they stand, however, I believe their subjects would readily recognize themselves.

The Chinese women and men whose life histories I collected lived through the dramatic changes of the last sixty years and also learned from others' memories about conditions of earlier times. Their experiences represent a side of Taiwan's history that is rarely written down and hence easily ignored: that of the working class. They saw economic, political, and social change from the point of view of people with limited power and resources and a very incomplete knowledge of the national and international events occurring around them. Like most people, they evaluated these by how they themselves were affected.

They sometimes misunderstood events beyond their immediate experience and usually emphasized those events in which they had special interest while ignoring others, or they simply omitted reference to painful or troublesome times. Sometimes, too, they may have misrepresented events deliberately. But all these things are done by anyone, even a historian: no one knows everything about the past or sees it from some abstract, inhumanly objective point of view. Indeed, it can be argued that an ordinary person's view of recent history is more balanced than that of a professional historian. For while society's elite (to whom most historians belong) may know next to nothing about the day-to-day realities of working-class life, working-class people like my informants not only know their own circumstances, but are also often well instructed, through schooling and the public media, in the "official" view of history and current events that their leaders put forward and which form much of the material for later historical studies. The views of ordinary people can therefore be quite complex, and sometimes contradictory. As a result, a life history is not a simple, factual description of the past that everyone would recognize as accurate, though it may superficially appear to be. Rather, it shows us both the impact of external events on a particular person, and an attempt by that person to construct a meaningful pattern out of those events. A single life history, taken alone, gives only a limited picture of anything beyond the individual who creates it; several overlapping lives show us something both of the individuals represented and of the shared experiences that make up a people's history and culture.

"What Is an Anthropologist, Anyway?"

Anthropology fieldwork, whether interviewing for life histories or collecting impersonal information about customs, kinship, economic activities, and the like, always begins with the anthropologist as a single human inquirer. She has a theory to test, or at least a plan of approach, and has acquired some prior knowledge about the people from whom she expects to obtain information. One of the biggest imponderables in the field situation is the response she will receive based on the kind and degree of knowledge her subjects have about "outsiders." With no training for cross-cultural

[17]

encounters, little information about foreigners, not much sense of cultural relativity, and often not even much curiosity about "their" anthropologist, the people about whom anthropological studies are written confront researchers as unprepared, and often unwilling, informants.

"What does she want?" "What will I gain if I give it to her?" "What can she do to me if I refuse?" are natural questions, as a strange-looking foreigner who speaks awkwardly and is generally deficient in politesse attempts to strike up a conversation, loiters to observe one's family funeral, or simply *watches*, scribbling foreign writing in her ever-present notebook.

Such a stranger is classified in the broadest possible terms at first. In some small-scale societies, it is even doubtful at first whether the anthropologist is even a human being, though this was not true in Taiwan. People unused to different styles of grooming and dress may find difficulty in determining something as basic as the visitor's sex. An American friend used to tell with amusement of how his elderly Taiwanese landlady had had to ask whether, despite his full beard, he was male or female, "because your hair is long, like a woman's." On being told that the beard should have been indicative, she shrugged, "American customs may be different, for all I know." In my case, my gender confused no one; I was clearly and disadvantageously a woman in a very sexist society.

My age, however, was a source of confusion to Chinese people unaccustomed to Caucasian faces. As a student and a married woman without children, I must be young, they thought, but I did not look it. Just as Americans often guess Chinese to be younger than they are, we look older than our age to them—a result of our "craggier" faces, deep-set eyes, and tendency (at least among graduate students) to premature wrinkles and gray hair. As age is an important status consideration for Chinese, this is a small advantage in gaining the respect due an adult. Its impact was lessened, however, by the apparent inconsistency between the "young" student and the "older" appearance, which gave people mixed signals about how to treat me.

My educational status, by contrast, placed me in a clearly positive light, for it suggested that I must be a person of elite status. The Chinese admiration for education exceeds that of most Americans; saying I was a student of their language and culture brought warmth and respect from nearly everyone. This familiarity with educational attainment did not, in general, include an acceptance of the anthropological position that the lives of ordinary people were worth studying, however. Even my educated Mandarin teachers disapproved of my taking time to study the Taiwanese language, which they saw as the coarse dialect of lower-class people. But, as I traveled around the city meeting people, I was always treated more helpfully when I revealed that I was pursuing, or, later, had attained, the lofty-sounding *bo shi*—Ph. D.—degree.

Furthermore, being identified as an educated person, I would, it was assumed, know some especially effective way to teach English. I was constantly besieged with requests to teach, formally and informally, and in fact did teach English in colleges, cram schools, government bureaus, and in my own living room. At first, I did so to finance my language studies, and later, as a service to friends. People approached me on buses and on the street with the frank suggestion: "Let's be friends, so you can teach me English." When for lack of time I turned down such requests, I knew I was perceived to be refusing to enter into a relationship. Only after some experience did I learn to respond as a Chinese would be likely to do, by agreeing to teach someone, so as to convey my openness to forming a friendship, but then to let the lessons trail off after only one or two meetings.

Though such matters are difficult to pin down, I believe that perceived relative social class status also affected my relationships with many Chinese (as it does in American society). Working-class people were typically less willing than "middle-class" ones to deny requests when I pressed hard, and may have hoped that my "higher" status might make me a useful contact for them. By contrast, Chinese whose education and class status was equivalent to or higher than mine were much harder for me to form relationships with. Perhaps this was because I had nothing much to offer in return for what I hoped for in the way of information and contacts from them. While it was unpleasant to recognize this, I came to conclude that I learned more about Taiwan's working class than about its elites largely because our relative prestige permitted me, at times, to inflict myself on some people but not on others. Many anthropologists must experience this biasing "advantage" in their work.

For the Chinese, whether new acquaintances or old friends, my most dominant characteristic, however, was my identity as an American. It was *Meiguo ren* (in Mandarin) or *Bikok lang* (in Taiwanese)—"American person"—that was shrieked at me by children in the streets, and only rarely the generic *da bizi* (big nose) or *yang guizi* (foreign devil), which distinguish race rather than nationality. It was as an American that I was introduced, discussed, described; the word for "friend" in Mandarin, *pengyou*, usually refers to non-Chinese only with a qualifier: a *Meiguo pengyou* (American friend) or a *waiguo pengyou* (foreign friend). American nationality was clearly my most salient and, for most people, my only significant identity.

A strong sense that the Chinese I was meeting responded more to their own stereotypes of Americans than to me pervaded my first field trip,

[19]

partly for the purely personal reason that in those years I acted more like an American. There was another important reason behind this stereotyping, however. Although it was not my intention, or my desire, to appear in this light, many Chinese saw me first and foremost as a representative of a country that has profoundly influenced Taiwan's society, often in ways of which they disapprove.

One powerful shaper of the perceived identity of any American in Taiwan at that time was the Vietnam war. The United States considered the Nationalist government an ally in that war, with the aims of which, as ardent anti-Communists, the Nationalists were in full sympathy. Under that alliance, the United States made massive purchases of building materials—mostly cement—from Taiwan's state-controlled cement company for the construction of bases and fortifications in South Vietnam. This gave a welcome boost to the island's export economy and made a small number of people extremely rich. The Nationalist government in return permitted the United States Army to use Taiwan as an official "R and R" (rest and recreation) post for its soldiers.

During the war years, Taibei swarmed with American soldiers looking for women, liquor, and souvenirs. Tourism and prostitution boomed, as did procuring of prostitutes by both officials and underworld gangs to meet the apparently endless demand. Pimps scoured poor hinterland villages for parents desperate or callous enough to sell daughters, many as young teenagers, into this ugly life. The sale of cement and women earned dollars but not admiration from thoughtful Chinese who saw the cost: the expansion of a corrupting underworld in which their government colluded. Military tourists were the Americans whom most Chinese encountered.

The Vietnam war, however, was only one facet of the decades-old relationship the United States has maintained with Nationalist China. I will explore this relationship further in the next chapter, where I examine the island's history and its resulting social organization. The long-term American-Chinese connection has left deep impressions on many Chinese minds, and many of these impressions are unfavorable.

The Chinese are a cautious as well as a courteous people, and do not commonly court confrontation by stating their resentments of Americans openly. Just once, in all my meetings with Chinese people in Taiwan, did I hear flatly and directly the hostile words that, because of the history of our national relationships, many Chinese people keep to themselves. These words were from a five-year-old girl.

Six months into my first stay in Taiwan, in early 1969, I was standing with my former husband, a tall, bearded, and, to Chinese children, somewhat intimidating "foreigner," waiting for a Taibei city bus. Riding back and forth

on a smooth stretch of red-tiled sidewalk was a very small and very energetic little girl, intent on steering her tricycle.

Greedy for opportunities to practice my Mandarin with someone who
could not immediately out-talk me, I opened conversation with a con-
ventional, "Little sister, have you eaten yet?"

Her only response was a sidelong and distinctly unfriendly look. I tried
again: "Little sister, come on over! I want to be your friend."

This provoked a response, and a remarkable one, as little Chinese girls
are usually very timid, especially before big, bearded foreigners.

Suddenly, but emphatically, she said, "I don't want to be your friend."

"Why not? We can be friends. I like you."

"Well, I don't like you. You're American, aren't you?"

"Yes, American."

"I *hate* Americans. Americans sold out my country to the Communist
bandits, so I hate all of you. My daddy says so."

Astonished as much by her vehemence as at hearing this level of political
discourse from a preschooler, I tried to persuade her that Americans and
Chinese were often friends. She was not to be persuaded; she was so angry
as to be quite unafraid; she hated me, she hated Americans, and she rode
away.

For once, I had heard an unmistakably honest voice on the subject of
United States–China relations. The opinions, of course, came from her
father, but she had heard them often enough, it appeared, to have them
firmly fixed in her mind. Her family had obviously immigrated from the
mainland, an assumption confirmed by her standard-accented Mandarin,
which a Taiwanese child of her age would not have mastered in those times.
How many Mainlander children have grown up in Taiwan hearing the same
sentiments—that the United States failed to back the Nationalist government strongly enough to assure victory over the Communists in the late
1940s, thereby condemning them to exile in alien Taiwan?

I have never heard such harsh criticisms from native Taiwanese, but they
too have their reasons to resent Americans. During World War II, when
Taiwan was under Japanese rule, American forces heavily bombed Taiwan's
cities. In addition, many educated Taiwanese blame the persistence of
unpopular Nationalist power under the leadership of Jiang Jieshi (Chiang
Kai-shek) on American support he received after fleeing to the island in
1949. "At the end of the war," goes a Taiwanese saying, "the Americans
dropped the atomic bomb on the Japanese, and dropped the Jiang family on
us. If they had only atomic-bombed us, and dropped the Jiangs on Japan!"

The dislike, and even hatred, that some Chinese feel for Americans is not
simply a direct response that grew out of experiences since World War II.

Before that time, the mainland of China had suffered very extensive economic and political colonization by foreign nations, including the United States. These had enforced humiliating unequal treaties that prevented the normal exercise of sovereignty by Chinese over their land, people, and revenues for decades. Generations of Chinese leaders grew up in a complex intellectual atmosphere of admiration for Western achievements, mixed with bitter resentment of the power that Westerners were able to exercise. On the mainland and later in Taiwan, the Nationalists actively taught a nationalistic doctrine glorifying the Chinese as a separate and superior racial group with undying hatred for the foreigners' unequal treaties. Such ideas, by the time I came to Taiwan, were a part of the education of every schoolchild and were widely propagated by the government.

Some of these attitudes are understandable reactions to the aggressive imperialism of the Americans, British, Russians, Japanese, and other peoples who colonized China. Because these are official party positions, they carry weight even with young people who have no personal experience with the war or the chaotic century that preceded it. As an American, I too was tainted with this heritage.

In spite of all this, many Chinese were willing to distinguish between abstract "Americans" and real-life examples, and to treat me as a person. Indeed, many Chinese have a good deal of admiration for some aspects of American culture—its technology, its lively popular entertainments, its generosity—which they had encountered as military men back on the mainland or as recipients of the post-1949 flow to Taiwan of United States economic aid and emergency relief. This admiration, although pleasant to experience, is, I believe, both narrow and shallow.

Whole areas of American life are as unknown and alien to Chinese people as their lives are to us, and their judgments about us are often based on "facts" that seem oddly distorted. Though the actual knowledge most ordinary people have about our society is, in fact, quite slight, Chinese people are not, in general, very curious about American life. In return for my questions about their lives, people asked what I paid for rent, clothing, and the like back home (all perfectly proper questions in Chinese society), and what I thought about popular figures such as presidents and movie stars, but they never displayed much interest in other subjects.

In addition, they wanted very much for me to affirm to them certain beliefs about American families which have gained currency in Taiwan. These ideas about our family life show us as a people who, by Chinese standards, lack the most basic morality. One belief that was constantly repeated to me was that when an American parent visits a married child, she or he is charged room and board, even if for only a single meal. Com-

[22]

monly, unsophisticated Chinese also believe that when our senior relatives die, we promptly forget them "as you would a dog," "because that is the Christian custom." At first I used to deny that this level of disregard was common, but I always found my hearers unconvinced. These beliefs about us contrasted so vividly with their own beliefs about themselves—that parents are always treated generously by married children and their spirits are remembered in family rituals long after death—that they had become incontestable evidence for a deeply felt sense of moral superiority of Chinese over Americans. Americans may have money and gadgets and Disneyland, but Chinese have the cultural formula for correct and enduring human relations, which are, ultimately, what really matters.

The people whose life histories I include here shared some of these mixed attitudes toward Americans, of course, for they permeate Taiwan's culture. If there is one serious drawback to my method of learning about Taiwan's working class through life histories, it is that because I am an American whose nationality has negative associations, the impact of the extremely important American influence in Taiwan was not easy for informants to speak about. People who knew me only slightly would think it an act of rudeness toward me as a person, and possibly slightly dangerous, to mention the military bombings, corporate exploitation, and interference in foreign relations my country has perpetrated on Taiwan.

As I pondered this problem in the field, I realized that nearly every American anthropologist is caught in the same paradox. When we study a society that has been strongly affected by American political, economic, and cultural influences, those who will speak to us are, by and large, those who do not see, or out of courtesy do not discuss with us, their negative consequences. Those who see them most clearly may avoid us, or be silent. What would an Indian anthropologist have heard from my Chinese subjects? How much of what I have learned stems from my Americanness, and how much from their Chineseness? I shall never know.

Fieldwork and Politics

For me, the most difficult part of becoming more like a Chinese was setting aside my interest in politics. Americans, I realized for the first time in Taiwan, discuss politics a great deal, treating an election, a government scandal, or the latest war as a subject for small talk, like the weather or the fortunes of a favorite ball team. Most Americans speak as though they believe their government is their personal business, about which they have every right to have opinions. Such outspokenness on matters of state shocks

Chinese people in Taiwan, where it is not only in bad taste but downright risky to criticize the government. An educated person is expected to know the government's position on important matters and to repeat it when necessary. Uneducated persons (and women) are expected to refrain from commenting on "national affairs" altogether.

Taiwanese men especially *do* discuss politics, of course, but much more cautiously than Americans, reserving their opinions for trusted intimates. A very large and efficient network of party activists, secret police, and paid informers is quite likely to pick up and report criticism of the authorities to those same authorities. Serious criticism is seen as evidence of Communism, and hence of treason. Investigation, blacklisting from government employment, prison, or death have been the well-known consequences of such treason, so people watch their tongues.

Taiwan's politics continued to fascinate me, however, and at first I probably contributed to the "pushy" image of Americans by excessive probing for people's "real" political opinions. I soon learned that most people were simply not going to trust me that far. The very fact that I had asked openly about such matters showed I had no political sense and might get my respondent into trouble. As I modeled my behavior to resemble that of a Chinese, I too learned to hold my tongue, waiting for the occasional quiet political confidence.

Becoming a Little Chinese

Despite an understandable strain of Chinese antipathy toward Americans, despite the cultural reticence of Chinese toward strangers, and despite my limitations as a fieldworker, time and my efforts to learn other ways of behaving have made me some good friends in Taiwan. At times, Chinese friends remark that I have treated them as a Chinese would; on a few occasions, in a dark taxi or on the telephone, I have been mistaken for a Chinese. From people who esteem their own ways so highly, this is praise.

But becoming a little like a Chinese has made me uncomfortably conscious of a contradiction between an acceptance of that intimacy and the anthropological goal of revealing a whole culture, not merely the smooth formal face it presents to strangers. Does one not betray trust by publishing friendly confidences? Friendship with such an end in view seems insincere: friends keep one's secrets, especially in China. Educated Chinese, knowing their society has held an internationally weak and culturally devalued position for over a century, sometimes resent the apparent "objectivity" that shows Chinese culture "warts and all" to the outside world.

I think the working-class people who have told me their life stories will be tolerant of what I have learned from our friendships, even if they were to disagree with my conclusions or object to my airing of some of their national dirty linen. Their tolerance comes from self-confidence, a class culture little affected by alien values, and from their clear-eyed attitude that Taiwan's current society has both its strengths and weaknesses, its points of pride and occasions of embarrassment. When I told them I wanted to write as honestly as possible, even about bad things, they agreed that only in that way can future generations learn from them.

[3]

An Island of Immigrants

Taiwan, a subtropical island 240 miles long by 90 miles wide, lies off the south China coast. It has been populated, and its history and culture shaped, by four great human migrations. The earliest immigrants, whose living descendants are known as the Taiwan Aborigines, began to arrive in the island as early as fifteen thousand years ago. Until the nineteenth century, small groups of potential migrants continued to land in Taiwan after sea voyages from the Philippines (de Beauclaire 1971:31). In earlier times, others came from the islands and coasts of south China, some of which are less than 100 miles away. Today, about a quarter million Aborigines inhabit the island's lofty, forested mountains and the poorer sections of its cities and towns. The next important wave of migrations, of southern Chinese from the provinces of Fujian and Guangdong, began about four hundred years ago. Arriving in large numbers from the early seventeenth century to the end of the nineteenth, their descendants, known today as the Taiwanese, are still the majority population, numbering, in 1987, about seventeen million. For fifty years, from 1895 to 1945, several hundred thousand Japanese came to labor, govern, and do business in Taiwan as part of the Japanese empire. Although at the end of World War II these migrants returned to Japan, Japanese influence on older Taiwanese and Aborigines remains strong. The last immigrants, also Chinese, are a mixed group who fled from the mainland of China to the island after losing the long Chinese civil war between supporters of the Nationalist party and those of the Communist party, in 1949. They and their children born in Taiwan, referred to as "Mainlanders," made up over two million people in 1987.

Each successive group has brought changes to those who came before, as old settlers and new struggled for resources and the power to control them.

Until the Chinese began to arrive in substantial numbers in the seventeenth century, those struggles were probably less intense, for the island had plenty of room to allow the small Aboriginal communities to follow their culturally diverse paths. Differences between older and newer arrivals—in population density, ecological adjustment, economic system, political organization, social relations, and beliefs—have shaped the culture that the immigrants have created for themselves. The Taiwan version of Chinese culture, and therefore the lives of the people in this study, are the complex products of the relations, peaceful and otherwise, among these differing peoples, and of the accommodations each has had to make to the others.

The turbulent coexistence of all four groups has been a vivid part of the life experience of older living islanders. Stories of war between Taiwanese and Aborigines were passed on to me by people who remember such times, or whose parents did; as late as 1930, an armed Aborigine rebellion against the Japanese revived old Chinese fears of their tribal neighbors. In this century, first the Japanese and then the Mainlanders have influenced Taiwanese lives through government and commerce. The Mainlanders themselves, recently arrived and uninterested in the island's history, are nevertheless affected by it and by the shock their arrival has caused the previous inhabitants. Since the beginning of Japanese rule in 1895, Taiwan's economy has been made increasingly complex and productive because of the interplay among peoples. By the 1930s the Japanese had replaced traditional agriculture with an early green revolution while, in the 1960s, the Mainlanders helped industry overshadow agriculture as the primary source of wealth. Tracing the experiences of the four groups of migrants reveals the historical background of our subjects' lives, as well as Taiwan's emergence as an industrialized country with a highly complex culture.

Prehistoric and Aborigine Settlement

The Chinese call Taiwan's Aborigines "Mountain People" because they now occupy the island's central mountainous regions. Once the only inhabitants, their ancestors first occupied the island fifteen thousand years ago, as proven by the archaeological discovery of stone tools from that time (Chang 1977:486). Such early inhabitants were probably foragers and fisherfolk, doubtless related to the people who left similar tools on the south China coast at about the same period.

Considerably later, by about 5,500 years ago (Chang 1977:85–91), people at Dapenkeng on the island's east coast were making and using a globular brown pottery marked with surface designs pressed into the wet clay that

[27]

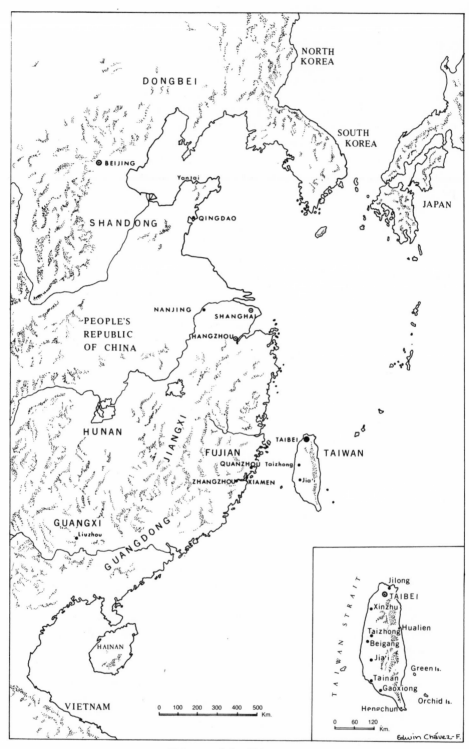

Taiwan and the China coast

looks a good deal like ceramics found on the coast of southern China and Southeast Asia. The cordage with which the pottery designs were made suggests a familiarity with rope making for other purposes—fishnets (there are stone "sinkers" as well) and lashings for canoes—while stone adzes for woodworking hint at the construction of boats. The folk of Dapenkeng may have been a seagoing people living on fish, wild plants, and, perhaps, on domesticated root crops like taro. If this is so, horticulture may have arisen one thousand years earlier in this region than in northern China. Such a pattern fits into archaeological and linguistic knowledge of the wider Pacific area to which contemporary Aborigines clearly belong. Their languages belong to the Austronesian family, which includes Polynesian and some Melanesian tongues, Indonesian, and even the language of distant Madagascar. It is even possible that this great radiation of Austronesian tongues may have had its source in Taiwan (W. Wang 1985).

After reaching Taiwan, the Aborigines did not cease to visit and exchange genes, crops, techniques, and ideas with their fellow Austronesians. Chinese historians record their voyages to the mainland and the Philippines late in the twelfth and thirteenth centuries (Davidson [1967]:563); contact with the Philippines seems to have been especially significant, continuing for some until the mid-nineteenth century (de Beauclaire 1971:47). Although there is little left at present of the seagoing tradition for most of the Mountain People, on offshore Orchid Island men still construct deep-sea canoes of lashed-together adze-cut planking in which they brave unpredictable winds and rocky coasts, after the custom of their fathers.

By a thousand years ago, these people were building stone terraces on the steep mountains in central Taiwan to grow millet and tubers (Triestman 1972:74)—a sure sign of population pressure on the more easily cultivated lowlands and of the abandonment by part of the population of a maritime existence. Another change in basic food production, which brought about the present-day reliance on the sweet potato, must have occurred some time after the Spanish transmitted that New World plant to the Pacific in the sixteenth century. The availability of sweet potatoes, which proved very productive in Taiwan, may have triggered a further rise in the Aboriginal population at just the time the Chinese began to compete with them for land.

Although the Chinese commonly lump the Mountain People together as a single ethnic category, they do not constitute a homogeneous group. The Dutch counted 293 local groups in the vicinity of their settlement in the mid-1600s (Davidson [1967]:562), which, like contemporary Aboriginal communities, were probably only loosely affiliated with their neighbors. In recent times, the Mountain People have lived in small kinship or residential communities that sometimes fought and sometimes allied themselves with similar neighboring villages. Their slash-and-burn cropping methods and wide-ranging hunting activities encouraged frequent group and individual moves and considerable cultural variation. With little social differentiation of rich and poor, or men and women, these were egalitarian communities with close ties to the natural world and an economic system based on reciprocity and mutual support. The generosity this culture teaches and values can still be seen in the open and hospitable ways of today's Aborigines, who cheerfully offer drinks from a common bottle of moonshine, invite strangers for a meal, and expect to share one's pack of cigarettes as they would freely do if the tobacco were their own.

Like other egalitarian horticulturalists living in autonomous villages, the Mountain People found it difficult to resolve some disputes, and in the past they were often at war with their neighbors. Bringing home the heads of dead enemies to display as skull trophies became a goal of war and a sign of bravery among men.

After millennia of slowly occupying the island, learning and using its resources, and creating patterns of social relations and beliefs that they still value today, Aborigines began to encounter competition for their land from entirely alien peoples. These were the Chinese and Japanese, who were impelled to venture forth by expanding populations and economies in Asia, and the Portuguese, Spanish, and Dutch, who were stimulated to exploration by the emerging capitalist economy of Europe.

Although the Chinese had first visited Taiwan in the seventh century, when they attempted to force local people to accept their overlordship, the island was apparently too remote to draw further Chinese attention until the sixteenth century. In 1564, in response to Taiwan-based Chinese and Japanese pirate attacks on China's coasts, the emperor of China claimed the island and settled a garrison in the south, near the present city of Tainan. Trade and colonists soon followed, beginning the process that has made Taiwan a part of the Chinese world.

While the Dutch were the first European colonists in Taiwan, other Europeans also explored its possibilities. The Portuguese, who merely visited in the early 1500s, described Taiwan as an *ilha formosa*—a "beautiful island," giving Taiwan its often-used alias, "Formosa."[1] The Spanish established a short-lived mission in northern Taiwan, from which they were driven by the Dutch in 1642.

1. The name Formosa, because it is not derived from Chinese, is the preferred English usage for some Taiwanese who advocate independence for the island and freedom from Nationalist Chinese rule.

The founding of a Dutch colony in 1621 was the result both of an increasingly aggressive Dutch policy in East Asia and of the Chinese authorities' desire to keep European traders out of their mainland ports. The Dutch, apparently satisfied with this foothold in a fruitful and strategically located island, set about building a base for their East Asian trade and for piracy against the trade of the Spanish and Portuguese. They were to remain in Taiwan until 1662, when an army of Chinese pirates seeking a safe haven drove them out. During these years the Dutch administered (to their considerable profit) the land and people—Chinese and Aborigines— of a large area of southwest Taiwan, encouraging a mainland trade in Aborigine forest products and in the rice and sugar that immigrant Chinese were beginning to produce.

The most enduring influence of the Dutch was, by fostering trade, to increase the flow of Chinese immigrants to Taiwan and to make the Chinese authorities more eager to control this dangerous outpost off their turbulent southeast coast. After the Chinese ousted the Europeans during the late seventeenth century, the Aborigines stood alone against China's vast pool of prospective emigrants, its complex economy, and its sophisticated methods of administration. While the Dutch had given them a short-lived religious tradition, some literacy, and firearms, the Chinese would give them their future.

That future, to make a sad tale brief, meant being pushed out of the low-lying plains and valleys, where Chinese agriculture was most successful, and into the forested mountains in a guerrilla war that lasted for centuries. As the Chinese population and economy expanded or foreign trade offered a price for upland products, the Aborigines lost ground, though they fought for every foot and decorated their villages with thousands of bleaching Chinese skulls. The hatred this bitter struggle engendered in the Chinese was most clearly expressed in the custom, common in the early 1890s, of cannibalism.

> One horrible feature of the campaign against the savages was the sale by the Chinese in open market of savage flesh. . . . After killing a savage, the head was commonly severed from the body and exhibited to those who were not on hand to witness the prior display of slaughter and mutilation. The body was then either divided among its captors and eaten, or sold to wealthy Chinese and even to high officials, who disposed of it in a like manner. The kidney, liver, heart, and soles of the feet were considered the most desirable portions, and were ordinarily cut up into very small pieces, boiled, and eaten somewhat in the form of a soup. The flesh and bones were boiled, and the former made into a sort of jelly. (Davidson [1967]:254)

In this century, modern administrations have controlled the Aborigines so that warfare is no longer practiced among themselves or against the Chinese. Limited education and social services have been provided for them, and their contacts with Chinese and others are carefully monitored. The Japanese forced them militarily into a vast reservation that they were not permitted to leave, though Japanese could enter, mostly as policemen and schoolteachers. Since the beginning of Chinese Nationalist control in 1945, Aborigines have been free to move down into the lowlands and cities, and the government has given many retired Nationalist soldiers land in the mountains. These men often marry Aborigine women, seriously limiting the marriage possibilities of Aborigine men. In the mountains, the Aborigines' old ways recede fast before the tide of economic development that brings more and more fruit growers, lumberers, power-generation workers, and military men to settle among them.

Those who move to the plains join a stream of earlier Mountain People who have assimilated to Chinese society by the adoption of Chinese languages, dress, and customs. They do not mix easily with the ethnocentric Chinese, who frequently stereotype them as "uncivilized" even when they adopt the majority culture. The Chinese surname that many "sinified" Aborigines were given in the past—Pan—is a character meaning "barbarian," with another beside it indicating the category "insect." While a few urbanized Mountain People have achieved fame as athletes or entertainers, most still experience social and occupational discrimination and poverty.

The Taiwanese: Pioneers from South China

The Chinese who migrated to Taiwan in earlier centuries have come recently to develop a sense of common identity as Taiwanese. Those who crossed the Taiwan Straits to settle the island, however, set out as women and men of Quanzhou or Changzhou or Xiamen cities, or as people of another of the many local communities of the south China coast. What they became in Taiwan was the product, in part, of the south Chinese culture they brought with them, of the pressure the Chinese state exerted on the remote island, and of the economy of the busy merchant cities of China's commercial coast. Conditions in China prompted, quickened, and at times controlled their emigration, and China remained a refuge for those who failed to adapt to Taiwan's rough frontier society.

But local conditions also shaped the Taiwanese: the violent contact with alien Aborigines, the distance from centers of state control, the new economic opportunities of a land not wholly monopolized by the rich and powerful. In this, they shared much with other south Chinese regional subcultures formed in remote mountain areas recently conquered from tribal peoples. Taiwan, however, differed from the outback of Guangxi or Yunnan provinces in being both well endowed for the production of valuable crops and well located to transport them to coastal markets. Its maritime position, exposing it to many influences, also made Taiwan more cosmopolitan than most parts of China. The Chinese government's desire to guard its frontiers against foreign encroachment; the Chinese merchants' search for profit from a rich agriculture, and the Chinese peasants' hope of acquiring land that would support their families might all be realized in this, the richest of the Qing dynasty's immense territorial conquests.

These motives brought a flood of immigrants to Taiwan during the seventeenth, eighteenth, and early nineteenth centuries. This was a period during which tendencies in government and economy converged to encourage the settlement of newly opened land by families working small landholdings with their own labor (Marks 1984:32ff.), a pattern that the Taiwanese saw as the ideal basis for a household. Some people, early in the migration or in a few favored locations, were able simply to strike out and pioneer as rugged individualists. The majority, however, settled as tenants on land that the government, attempting to encourage Chinese occupation, had sold or granted in large blocks to land speculators for further subdivision into family farms. Although the landlord held rights to the subsoil, the tenant had a permanent right to his parcel of land, from which he could not be evicted as long as he paid his rent (Wickberg 1981:212–13). Such tenancy was not quite ownership, but it was close enough to be very attractive to the many land-poor families of Fujian's sandy coast. Large areas were opened up by tenants brought in by land dealers, so that settlement of a new area was often rapid and the settlers were homogeneous in regional background. Some areas were settled through government grants to troops demobilized in Taiwan after having served in the military garrison.

Subcultural or ethnic variations among the immigrants were maintained or even accentuated by the discontinuous pattern of settlement and varying ecological adaptations they made in Taiwan. The Hakka minority, for example, found their niche in the foothill regions, where they specialized in upland agriculture, forestry, and skirmishes with the Aborigines. Such Hakka had little in common with the Hoklo (lowland, Fujianese) immigrants.

Increasingly, as Chinese settlement encountered Aborigine resistance, pioneering families banded together in fortified villages to clear and keep land. Often the ties that bound them into cohesive communities were

[33]

based on kinship or, if there were few kin ties among a group of migrants pioneering together, on fictive kinship that assumed a common ancestor for everyone sharing one of the few Chinese surnames. These ties were extended agnatically, creating strong kin groups in which men played all major roles. The strong tradition of patrilineality, long part of Chinese culture, was strengthened further by the constant need for physical defense on the frontier. A common mainland place of origin served as a bond to organize groups that had no basis for forming lineages, familiar local accent and custom supplying the necessary sense of connectedness.

Although lineages and villages of people of similar mainland origins needed a sense of solidarity to take and hold Aborigine land, they needed it as well to create effective work groups to clear the luxuriant forests and build the irrigation systems necessary to grow rice and sugar (Pasternak 1972). Taiwan's western plain is crossed by many short rivers falling rapidly to the sea which become raging torrents in the rainy season. Typhoons, with their destructive winds and flooding downpours, frequently wreak havoc in autumn on what has been built that year. Building and maintaining networks of canals with their necessary dikes and sluice gates required substantial numbers of coordinated, cooperative workers. Even running an irrigation system in good working order meant sharing the available water equitably and finding ways to resolve the disputes over land, water, and labor that inevitably arose.

Because the Chinese government apparatus was weak in most parts of Taiwan, and because in any case the state discouraged the use of its courts for local conflict resolution, Taiwanese pioneers generally depended for their rights on the strength of their village or kin group. While mediation could often resolve difficulties within a community, disputes among communities frequently led to feuds and to outright warfare (Lamley 1981). The men of one or several allied villages were quick to turn their strength to defending their land and water or to attacking those of others. Local alliances of lineages or villages were the strongest political bodies in the countryside, fighting, making peace, controlling important economic activities, and defining the rules by which their members lived. A family that did not belong to such a group was in serious danger.

Occasionally, the Chinese state attempted to exert the authority it claimed over these independent people, who then rebelled, raising arms against the imported mainland troops sent to "pacify" them. Rebellions resulted, too, when official corruption, completely uncontrolled by the distant central government, became intolerable. Especially during the eighteenth century, when rebellion was virtually continuous, Taiwan was known in Beijing, China's capital, as a hard-to-govern region with "an outbreak every three years and a rebellion every five."

In 1722 one of the greatest of these uprisings was sparked by the immigrant Zhou Yigui, who led the many people who were angered by a new government monopoly on camphor production. Together they drove all the officials out of Taiwan, crowned Zhou emperor of Taiwan, and began to set up a presumably more just system of government. In response, a large mainland army crushed the rebels, sent Zhou back to Beijing in a cage to be crucified, and laid waste the countryside. The devastations of war and the diseases that followed it were worsened by the unlucky chance of a violent typhoon that, in 1723, left "scarcely a building uninjured in the settlements near the coast" (Davidson [1967]:73).

In 1784 an even larger rebellion lasting nine months and killing a hundred thousand people grew out of a feud between Changzhou and Quanzhou branches of an immense secret society. It too was brutally put down—its leader was executed by being cut into a thousand pieces—and the countryside ravaged in "an exhibition of severity the like of which the island had never seen" (Davidson [1967]:78). Lesser episodes, with their recurring demands for independence from the Chinese, continued well into the nineteenth century.

Despite the frequent violence, peasants continued to plough their land, growing rice, sugar, and other valuable crops for export to Fujian's coastal cities. Most of the sugar consumed in northern China, and much of the rice eaten in Fujian, was grown in Taiwan, as was the "oilcake" of pressed-out peanuts used for fertilizer in Fujian (Davidson [1967]:66). Well-armed men harvested valuable timber and other forest products, from textile fibers to herbal medicines, and in the late nineteenth century more and more Chinese woodsmen distilled camphor from huge camphor trees for a growing Japanese market. At the same time, increasing American demand for green and oolong teas made this a profitable crop in north Taiwan. As tea grows best on cool, misty hillsides, more Aborigine forests were cleared for its cultivation, more small peasant families sharecropped on the edge of Chinese civilization, and more big landowners and tea merchants drew profits from Aborigine land and Taiwanese labor.

From the beginning of large-scale Chinese immigration in the seventeenth century, most peasant migrants were firmly embedded in an embryonic capitalist economy run by a class of state-aided entrepreneurs. Before a peasant family could secure its own subsistence, it was obliged to pay out rent or taxes, in money or in kind, for the use of the land. In Taiwan, local community power was sometimes great enough so that weak state agents were unable to collect taxes; it was this power, perhaps, as much as the island's natural agricultural advantages that allowed immigrants to flourish there. But landlords with their private armies could usually collect rents, siphoning off much of the wealth created in Taiwan's countryside.

Because Taiwan's economy was built on land speculation and exports, the use of money and the habit of calculating the costs of land, labor, and goods permeated the way of life of settlers even in remote valleys. As confrontations between Chinese and Aborigines became less those of war and more those of business, Chinese familiarity with money, officially sanctioned land transactions, interest on loans, and wage labor enabled them regularly to gain over the tribal people. Although capitalist relations often operated to the peasants' disadvantage in their dealings with landlords and merchants, the Taiwanese could profitably apply what they knew of such relations in their dealings with their former enemies.

Taiwanese sophistication in an economy with some capitalist patterns also gave the island's people an advantage when they began to produce for international markets. During the early nineteenth century, European capitalists had chafed at the restrictions the Chinese state imposed on their trade with China. When they could gain no entry diplomatically or economically, the British, in the 1840s, began simply to bombard coastal cities until the Chinese agreed to allow their trade—the British wanted especially to market opium in China—to be undertaken on British terms. Once China was "opened," European and American interest soon turned to Taiwan's small tea trade. Here, capitalist elements of Chinese tradition, which were especially strong in Taiwan, enabled island Chinese to organize rapidly to meet the new demand and to maintain control over a good deal of the profitable new export trade. Although Europeans and Americans entered Taiwan as tea merchants, they did not gain the kind of dominance that would have enabled non-Chinese to drain all the tea profits back to their homelands. Foreign merchants interested in other Taiwan commodities generally found they could not compete profitably with the already-established Chinese system. In the long run, it was more to the advantage of the peasant majority that the merchants and landlords who gained from their work were Chinese. Unlike foreigners, they might invest their gains in Taiwanese business, establish local schools, improve the roads and bridges, and be accountable in some measure to local pressure.

To meet both island and export needs, many small industries and commercial enterprises grew up. Sugar had to be refined, rice milled, camphor distilled, and indigo made into dye paste. As steam shipping became important, coal mining was added to the extraction of gold and sulphur from the island's mountains. The Taiwanese drew on a long and rich Chinese tradition of practical science and engineering that enabled them to accomplish these and many other industrial tasks with a minimum of equipment, though with much labor (Hommel 1937). When new problems presented themselves, Chinese craftsmen invented ingenious solutions. One observant visitor described the extremely simple and clever manufacture of lead linings for tea boxes in these words: the visitor

> will find the chief workman standing beside a pot containing molten lead, and on the floor may be seen . . . two tiles, one on top of the other. Commencing operations, the Chinese with one hand lifts one side of the top tile up slightly, and with the other hand dips a little of the molten metal out of the pot and with a dexterous movement dashes it in between the two tiles; then, instantly dropping the upper one, and stepping upon it, he applies sufficient pressure to force the melted lead to spread over the tiles. The metal hardens in a few seconds; the upper tile is again lifted . . . these plates, after having been trimmed, are soldered together in the shape of a box. (Davidson [1967]:386).

The tea trade alone required many specialized workers: farm families who planted and cared for the bushes; tea-picking girls and women who selected the correct leaves; carriers who rushed them down the hills for processing; owners and laborers in small tea-drying factories; makers of sacks, baskets, lead liners, and wooden boxes for manufacture and shipping; porters, clerks, and buyers to bring the finished tea to the big urban merchants; and sailors to start it on its journey to American tea tables. Taiwanese labor was supplemented in busy seasons by throngs of migrant laborers from the mainland (Davidson 1903:55), who were housed and fed by local boardinghouse keepers and "entertained" in teahouses and brothels. Other agricultural, industrial, and mining activities produced similar arrays of occupations and opportunities for small business. Not all business was small, however, and Ng observed that "in a frontier and migrant society such as Taiwan, merchants wielded greater influence in the urban communities than their counterparts in the mainland" (1983:182).

Many Taiwanese, then, engaged in wage work or small-scale commerce and industry, often combined with agriculture. There was no sharp break between a purely agricultural life in the countryside and a commercial existence in the towns and cities, though towns housed fewer farmers and more families who provided services and luxuries for the relatively rich who clustered there. Competition, shady practices, the attempt to profit on a deal at another's expense were a part of the daily lives of the people enmeshed in this small-scale capitalism, although generosity to acquaintances, paying one's debts, and a desire for a reputation as an honest

[37]

businessperson probably helped keep these antisocial tendencies in check then, as they do today.

Many of the occupations the Taiwanese pursued in these early centuries, as in the present, were carried out by families, with the assistance, in larger enterprises, of hired labor. Every family must have hoped at least to achieve a stable balance between having sufficient means of production (land, production equipment, etc.) to support a family, and enough labor in the form of able-bodied family members to use them efficiently. Families then as now hoped that their capital and labor would earn them the money to buy more means of production and raise larger, multigenerational families modeled after the households of merchants and landlords. While this sometimes happened, for many just keeping a balance between resources and people required both hard work and good fortune. Too many daughters and too few sons, a parent's early death, or an infertile marriage might spell poverty as surely as loss of land to a moneylender or the destruction of the family fishing boat in a typhoon. Whether they were at war or competing in the market, life meant struggle, confrontation, and a constant search for security.

As Taiwanese people shaped their culture to meet these challenges, they came to rely very heavily on two institutions: the local community, defined either by lineage ties, common origin, or simple coresidence; and the patrilineal coresident family. From the abundant evidence of present-day religious beliefs and activities, we can reconstruct something of how Taiwanese people themselves must have perceived these institutions and their place in organized society.

Taiwanese popular religion has long centered on rituals performed for three categories of spiritual beings: ancestors, gods, and ghosts (A. Wolf 1974). Family ceremonies, even when they focus on the living, always include references to the dead men and women ancestral to the family. In many households, these honored dead receive prayers and offerings daily at handsome living-room altars. The worship of ancestors, representing a family's deceased patrilineal kin but also representing, abstractly, the orderly structure of family life, focuses people's attention on the importance of belonging to a well-defined and well-organized family. Worshiping their ancestors situates people clearly in history and in society and emphasizes the ongoing rights and responsibilities of living members of families toward one another.

Gods, by contrast, are worshiped in elaborate, community-built temples—colorful, cool, and fragrant with incense—that were at one time the most beautiful places ordinary, hard-laboring folk ever saw. Imagined as a hierarchy of heavenly bureaucrats who rule the ordinary world, gods also

embody the social power of the officials and the wealthy. There are benevolent and vindictive gods, compassionate and grasping ones, mighty ones
and those of limited power, just as in society the ordinary person might
observe good and corrupt officials, men of great wealth and power, and
lesser lights.

A community, whether a whole village or one of its parts, a town or a
city neighborhood, typically sets up a temple for the worship of the god or
goddess who acts as its patron and protector. Community temples are social
centers, used not only for worship and ritual celebration, but also as
playgrounds for children and meeting places for the elderly, and, in the
past, as classrooms, for military practice, and for the storage of arms. Local
gods are expected to guard against war, sickness, and disaster; in prayers
one petitions them first for *pieng an* (T) (peace and quiet). Such deities—
powerful images of local solidarity—represent the community itself.

In addition to the ancestors and gods, elegantly housed in lineage halls,
altars, or their own temples, Taiwanese pay ritual respect to ghosts, symbolically represented as homeless, and worshiped only out of doors. These
are the spirits of the dead who linger on, hungry, filthy, and malicious
toward the living, because they died outside of society's important institutions. People with no descendants to care for them as ancestors become
ghosts after death, as do soldiers killed in battle far from home whose bones
lie unburied. The drowned, the suicides, the girls who die before marriage makes them at least potential ancestors, and many others whose lives
do not fit the tight patrilineal/communal model are all doomed to a wander-
ing and dangerous existence after death. Ghosts symbolize, too, those
living people who have neither family nor community: beggars, the homeless, drifting migrant workers, strangers of all kinds (Weller 1985). The
social world of past and present Taiwanese is divided symbolically into one's
own and similar properly organized families, enduring and reliable, symbolized by ancestors; the powerful worldly authorities, who might punish
but who can be persuaded and sometimes bribed to benevolence, symbolized by gods; and strangers of unknown background, objects of suspicion
and dislike, represented by malevolent ghosts.

The Japanese: Taiwan as a Sugar Colony, 1895–1945

Toward the end of the nineteenth century, Taiwan began to feel the force
of expanding imperialism in East Asia. In the face of this threat, the
emperor raised the island to the rank of a province and entrusted it to an
unusually progressive governor, Liu Mingquan, to strengthen Chinese

administrative hold on the population. Liu built China's first railroad and a telegraph system, introduced electricity to the new provincial capital of Taibei, and pioneered a modern, state-run coal mine, along with many other reforms. Liu's efforts were insufficient to avert the many pressures that foreigners were bringing to bear on China, however. As foreign shipping increased in the Taiwan Straits, so did shipwrecks. Aborigines, ever more hostile to intruders, began to massacre survivors who landed on their shores, provoking outraged foreign ambassadors to demand that the Chinese control "their" natives. As the Chinese clearly could not do so, and as Taiwan was in any case a promising acquisition for any imperializing nation, it was only a matter of time before one of them attempted to include the island in its empire. Eventually, the Japanese outmaneuvered the French, British, Americans, and others interested in carving off slices of China, securing sovereignty over the island through the Treaty of Shimonoseki in 1895.

Taking possession was another matter. With Beijing's encouragement, members of the more prosperous class in Taiwan proclaimed an independent Republic of Taiwan, hoping that some republican Western nation would therefore be motivated to save it from Japan. The Republic lasted only a few weeks, for its leaders were not committed to its cause. Their followers, drawn from the many Taiwanese who were always ready to oppose outside authority, fought the Japanese entry into the island and remained as pockets of resistance (and banditry) for several years. Women joined in some of the early battles and served as spies for the resistance (Davidson [1967]:328–30). Aborigines continued sporadic opposition into the 1930s as the Japanese systematically invaded their territory with heavy modern armaments (Bodley 1982:56–59; see also Ch'en 1977).

The Japanese who came to rule Taiwan were riding the crest of an extraordinary accomplishment. In the previous thirty years, an alliance of samurai and merchant classes had turned Japan from an archaic, agricultural backwater into a strongly centralized, rapidly industrializing nation aiming for international equality with advanced capitalist countries of the West. Such nations had official or unofficial empires that supplied them with cheap raw materials, markets for their consumer goods, and an income from colonial taxes. To compete, Japan needed the same advantages, and China was the obvious target. Fresh from the successes of reorganizing Japan, these empire builders set out to make Taiwan not just a profitable but a model colony that would show the world that Japanese culture was as powerful and progressive as any.

Economic development would be the foundation. The Japanese home government invested large sums in Taiwan's future productivity: railroads, harbors, and other transportation and communications systems were built, agricultural research and extension work was undertaken, the health and skills of the population were improved through medical and educational services. Japanese capitalists began modern food processing, mining, and other industries based on local raw materials. Trade was redirected to or through Japan, with cheap Taiwan rice enabling Japan to shift much of its own population from agriculture to industry. Newly wage-earning Japanese eagerly bought cheap Taiwan sugar grown in new irrigation systems paid for with Taiwanese taxes. Built to meet Japan's needs, it was an economic system operated by capitalists and state functionaries in smooth cooperation. While business profits went mostly to Japan, much of the tax collected in Taiwan was spent there on the infrastructure and administration that had made increased productivity possible. For Taiwanese peasants, life became much safer, healthier, a bit more comfortable.

The new political system, tailored to the needs of the economy but also to Japanese ideas of justice, also hastened the colony's rapid development. Efficiency and fair regulations and laws were fostered by well-trained and dedicated civil servants, police, military forces, and schoolteachers. Soon, except for the Aborigines, some of whom were treated very harshly, the population rapidly accepted Japanese officials, flocking to the incorruptible new courts with old and new grievances, and allowing Japanese officials and civilians to live safely among them (Davidson [1967]:594). Japanese officials are remembered today as strict but fair. "When the Japanese caught a thief, they'd put him in a box, all bent over, for the night. That would fix him! We hardly ever saw thieves in those days. *They* knew what they were doing!" an old gentleman once cackled to me when he saw a policeman.

Enforcement of the laws was much simplified by the system of household registration the Japanese had perfected for their own use. Still in operation today, the law requires every family to register with the police, giving information about all current members, including name, age, sex, relationship to household head, marital status, educational level achieved, occupation, and numerous other details, and to update that information yearly. Such data are invaluable for government planning purposes, and were and are of great utility to the police in controlling both crime and political opposition.

Whether out of respect for what was, after all, a somewhat similar culture, or simply to lessen the possibility of resistance to their policies, the Japanese did not attempt to alter radically Taiwanese culture and social structure. Landlord-tenant relations, patterns of inheritance, customs of marriage and adoption, and religious practices were permitted to continue largely unchanged. Indeed, as many Taiwanese customs were now upheld

[41]

by a functioning legal system, Japanese tolerance may be said to have fossilized them at a time when many practices might have been expected to change with the times. Despite the innovations of the Japanese regime, it had a generally conservative influence on basic institutions.

Even so, significant changes took place. Whereas in some parts of northern Taiwan about 70 percent of girl babies had previously been adopted out to other families as future wives for their sons, by the 1930s, after greater job opportunities for young people gave them more voice in their own marriages, girls and their adoptive brothers began to repudiate such arrangements. The adoption of baby daughters-in-law declined sharply thereafter (Wolf and Huang 1980:129, 193). Japanese officials prohibited some customs they found too distasteful. Footbinding, for example, was forbidden in order to protect the health of little girls, who sometimes died of gangrene from the painful and crippling process. An American who surveyed people in the sugar-growing Jianan Plain in the early 1950s noted that they still remembered warmly the Japanese engineer who designed the region's irrigation system, and that in consequence of their respect for the project, they were more reliant on science than on tradition and ancestor worship in their daily lives (Raper 1953:165).

Although the Taiwanese were treated fairly and equally among themselves, they were not accorded equality with the Japanese. Racism, an inevitable by-product of imperialism, set limits to the role the Taiwanese could play in society. In the early decades of Japanese rule, they were excluded from political participation and even from the study of law, ignored by Japanese businesses except as low-level manual workers, and forbidden to marry Japanese. Unlike Japanese, they could receive flogging as a legal punishment. Although some of these forms of discrimination were ameliorated during the 1930s, none was forgotten. As many Japanese lived in housing built by their government or business employers, a residential segregation emerged that could still readily be seen in the 1970s in the discontinuous pattern of Japanese-style and Taiwanese-style housing in cities. The educational system, intended to create a more literate and loyal population, was initially segregated, though nothing prevented well-to-do Chinese from sending their sons to school in Japan. After 1922, Japanese-speaking children of either group could enter the better Japanese schools on the island. Taiwanese who studied beyond elementary education were channeled into teaching and medicine, "safety-valves" for the few Taiwanese allowed upward mobility (Tsurumi 1977:77).

A small stratum of elite, Japanized Taiwanese emerged either from wealthy families who could afford education or from families for whom the new schools were a path out of poverty. They taught the Taiwanese children, doctored the Taiwanese sick, ran small businesses, and slowly came to fill in the lower ranks of technicians in larger, Japanese-run concerns. Only the most Japanized of these, however, fully assimilated into the Japanese community.

Japanese discrimination had numerous causes. The Japanese clearly detested some Chinese habits: a government publication aimed at showing the English-speaking reader the best of *Progressive Formosa* described the state of local markets as "more than enough to make any Japanese instantaneously sick" (Government of Formosa 1926:79); they punished the near-unconscious Chinese custom of spitting in the streets so severely that many urban Taiwanese still think it disgusting, too. Discrimination had a class basis as well: the majority of immigrant Japanese were urban and middle class, while most Taiwanese were peasants, and elite Japanese felt far superior even to Japanese peasants (Hane 1982:8). The Japanese were especially ethnocentric and ultranationalist at that time as the only Asian society to be holding its own with Europeans. But, whatever the superficial reasons for Japanese discrimination might be, the logic of colonization required that if Taiwan was to be a colony that sent more wealth to Japan than it got back, its people would have to be seen as, and to believe themselves to be, inferior to the Japanese.

Not all Japanese, however, wanted such a relationship. Especially in the 1920s and 1930s, more liberal and democratic Japanese favored greater equality, including full Taiwanese political participation, home rule for the island, and economic reforms that would assist the peasants. These ideas appeared in Japanese publications in Taiwan and were encountered directly by the many Taiwanese who traveled freely to Japan. Socialist and Communist ideas circulating widely in Asia gave ideological focus to working-class and peasant movements for higher wages and lower rents. In these decades, Taiwanese people also became aware of the ideological struggles in south China between the Chinese Communist and Nationalist parties. Educated Taiwanese experienced an exciting sense of both reformist and radically new possibilities for the future, and their feelings toward the country that had freed them intellectually while oppressing them politically and economically were deeply ambivalent.

Developing pressures for democracy in Taiwan were sharply curtailed in the late 1930s by militarist and extreme nationalist responses to similar pressures in Japan. As the empire geared for war, first with China and then against competing European and American imperialist forces in Asia, Taiwan's people were pushed harder to sacrifice for the emperor, take Japanese names, and be fully loyal. Traditional religious celebrations were abruptly suppressed, and people were ordered to worship Shinto deities in public

ceremonies and on their home altars. Opportunities for expressing dissident views or organizing political opposition vanished, creating resentment
and a deepening sense of oppression.

The war between China and Japan, which lasted from 1937 until 1945,
brought a resurgence of Chinese nationalism to many Taiwanese, while the
sufferings and privations of that war created widespread discontent. Of the
two hundred thousand Taiwanese who served the emperor in the war, more
than thirty thousand died (*Free China Journal* August 5, 1984:1). American
forces bombed Taiwan's cities repeatedly, cutting off vital supplies in the
last months before the atomic bombing of Hiroshima and Nagasaki ended
the war. By time of the surrender, many Taiwanese were disillusioned with
the Japanese empire, others had become more Japanese than ever, and the
rest simply did not know what they felt.

The more than three hundred thousand Japanese civilians, some of them
farmers and ordinary workers, but mostly clerks, schoolteachers, businessmen, and bureaucrats and their families, were rounded up and, within
weeks, were off the island. Many had been born in Taiwan or had lived most
of their lives there. Some, who had never been to Japan, had no real home
to return to. These refugees, forced to leave Taiwan for the rubble of
postwar Japan, must often have longed for their peaceful and prosperous
days on that lovely island; Taiwan remains today a favorite vacation spot for
Japanese tourists.

Even before the war was over, an agreement among Franklin Roosevelt,
Joseph Stalin, Winston Churchill, and Jiang Jieshi (Chiang Kai-shek) set-
tled Taiwan's future. It was to be restored to Chinese sovereignty; the
Taiwanese were not asked for their opinion on the matter.

Fifty years of Japanese rule had had a profound effect on the island,
nearly doubling its population, to six million, and multiplying its productivity manyfold. They had engendered from its mainly agricultural population
a modern-educated middle class with a cosmopolitan outlook and an identity as a people who were not just descendants of regional Chinese immigrants, but not exactly Japanese, either. There must have been a moment
when, knowing they would soon be under Chinese rule again, Taiwanese
could assume themselves simply to be Chinese. That moment lasted until
shortly after the Mainlanders arrived.

The Coming of the Mainlanders, 1945

October 25 is now a national holiday in Taiwan, known as Retrocession
Day—literally a "Day of Brilliant Return"—commemorating the ceding

[44]

back to China of sovereignty after Japan's surrender. In December 1945, when Chinese troops landed in Taiwan to take possession of the island for the Nationalist government, Taiwanese turned out by the thousands to welcome them. The welcome quickly soured as the Taiwanese, used to well-disciplined Japanese soldiers, encountered an ill-equipped and disorderly mob, draped with cooking equipment and often bare-footed, who represented the new regime. Such troops had terrorized the mainland Chinese countryside through which they passed—raping, looting, killing people and animals, and shanghaiing young men as soldiers or porters. They saw no reason to behave better among people who had been part of the hated Japanese empire. Mainland troops ran riot in Taiwan for the next several years; they were armed men against whose insults and injuries there was no reliable redress.

It was not only the foot soldiers who treated the Taiwanese, in the words of a recent Taiwanese historian, as "slaves without a country" (Shi 1979:706). The Nationalist official in charge, Chen Yi, quickly seized all Japanese property, public and private, which the Taiwanese had hoped would revert to them, and considerable Taiwanese private property as well. He and his underlings shipped large stocks of raw materials, factory machinery, Japanese military supplies, and even metals from public buildings and the telegraph system to Hong Kong and Shanghai, where they sold them at large personal profit. They held wealthy Taiwanese for ransom (Kerr 1965:191–93) and stole outright from the poor.

On February 28, 1947 (known as "2:28"), rebellion against these extortionist tactics burst out after Mainlander soldiers shot a woman peddler for selling cigarettes illegally. With Japanese Imperial Army swords, Taiwanese men roamed the streets of Taibei, taking Mainlander heads, while Nationalist soldiers machine-gunned bystanders at busy crossroads (Kerr 1965:250–300; see also Shi 1979: 749–80). For a few days, by a coordinated effort, the Taiwanese seized many of the important urban centers, with high school and university students and their elders in the Japanese-educated professional class providing much of the leadership.

Soon, however, military force and deceptive promises from the Nationalists persuaded the Taiwanese to lay aside their arms and to open negotiations. As a participant told me bitterly, "Under the Japanese, we learned to trust the word of the authorities. The Nationalists betrayed that trust; they will never have it again." Between ten and twenty thousand activists were rounded up and shot—by the sides of roads, from bridges, at a large open racetrack. The Nationalists hunted down the survivors of this bloodbath during the following months, sending many more to torture and jail. In a few weeks, the liberal-minded, educated, and generally pro-

Japanese new middle class was virtually destroyed. People whose father, brother, or aunt had been implicated in the events of 2:28 were barred from government work, including schoolteaching, and remained under a dangerous cloud of official suspicion for decades. The government's violent response to the 2:28 uprising eliminated much of the potential Taiwanese leadership, terrorized the population, and left the Mainlanders firmly in control.

In the autumn of 1949 the island's reeling social system was shocked again as the Nationalists were driven by the Communists off the mainland of China into Taiwan. Another purge followed, in which the supporters of the Nationalist clique headed by Jiang Jieshi hunted down "Communists"—that is, anyone he suspected of disloyalty to him. Taiwanese distrust of the new government deepened.

To understand why these latest Chinese immigrants entered Taiwan so violently, we must briefly examine the events that led up to the Communist success and Nationalist failure in China. For, while Taiwan under Japanese rule was peacefully becoming a safer, more prosperous, and more technologically advanced place in which to live, the people of the China mainland were experiencing imperialist attacks, civil war, and social chaos on a staggering scale.

China's last imperial dynasty, the Qing, fell easily from power in 1911 after a century in which population pressure, foreign invasions of its economy, and governmental inflexibility had lost it any popular support. The empire segmented into many natural economic and political regions headed by various parties and warlords. As all thinking Chinese could readily see, these smaller units were even more vulnerable to foreign penetration than the tired old empire; foreigners, seeing it too, expanded their activities. This brought wealth to a tiny number of Chinese landlords, industrialists, and financiers and increasing poverty to the peasants, textile workers, and servants whom they employed. Class differences, always wide in traditional China, became even more so in the capitalist-dominated coastal cities, where some Chinese could afford any imaginable luxury. At the same time, women and girls were worked to death in the silk mills, and young union organizers were unceremoniously shot in the street (Burchett 1976:54). As landlords moved to high-rolling cities like Shanghai, peasants were pressed harder for rent and given fewer customary protections against bad harvests or disasters. An intellectual gap grew between reactionary Chinese, who thought the teachings of the past were sufficient for the present, and those who believed that scientific thinking was necessary to compete with the West. Riven by regional, class, and ideological differences, China lost the capacity to maintain orderly social life and a minimal standard of living for its people.

Two political parties, the Nationalists (Guomindang, Kuomintang, or KMT) and the Communists emerged as the two competing political centers around which different classes rallied. The similarities between these parties are worth noting. Both were modeled in their organization after the Leninist Communist party of the Soviet Union, which sent advisors to both sides at various times. Both assumed it was the role of the party to guide society and the state, and that popular democracy must subordinate itself to that guidance. Both believed that only with national reunification—*one* China, with *one* party and *one* government—could the Chinese throw off foreign control. Neither would accept a divided China, or a two-party government in a united country.

But the differences between the two ultimately settled their conflict over which of them should rule. The Communists acted on the basis of a sophisticated analysis of China's problems—Marxism, supplemented by the ideas of such Communist leaders as Mao Zedong (Mao Tse-tung), and with the support of intellectuals and much of the huge peasant and worker population. The Nationalists, who controlled a larger area until the late 1940s, had no clear-cut theory or social program and drew their support mainly from a tiny proportion of the Chinese people—the merchants, landlords, and industrialists of the coastal regions. While the Nationalists did little to alleviate poverty and injustice, depending increasingly on military force to remain in power (Ch'ien 1965), the Communists developed economic reforms and the political techniques that persuaded people to practice them.

The struggle between the parties was complicated and prolonged by the aggressive expansion of the Japanese in China beginning in 1931. Responding to popular anti-imperialist, pronational sentiments urging cooperation on the contending parties, the Communists began guerrilla resistance when the Japanese expanded in the North China plain in 1936. The Nationalists, however, reluctant to expend on the Japanese resources they hoped ultimately to turn against the Communists, held back. Finally, in 1937, with American assistance, they too began to resist the Japanese takeover. Their failure to put national defense before internal political goals lost them the support of many, especially students.

During these years, the corruption the Nationalists had allowed among themselves grew worse. Their leader, Jiang Jieshi, his family, and three closely allied families had gained control of China's main banks, the national revenues, and sources of foreign aid by using their power to manipulate

[47]

currencies, speculate in import-export deals, and divert government funds to build their private fortunes. Lesser civil and military officials did the same. Generals, for example, held up their troops' pay to play the stock market, so troops were often paid weeks or months in arrears. Soldiers scrounged and stole from the peasants to survive. Civil servants committed grave abuses—collusion between government officials and landlords sometimes multiplied peasants' taxes by a factor of five (Eastman 1984:64). Nothing could be accomplished in government without gifts and bribes, and the lavish and blatantly immoral life style of many Nationalist officials was an international scandal. Thus, popular support dwindled further.

Many people remained in the Nationalist orbit, however, continuing their loyalty to Jiang Jieshi. Capitalists, big and small, especially landlords, feared a Communist government, and the huge army of Nationalist party members, civil servants, and military officers living at public expense— sometimes very well—also preferred the status quo to the reforms the Communists were making in the north. Nationalist propaganda also frightened many; and Jiang, a leader with a certain charisma, managed to persuade many Chinese that he, at least, was above corruption.

From the end of the war with Japan in 1945 to the final Communist victory in 1949, the Chinese endured civil war. The Nationalists, with American help, and the Communists, aided much more sparingly by the Soviet Union, fought major battles over the provinces known as the Dongbei, or Northeast, which the Japanese had developed agriculturally and industrially since 1931. After their failure to hold the north, Nationalist troops began to desert to the winning side by whole armies at a time.

As the Communists accomplished their final, triumphant mopping up in the autumn of 1949, Jiang brought the central and provincial governments of China (with their treasuries), as much of his army as he could ship over, and a panicky group of military dependents and civilians from coastal cities to Taiwan. Among them were Shanghai textile mill owners, some with the basic equipment from their factories, small merchants from Fuzhou, and members of the Shanghai underworld who had acted as Jiang's enforcers in coastal cities. At least a million were military men (the exact figure is still secret), the core of an army with which Jiang hoped later to retake the mainland. Altogether, between one and one-half and two million Chinese made the crossing to what was hoped would be a temporary refuge.

Until that crossing, Taiwan had been very much a sideshow to the main events on the mainland. Chen Yi's atrocities on the island after 1945, which precipitated the 2:28 uprising, were no worse than similar acts of oppression against dissident populations throughout the Nationalist rule. The stripping of Taiwan's resources and the liquidation of its middle class were, and still are, justified by the Nationalists as necessary for the prosecution of the war. With their attention fixed on the calamitous defeats of the civil war and their own status as refugees, most Mainlanders saw Japanized Taiwan simply as the alien and inconsequential backdrop to their own tragedies.

[4]

The Changing Political Economy under the Nationalists

With the arrival of the Nationalists, the island's closely linked political and economic systems underwent major changes, which kept Taiwan poorer for fifteen years than it had been in the prosperous thirties under the Japanese. Between 1945 and 1950, economic goals were first reoriented away from the Japanese empire and toward China's mainland. Then, with the collapse of Nationalist power there, the system floundered, surviving on American aid and a limited range of indigenous products and markets. Both Taiwanese and low-ranking Mainlanders remember these mostly as hard years, though for a few, money flowed freely from smuggling, graft, or postwar rebuilding.

Economic Development

Among the immigrants who arrived in Taiwan after 1949, some pressed for reforms, particularly in agriculture. Under pressure from the United States, Jiang gave these land reformers permission to reorganize Taiwan's landholdings under a program that liberal Nationalists had long advocated for the mainland, though never put into action. Under the reform, complete by 1953, farmland in excess of three hectares (7.2 acres, enough for a family farm) was bought from landlords by the government, paid for with government bonds and stocks in government companies. It was resold on ten-year mortgages at an annual rate of 37.5 percent of its annual crop value to families with less than that quantity of land, tenants being given the first right to purchase (Chen 1961; Yang 1970). Landlords hated the policy, for government investments seemed very shaky in the early 1950s; frightened by the events of 1947, however, they did not protest. Nevertheless, they thought up as many schemes as they could to avoid having to sell their land, such as dividing it up legally among many family members. By contrast, the reform was popular with tenants and greatly improved the prestige of the Nationalist party in the countryside. The land reform secured Nationalist rule in Taiwan both by undercutting the power of landlords and by ensuring support from the much larger group of new owner-operators.

This major change in ownership of the primary means of production greatly affected rural life in Taiwan. Farmers did not become rich from owning their own land, for Nationalist taxes, direct and indirect, soon ate up most of the gain made on rent; but about two-fifths of former tenants built new houses, many families ate a bit better (Yang 1970:276–88), and some found the capital to go into small businesses that did produce a higher income. The reform, moreover, had other important long-term consequences. By keeping landholdings small, the policy meant that many farm children would have to leave the land and go into other occupations. This created a pool of cheap labor for industry when it began to expand. The small size of farms meant also that their mechanization was difficult, constraining most farmers to continue to rely on the cheapest and most available of labor, their own large families. These pressures and government tax and pricing policies kept farmers poorer than the rest of the population, made young people want more than ever to escape farm life, and encouraged explosive population growth in Taiwan during the fifties and sixties (Hsiao 1981; Huang S. 1981). By the early seventies, many farm households depended heavily on nonagricultural income to get by (Wang and Apthorpe (1974:13).

While the land reform brought some immediate benefits, the Nationalist-run economy did very poorly in Taiwan beginning with their arrival in 1945 until the early sixties. Chinese rule brought terrible inflation to the island which did not stabilize until the mid-fifties, destroying people's savings and making business dealings risky. Between the wartime inflation of Japanese money and the unprecedented Nationalist expansion of currency, staple foods that cost one yen in prosperous prewar 1937 cost 72,262 units of Chinese currency by May 1949, and building materials inflated from one unit to 93,563 over the same period. Between January and June of 1949, the cost of living rose ten times (Kann 1955, IV:689). This was the result not only of "normal" wartime inflation, but of "the forced

[51]

requisitioning, from August 19, 1948, onward, of foreign monies, gold and silver, against almost worthless paper, under false pretences, . . . a crime against the people" of China (Kann 1955, I:595).

In Taiwan the government staffed large state enterprises with Mainlanders, who knew nothing about the businesses, as a reward for their services. These state enterprises lost money and were sources of corruption. Extremely complicated governmental control of trade slowed exports and imports, making it difficult to obtain raw materials. Access to large quantities of capital and credit depended on personal ties with the banking establishment, which eliminated most Taiwanese from competition. The heaviest burden on the economy was the huge military force that Jiang maintained in the ever-diminishing hope of retaking the mainland. Four-fifths of government income including the very large commitment of American aid to Taiwan in these years, went to the military, keeping the inflation rate high through the early sixties (Morgan Guaranty Survey 1962), and leaving little for social or economic development (Jacoby 1967:109).

In the 1960s Taiwan began to move to an industrial economy that soon successfully exported textiles, footwear, plastics, and electronics to the United States. This dramatic reversal was brought about by changes in leadership, by the cutoff of much of the American aid on which the Nationalists had long depended, by fears of being surpassed by the then-plausible gains of the Communist Great Leap Forward, and by a boom in foreign investment that brought private capital from the United States and Japan. Taiwan advertised itself abroad as having plenty of cheap and docile labor that was forbidden to strike. By the seventies, companies like Westinghouse, Sanyo, and Texas Instruments were well known in Taiwan, employing thousands of young men and women at wages of a few hundred dollars a year. Smaller businesses expanded in association with them, often capitalized initially from the earnings of workers in one of the big enterprises. Economic growth faltered occasionally, for the new dependence on exports has made Taiwan vulnerable to changes in the world—and especially the American—economy; but in general, growth has been both high and constant since the sixties. And in the early 1960s, urbanization brought so many people out of the countryside that more people were now living in cities than in rural areas.

As life became more prosperous, a consumer economy began to grow. By 1982, nearly 70 percent of Taiwan's households had telephones; these had required an installation fee equal to a worker's yearly wage when I arrived in 1968. Ninety-five percent had refrigerators, which only the salaried middle and upper classes could afford in 1968 (and which they then displayed proudly in their living rooms.) Eighty-five percent had color television, 90 percent had motorcycles, and over 7 percent owned private cars—a luxury in a country where the public transportation network is so complete (*Free China Journal*, July 1, 1984:4). People ate noticeably better, bought Japanese-styled "Western" clothes, supported more children through longer educations, and had more money to save and invest.

Life in Taibei astonished me when I arrived in 1980 and compared what I saw with pictures and memories of 1968 and even of 1975. My first impression (and the only impression for most visitors) was of great wealth. I saw young men playing ice hockey in a twelfth-floor amusement complex, immense traffic jams of private cars, dresses costing hundreds of dollars in chic boutiques, and street after street of expensive, brand-new condominiums. Billboard ads offered villas in the mountains, and pricey Japanese-style restaurants were flourishing. Where in 1968, on a very small student scholarship, I had been able to afford a comfortable bungalow with its own yard, a full-time housekeeper, and occasional visits to the best restaurants in the city, now as a full-time university professor I found that many of these things in Taibei, as in New York or Tokyo, were quite out of my price range. It was an interesting reversal.

When I began my interviewing for the life histories, however, I soon discovered that for some of my old friends life had not changed much. A few had become fairly well-off and moved to fancier neighborhoods where they worried about parking and getting their youngsters into the "right" schools. Most, though, lived much as they had, their biggest acquisitions being better diets, a few more clothes, a color television, and a motorcycle. They still experienced crowded quarters, long hours of work, little economic security, and what most Americans would consider a very simple life style. They talked with me a great deal about the wealth they saw in their city, and sometimes lamented that they had not had the luck or cleverness to get rich. Chinese people love to poor-mouth themselves, so I did not take some of their complaints literally—it often turned out they had significant sums in the bank or lent out at interest—but it was clear as I reexplored the city and countryside that there were many people who had benefited very little from the economic miracle. As they said, "*kun do li ci*" (T)—"We get by."

Another side of life that has not changed greatly is politics. The rule of the Nationalists in Taiwan was harsh in the beginning both because they had developed a repressive style of government on the mainland, and because their main goal—to retake the mainland—required the subordination of the needs of the island's people to those of high Nationalist leaders for power over resources. By continuing to maintain the fiction that they are the government of all China, even their representative elective institutions have remained biased against native Taiwanese participation and power

[53]

holding. Strongly repressive measures are necessary to preserve this un-equal situation against the pressures of the large and increasingly pros-perous Taiwanese majority.

Ethnicity and Social Class

Although the social fracture between Taiwanese and Mainlander has healed somewhat, especially among those born since the economic boom began, Taiwanese at all levels of society resent their political inequality and the harsh measures used to maintain it. Those who would actively oppose the Nationalist claim of being a central government for all of China were long forbidden to put forth an alternative political position or to form an opposition party. In 1986, Taiwanese oppositionists formed such a party, although its legality remains open to question. But though it has been difficult to institutionalize the ethnic distinction in politics, working-class people remain conscious of their own and others' regional origins in daily life as they speak different languages, follow different customs, and link into different social networks. Ethnicity remains a meaningful category for most people. Social class distinctions, though less well articulated, also operate in Taiwan. To be born working-class or elite, Taiwanese or Mainlander, makes a considerable difference to an individual's life circumstances and future fortunes.

The existence of classes and ethnic categories in a society creates a degree of cultural complexity much greater than that seen in egalitarian, small-scale societies. For social scientists, therefore, ethnicity and class are important concepts, but they are also complicated and controversial ones because they are among the commonest means by which people in complex societies are manipulated politically and economically, and by means of which they resist such manipulation. Individuals, social groups, and power-ful organs of the state have interests in shaping what ethnicity and class will mean, and in using these concepts for political ends. On these matters, there is no such thing as an "objective" viewpoint, even for an outsider; *any* viewpoint has political implications.

Ethnicity does not derive only from the persistence of historical cultural elements in an ethnic group, even if that group's members perceive these as badges of identity. Some groups, in the process of adaptation to new conditions, abandon virtually all customs, traditions, languages, and characteristic forms of social relations that historically marked their culture of origin, as the great majority of Americans have done. Nevertheless, ethnicity may persist as a matter of self-identification, as for the large numbers of completely assimilated American Irish, Jews, and Poles. Such people enjoy a sense of being connected to the past which, however, affects their cultural behavior hardly at all. And under some circumstances, such ethnic identities are optional: by changing a surname, Americans of European background can, if they choose, drop their ethnic identity and join the cultural mainstream. (This is obviously much more difficult for Americans whose physical appearance suggests a non-European origin.)

Ethnicity has a very different meaning in societies where it has become an official identity, and where ethnic groups do not receive equal treatment under the law and in society. Although the limitations imposed on Taiwanese to the benefit of Mainlanders are less serious than those placed on Jews by Germans under Hitler or on Blacks by precivil-rights-era Americans and in contemporary South Africa, they have nevertheless made ethnicity an important and persistent factor in Taiwan's social organization.

Each of Taiwan's citizens inherits a hereditary identity based on province of origin from his or her father—the mother's identity is irrelevant except in cases of illegitimacy. This provincial identity is indicated in household registrations and on the identity card that every adult must carry when in public. Until the sixties, children in school were often asked at the beginning of the school term to indicate their provincial identity for their classmates. Asking after a new acquaintance's "old home" is a common conversational opener. Many people identify themselves as soon as they speak, by language or accent, and even certain haircuts and clothing styles are associated with particular groups. Ethnic identities are thus frequently apparent in ordinary life, and older people are generally highly conscious of their own and others' ethnicities. Because Mainlanders are in substantial numerical minority (about one-tenth of the population), the Taiwanese usually collapse them into a single category; among Mainlanders, however, the distinctions between for example, a Cantonese and a Shandongnese are still significant.

The authorities continue to identify persons by their provinces of origin in part because the Nationalist government, still claiming to be the government of all of China, wishes to remind islanders that their government represents the mainland as well. There have been practical reasons, too, for some people to adopt strong ethnic identities and impose them on others. In the early years of Nationalist rule in Taiwan, being a Mainlander gave one a distinct advantage in getting government jobs, while being Taiwanese often sufficed for being fired from one. Mainlanders today justify their earlier, harsher discrimination by noting that Taiwanese were ignorant of the national language in which government business was transacted. This is reasonable enough, except that a good many Mainlanders from the south also speak Mandarin almost incomprehensibly, or not at all. In any case, a good deal of technical business in government departments where Taiwanese were able to hold their jobs continued to be conducted in Japanese into the seventies. More important than language skills was the reality that Nationalist leaders retained the loyalty of those who had followed them to Taiwan by giving them government jobs, preferring their minority government to be in the hands of their own people instead of those of the increasingly hostile Taiwanese. The number of Taiwanese that the government employed decreased steadily from 77 percent in 1946 to its lowest point at 61 percent in 1962 (Gates 1981:257). As long as government and military positions remained in Mainlander hands, the Taiwanese could be controlled.

But government work, schoolteaching, post-office jobs, and the like constituted the choicest occupations in Taiwan during that stagnant period from the destruction of the thirties' prosperity to the new industrialization of the sixties. Mainlander discrimination kept the Taiwanese confined to agriculture and small business in the forties and fifties, a situation that perpetuated Taiwanese resentment and sense of separation.

While Mainlanders effectively monopolized official occupations, a stereotype arose that commerce and industry were the special occupational niche of Taiwanese because their many small businesses, and a few successful large ones, were so visible. In fact, Mainlander businesses founded with the capital, machines, expertise, and political contacts of Shanghai capitalists also flourished, giving Mainlanders a disproportionate share of the private enterprises, almost one-third of the largest one hundred corporations in 1973 ([American Embassy Staff? 1973?]). Perhaps because Taiwanese business expanded so rapidly after the sixties, and perhaps, as Mainlanders argue, because the Taiwanese owned the land, they came to be seen as people with money, or at least as having the means of making it. Ethnic identities became strongly tinged with assumptions about occupation.

Linked patterns of language use and education also promoted the separation of Taiwanese and Mainlander ethnic groups. When the Japanese moved out of their elite neighborhoods and schools in Taibei, Mainlanders moved in. Although schools were never legally segregated by provincial origin, Mainlander communities often had their own schools, either inherited from the Japanese or specially built for military families, where all the children were Mainlanders learning standard Mandarin from Mandarin-speaking teachers. This handicapped the non-Mandarin speaking children in their pursuit of education. With the shift to Mandarin, it became difficult for Taiwanese to transact official business because of the language barrier.

On my first visit, I sometimes heard teenage girl ticket takers on the public buses scold elderly Taiwanese men simply for trying to purchase tickets in the wrong language. Taiwanese culture was seen as lower class and in need of reform—a view that some Taiwanese accepted humbly and others resented deeply because it came from authorities who at the same time insisted that the Taiwanese be loyal Chinese.

As time passes, the government increasingly plays down the distinctions between Taiwanese and Mainlanders. People accustomed to thinking politically—mostly the educated elite—are intensely aware that to stress the distinction casts doubt on the unity of the population behind its largely Mainlander government. To suggest that the population does not support the government comes extremely close to disloyalty, so discussion of Taiwanese-Mainlander differences is avoided. This does not mean that the distinction has become unimportant. In the life stories of my working-class subjects, being Taiwanese or Mainlander constitutes part of each person's primary identity; the language barrier alone causes feelings of separateness among older people, as do their different attitudes toward the Japanese, the Nationalist government, and many local customs. At the same time, the life histories contain examples—such as Miss Guo and her "old lover"—of married couples who have managed a lifetime and several children together despite ethnic differences. There are many such families.

Younger people, born in Taiwan, have a less clear-cut view of these ethnic identities, especially those born to mixed Taiwanese and Mainlander parents. But the stereotyped beliefs that Mainlanders have an easier road into the upper levels of government service, the military, and academic life while the Taiwanese monopolize commerce and industry are not without foundation. Mr. Zhang and Mr. Kang, after a life spent under the shelter of government service, would feel demeaned to work in a Taiwanese business, even if they could find a Taiwanese who would hire them; and there are no Taiwanese dead among the hundreds of young Air Force officers with whom Mrs. Zhang's son is buried.

When we turn to the understanding of social class in Taiwan's society, we face a more complex problem than that of ethnicity. "Class" means many things in social science, sometimes referring to a stratum in a kind of social layer cake hierarchically arranged by either wealth or prestige. Layer-cake analyses are always flawed, for in a society that is undergoing any change at all, rankings by wealth and by prestige often do not coincide. An even greater drawback of the layer-cake approach to class is the reality that ranking people in society by wealth and prestige is a closed exercise. Such rankings, in and of themselves, tell us nothing about why some groups rank higher than others, why change occurs in such systems, or indeed anything

[57]

else at all about the society in question. Understanding class categories should generate insights about the dynamics of the relationships among these unequal categories: how social inequalities emerged, are maintained, and may be reproduced.

To analyze social class, one may employ the cultural categories used by the people themselves. In Taiwan, although ethnicity is a much-used cultural category among working-class islanders, social class is not, although people do refer frequently to the rich and the poor, and to those who have or have not "received education," as different and unequal strata in society. For some social analysts, the fact that these people do not explicitly define classes within their society and identify with one of them—that they have no "class-consciousness"—means that Taiwanese society cannot be said to be organized into classes. Such an approach is unhelpful because the analyst expects, unrealistically, that the people under study will discuss their own society perfectly freely and in social-science terms. These life histories, however, reveal their subjects to be conscious of social categories—rich and poor, educated and uneducated, Mainlander and Taiwanese—that clearly imply organized inequality even though they do not describe it in terms of "class."

Additionally, people in Taiwan are *not* free to analyze their society in class terms, because this is what the government's great rivals, the Communists, do. Careful censorship of the written word and school classrooms has effectively deleted the term from discourse.

A different line of argument holds that Taiwan's people *are* conscious of class, but in a distorted way. Because ethnic differences are so apparent and the conflict between Mainlanders and Taiwanese has sometimes been so sharp, many people see ethnicity as the dominant form of inequality in their society, while class relationships are less clearly seen. Many of the people in the life histories, both Taiwanese and Mainlanders, made it clear to me that they believe their society is structured into two ranked categories, with their own ethnic group the victim of the other (Taiwanese feel oppressed by Mainlander domination of government and military, Mainlanders by Taiwanese wealth and business prominence). Each sees the other as "rich" and powerful, unlike themselves. This comes very close to a view of Taiwan's society as one in which ethnicity and social class coincide. However, it is also apparent from the life histories that the working class contains people of both ethnic groups, as does Taiwan's elite—and that everyone knows this.

Although Taiwan's society may indeed have been organized into two unequal ethnic strata just after Retrocession—since the mid-sixties when opportunities began to expand for everyone—this is no longer the case. It is not surprising that working-class Taiwanese should remember the former Mainlander dominance, while working-class Mainlanders are struck by the way Taiwanese have come up in the world of business.

Although both Taiwanese and Mainlanders sometimes speak of their own group as if it were homogeneous and are therefore likely to see social relations in ethnic terms, they are also conscious of a kind of ranking that crosscuts ethnic categories—"rich people" and "educated people" versus "poor people" and "uneducated people." Miss Guo is quite explicit that "rich people" would be unwilling to invite people like herself to join rotating credit clubs, for example. Mrs. Zhang sees her fellow Shandongnese employer as rich, powerful, and educated compared with herself, despite their common ethnicity. Although neither would use the term "class" to make this distinction, they make the distinction nonetheless. Taiwan's people, it seems to me, are conscious not only of ethnic hierarchy but of class differences as well, though working-class people often assume the two coincide.

Attending to what these people say about social inequality in Taiwan is essential to understanding that society, but native views alone can fruitfully be supplemented with other forms of analysis which will link patterns of inequality to other aspects of the culture—if we are careful to specify what we mean by class.

The concept of class has its greatest utility when we use it as Marxists do to categorize people's relationships to the society's political-economic system. Fundamentally, this approach asks: How are people connected to society's most basic resources, the means of production? In an industrial capitalist society, the means of production include land, tools, factories and their productive machinery, raw materials for industrial use, and money capital. People in such societies either own these means of production, and can be called the capitalist class or bourgeoisie, or they own no means of production but sell their labor to those who do, and can be called the working class or proletariat. The part of the working class that labors in modern, technologically advanced industry is particularly significant because the greatest wealth and economic dynamism are concentrated there. The relationship between workers and capitalists affects the course of history most deeply because the owners of capital struggle to control the workers, and the workers struggle to control their own lives.

These, therefore, are society's most significant classes. There are, of course, other categories of people—white-collar workers, an underclass of permanently unemployed and criminal elements, intellectuals, and so forth, but they are peripheral to the real issue: Who will control society's most productive resources—capitalists, whose primary goal must be the expansion of capital by the making of profit, or workers, whose primary goals are secure employment and maintenance or improvement of their families' lives? Other groups, whatever their rankings in wealth or prestige, do not matter very much except as they line up on one side or the other of the power struggle between the workers and the capitalists. We need not build a layer-cake model that includes all social groups to understand class relations in a particular capitalist society; we must only pinpoint who, in that society, owns the means of production and lives from profit, and who sells the labor that operates production and lives from wages.

This model of society and its fundamental source of change is not a perfect one, especially for countries with governments that employ many people independently of private capitalists. In Taiwan, with its overscaled national government (intended for all of China) and military and its many state-run enterprises, the state itself is a major owner of important means of production; the petroleum, coal, electric, railroad, cement, and sugar businesses, to name a few, are state enterprises. Workers in such businesses—civil servants, schoolteachers, and career military officers—have a strong interest in the maintenance of the public power that protects private and public enterprises against other workers' attempts to gain power.

The model of social class that depends heavily on defining each group's relationship to the means of production also applies with difficulty to the myriads of small business people and farmers who form a large part of Taiwan's population and an important part of its economy. Are they capitalists or workers? They own their own means of production, but they also provide most of their own labor needs, so they do not, as capitalists do, live from profits drawn from the work of others. And, in Taiwan's complex, mixed economy, small business people need access to important means of production which they do not control. Where, for example, a family subcontracts to a large factory to finish sweaters, its members differ from the factory's own workers only in that they supply their own workplace, perhaps purchase some of the necessary raw materials, and work according to their own schedules. Otherwise, they are simply selling their labor—usually rather cheaply, saving the factory owner his overhead costs.

In nineteenth-century European societies of the early industrial revolution, this "petty bourgeoisie" of small producers and shopkeepers was likely, in the political struggle, to line up with the big capitalists, and to be political enemies to the workers' cause. In Taiwan, the alliances seem to be different. Small business people, especially among the Taiwanese, form their closest ties with their laboring neighbors through kinship, neighborship, and community rituals. Members of small business families often work in factories or other clearly "working-class" jobs. People in this class are fully aware that they are "little people" in a society that also has wealthy and powerful people far "above" themselves. On the other hand, even the smallest entrepreneur sometimes dreams of making it big and rising into the class of big capitalists, and laborers dream of noodle stands of their own. Neither, in my opinion, would politically support the elimination of the opportunities they believe capitalism offers them, but both, in their daily lives, identify strongly with the "poor" and "uneducated" that comprise most of Taiwan's working class.

In short, in this society where relatively few people own or control major means of production, the ownership of a tiny shop or business does not separate a family enough from its laborer neighbors to cause differences in political orientation, although many older Mainlander immigrants still identify more with their fellow-ethnic government employers than with the working-class majority. At the same time, the gap in productivity between working-class people and those who own, control, or manage large-scale modern industries is a large and real one that ordinary people perceive as the result of differences in wealth and education.

Societies such as those in Taiwan, imperial China, and the United States are variously described as "state level," "complex," or "class" societies. Their distinguishing characteristics are the persisting inequalities between classes (and, sometimes, ethnic groups) and a centralized government with the power to set many of the political, economic, and cultural conditions under which these unequal segments relate to one another. Class societies vary greatly in the degree to which individuals and families can move from one class to another, and in the degree of forcible control that the government exercises to maintain a pattern of relations among classes. Nevertheless, because class relations and state power always shape class societies, politics at the national level, and possibly the international level as well, are directly and immediately relevant to their cultures. This is so even when many members of that society, as in Taiwan, take little part or interest in politics.

Most of Taiwan's people are clearly materially better off now than they were during the best of Japanese times; many more have found nonmanual jobs; and a smaller number of workers than in the past now perform the most grueling kinds of manual labor. Social mobility has been both relative and absolute, and people know it. At the same time, inequalities persist. Differences in wealth, often a good indicator of other forms of inequality, are vast, ranging from the Jiang family, which had grown rich on the mainland through political influence and continued to do so in Taiwan, to families like Miss Ong's, whose ancestral land became valuable as the result of urban growth, to such men as Mr. Kang, who after a lifetime of service

[61]

and labor will not have enough to live on when he retires. Yet there are few overt signs, especially among the working class, that people resent or wish to eliminate these inequalities through political action.

A group's apathy rather than activism toward political processes that ultimately affect them requires considerable explanation. Anthropological studies show that people in cultures without social classes and centralized power typically participate vigorously and enthusiastically in their societies' decisions. When a significant proportion of a class society's population refrains from involvement in politics, we may at least suspect that the power of the state or of a dominant class discourages them from involvement.

Repression and Resistance

The most rapidly growing segment of Taiwan's economy since the sixties has been its industries. In modern industry we can see most clearly the connections among economic development, social class relations, and political power. Where a class confrontation between industrial workers and factory owners over wages, working conditions, and other mutual interests might have taken place, as it has in many industrializing countries, the Nationalist government interposed martial law, making it illegal to strike or to form independent unions. It is illegal to hold meetings of any kind without police permission, or to meet in educational groups to study socialist solutions to laborers' problems. Working people, who through experience in the new factories might have developed a consciousness of their own importance in the new industrial economy and tried to gain leverage from it, have not done so as industrial workers have done in less repressive industrial countries. Taiwan's industrial growth was built on cheap labor, which remained cheap because state power limited workers' power to organize in their own interests.

One can argue that, since cheap labor was very nearly the only resource Taiwan's battered fifties economy had to put on the international market, only by keeping the price of labor low did the country achieve the present greater prosperity. But Nationalist antiworker policies long preceded their 1960s seduction of foreign investors with promises of low labor costs in Taiwan. Having been driven out of China in 1949 by a coalition of workers and peasants, the Nationalists had learned to fear working-class strength. The government, committed not to democracy but to the concept of "political tutelage" of the population by the Nationalist party, found reasons to suppress, limit, or control virtually every kind of popularly developed social organization except for those focusing on kinship and folk religion—and even some folk religions are outlawed and suppressed (Jordan 1972). Taiwan's police, secret police, intelligence, and other surveillance organs, large and ubiquitous, have received excellent training by American specialists and they now themselves train Salvadoran police in "population control." The island is small, escape routes few, and the household registration system enables the police to exert great pressure on relatives of fugitives to turn them in.

The Nationalists' profound distrust of social groups or movements they do not control has led to the banning of publishing groups, the imprisonment of students and teachers meeting privately to discuss politics, the infiltration of informers into all kinds of organizations, and even the suppression, in the mid-seventies, of a naively patriotic students' movement that favored Chinese control over some islands off the Vietnamese coast. The government approved of the students' objectives, but it simply would not permit organizational independence. Workers stand a poor chance of educating and organizing themselves under these conditions. As a result of this close control, the government benefited politically and big corporations benefited economically from the Nationalists' antiworker policies.

Taiwan, under martial law until 1987, does hold elections in which many working-class people participate as voters and, occasionally, as candidates. But elections do not give working-class people (or, indeed, most of the rest of the population) much voice in government for three reasons. First, a great deal of government power lies with the organs of the central government (those for all of China) rather than with the provincial and lower levels of government. Real power concentrates, therefore, in the hands of a very few Nationalist leaders close to the Jiang family, and the rest belongs to a representative body whose members were elected on the mainland in 1948. In the seventies, as more and more of these aged legislators died in office, a few "at large" seats were permitted, which gave the majority Taiwanese population some additional seats. In the elections of 1980, however, about 85 percent of the seats were still held by persons who represented mainland provinces and were generally out of touch with Taiwan's current conditions.

The second limitation on the democracy of Taiwan's elections is the prohibition against forming new political parties. Until 1986 the Nationalist party permitted only its own existence and that of two very small parties left over from Chinese mainland politics of the forties, which the Nationalists subsidize to avoid being called a one-party state. Candidates registered and ran as "outside the party," but were not permitted to support each other's candidacies even by appearing on the same platform. The fate of the new

Democratic Progressive Party, which emerged from this coalition, is still uncertain. Most outside-the-party candidates and voters are ethnically Taiwanese, while Mainlanders, even working-class ones, generally vote Nationalist.

Third, it is widely believed in Taiwan and reported in the international press that the Nationalists manipulate election results by ballot-box stuffing, vote buying, and intimidating popular candidates from running for election. Mr. Go, who does not like to discuss the matter, is believed to help in rounding up the local Nationalist vote in his neighborhood by distributing small payments; he is also known to have some muscle at his command, which makes people think twice before double-crossing him. A would-be outside-the-party candidate whom I knew slightly thought better of running against an unpopular Nationalist after his mother was threatened—not an uncommon sort of occurrence.

Elections, therefore, have proven a slow and fairly ineffectual means by which groups outside the inner circle of Mainlander elites may gain power. Although some Taiwanese have moved into high-ranking government and party positions in the 1970s and 1980s, they are usually party stalwarts and members of the economic upper class who do not represent working-class interests. The usual channels through which workers can come to understand and to affect the political system—unions and electoral politics—are blocked.

Nonetheless, resistance to Nationalist power repeatedly surfaces—sometimes clearly focused against the party, sometimes as a diffuse resentment of Mainlanders among Taiwanese. Resistance often takes apparently apolitical forms, such as antipollution demonstrations, which emphasize the solidarity of local communities and of the Taiwanese as a native-born ethnic group. Serious Mainlander opposition to the government, which has never been great, was suppressed by purges in the fifties and early sixties, though occasional defections of airplane pilots to the People's Republic of China, or complaints by poorly cared-for veterans of Jiang's original army, show that not all Mainlanders support the Nationalists.

Dissidence among intellectuals often takes the form of setting up a magazine to publish articles critical of the government until authorities crack down, ban or confiscate the publication, and send the most outspoken writers to jail. In the eighties, such intellectuals began to cooperate in increasing numbers, forming an opposition party. Novelists and short-story writers produce works of fiction that, by describing the lives of working-class people, criticize the system more indirectly. Some young people, while studying abroad, acquire a greater understanding of Nationalist history, the utility of class analysis, and the socialist experiments of the

People's Republic of China. Disillusioned, they respond differently to government and party when they return home (see Huang M. 1976).

Those who stand for the idea that Taiwan *is* a separate country and that all of its people should decide its political and economic future are labeled traitors and seditionists and punished accordingly. The Taiwan Independence Movement is therefore very much underground, or carried forward by small numbers of Taiwanese who have emigrated to Japan or the United States. Safely abroad, branches of the independence movement criticize the regime, attempting to persuade overseas Taiwanese to seek power at home and retain their Taiwaneseness while away. On one occasion, members of this group attempted to assassinate Jiang Jingguo (Jiang Jieshi's son) when he visited New York.

People who cannot be considered intellectuals yet who have considerable educational attainments, like Mr. Kho, sometimes find oblique ways of expressing their alienation from Taiwan's power structure. At some risk, Mr. Kho, who regrets the change from Japanese government, has rejected Mainlander reimposition of Chinese symbols by adopting a Japanese religion. Some Taiwanese symbolically reject Chinese authority by joining Christian churches with a reputation for sympathy with Taiwanese aspirations for greater local power.

But most working-class resistance takes different, less bookish, and less focused forms. The strength of working-class Taiwanese ethnic identity owes much to the people's participation in folk religion, which explicitly links the natives to the soil and history of the island. In 1980 I was told of the ever-growing presence at religious celebrations in the south of dozens, perhaps hundreds, of spirit mediums who show their spiritual powers by feats of self mutilation—piercing cheeks with skewers, beating backs with spiked balls, climbing "knife ladders," walking through hot coals—which left them uninjured. These practices are not new, but great gatherings of mediums drawing thousands of spectators represent a new trend. When mediums perform their bloody, horrifying acts, one thing they may be "saying" through their ritual is that Taiwanese have a kind of power that makes them invulnerable to mere physical force. Such symbolism is common in millenarian movements throughout the world, including China, as peoples who feel themselves oppressed seek the strength to reassert their power and reshape their societies (see, for example, Naquin 1976:30). The avid crowds who watch these spectacles are reminded that a society can draw on many different kinds of power, including those of numbers, group solidarity, and belief in themselves.

Resistance in Taiwan can assume more mundane forms as well, as Mr. Kang's description of what goes on in Taiwan's political shadows indicates.

[65]

Were the caches of guns and knives found by the police, which he mentions, intended for an underground resistance, or were they just gangsters' weapons? When Miss Ong's husband speaks mysteriously of the role his martial arts friends some day hope to have in "making life better for the poor," is politics involved, as there often is with Chinese gangs, or is he just, in the local phrase, "blowing cow?" I once heard a taxi driver deliver a very polished anticapitalist speech to my Taiwanese companions, who were amazed at his obvious attempt to involve them in something subversive. Sometimes an electric power plant or a government official is blown up, or a bomb is found on a bus. People have been told by the government that spies are everywhere, and I have myself met people who live beyond the edge of political safety, hoping only to accomplish a little more before being caught and sent to the infamous political prison on Green Island. And, in addition to local sources of dissent, it would be surprising if the island had *not,* in all these years, been infiltrated by Chinese from the Communist mainland, who have every reason to want to keep tabs on their old enemies.

The political situation continues to be further complicated, as it has been since 1945, by the stated goal of the Chinese Communist party of reunifying China by reincorporating Taiwan into their nation. This possibility makes nationalist and independence advocates alike uneasy, for they assume that only a strong government armed with the latest in American military technology can prevent it. For many, anti-Communist fears excuse the dictatorial martial law that is often turned against the government's liberal critics. In response, the great majority of working-class people avoid national-level politics and political discussions, which they have been plainly told is none of their business. In the seventies and eighties, however, ordinary people have rioted against Nationalist vote fraud, burning police cars and demanding fairness for Taiwanese candidates. Recent elections have shown that for most voters, the real issue is not the choice of candidates, but the dominance of the party itself.

Politics in Taiwan is full of unanswered questions, or rumor and conjecture. Long-term American residents offer tips on how to recognize secret agents and how to get mail and manuscripts out of the country unread by the authorities; Chinese friends offer cryptic advice about speaking cautiously, or mention the oddities that intrigue Mr. Kang. A close associate pointed out the building where, in 1947, he had been tortured before a long imprisonment. The rumors give the island's atmosphere a taint of anxiety, even of paranoia; living there, one comes to fear there are horrid secrets that would be dangerous to know, acts or words that would result in swift and awful punishment. So while some resist, most keep silent, speak of other things, and construct for themselves little worlds of self-employment, neighborhoods, and families, where the dangerously "complicated" society can be kept at bay.

And so, in the 1980s, Taiwan balances economically between its own needs and those of America and Japan. Politically, it balances on shifting relationships between the United States and the People's Republic of China, and on those between ethnic groups in its own population. Its future is more uncertain than that of most countries, though uncertainty is the human condition everywhere. Many Mainlanders who can do so emigrate, usually to the United States, and even some Taiwanese legislators are believed to hold U.S. "green cards" for permanent residence here, in case of a takeover from the mainland. The ordinary folk of Taiwan, more than ever, live in the present, planning from decade to decade, or year to year— "getting by."

[5]

Working for a Living

This chapter begins with a description of working-class occupations in Taiwan and then introduces two women, Guo A Gui and Lo A Lan. After I give brief sketches of these people as I saw them, each recounts her own life history. Miss Guo and Mrs. Lo, chosen to illustrate the theme of "working for a living," have held many manual and service jobs but have never been employed in any of the more secure and well-paid worker occupations. Other life histories will reveal additional work experiences, just as these two inform us about family life, female-male relationships, and other themes taken up in later chapters. The lives of Miss Guo and Mrs. Lo are particularly appropriate as illustrations of work life, however, because they show so effectively the poverty that punishes weakness, failure, or ill fortune in societies like Taiwan's. Fear that they or their children might find themselves in such a position motivates much of the industriousness with which most Chinese approach their work.

Business and "Bitter Labor"

Work is essential to life for most of Taiwan's people. Many shopkeeping households are open for business from early morning until everyone goes to bed at night; some never take a holiday, even at the New Year. Factory workers put in six or seven days a week, often at more than eight hours daily (Diamond 1979:322)—eighteen in some small owner-operated factories (Niehoff 1987). Taxi drivers drive till they drop, often for sixteen hours in heavy smog and dangerous traffic. Much manual work is either physically exhausting, like the pedicab driving, which, until the late sixties, provided

[68]

much public transportation in Taibei, or it is deadeningly boring, like the decoration of millions of sheets of imitation paper "spirit money" burned at religious celebrations, or the factory assembly of microscopic electronic parts. Work, for the poor, takes up most of each day, and often pays badly. Although workers know they must work, and hard, they cannot be said to value work for its own sake. People, when they have choices, choose jobs for their rewards: ample leisure, if possible, a good wage, few physical demands, and the opportunity to control their own time and effort (Harrell 1985).

Although the growth of mining, the handicraft industry, and commerce slowly created more varied jobs in the nineteenth century, agriculture remained the main occupation of more than half of Taiwan's people until 1958 (computed from DGBAS 1974: Tables 18 and 22). The modern industrial boom of the 1960s tipped the balance from a primarily agricultural to a primarily nonagricultural economy. By 1983 only about one-third of families were registered as farming households (DBGAS 1981, Supplementary Table 11), and many of their members worked at nonagricultural jobs.

Until recently, most farmers in Taiwan grew rice or a combination of rice and sugar, with a few subsidiary cash crops. Unmechanized rice and sugar agriculture uses a great deal of labor under extremely uncomfortable conditions. Wet rice growing requires many hours spent knee-deep in muddy water: planting, weeding, spraying with dangerous insecticides, adjusting water levels, and mending irrigation dikes. When harvest is near and the fields are dry, hand cutting, carrying, threshing, drying, and storing of grain call for major physical efforts, especially when rain threatens the harvest. Sugar growing is notorious for extremely heavy labor in cutting and carrying huge bundles of cane from the fields. Taiwan's generally high heat and humidity make such labor even harder, adding the dangers of heat prostration to other work-related ailments such as hernia, varicose veins, back trouble, and snake-bite. It is not surprising that many people prefer other kinds of work when it is available.

The economic rewards of farming depend on the relationship of the worker to the land. A day laborer working for wages, a tenant who share-crops for someone else, a family that owns enough land for its own members to work, and a landlord who employs others or leases land to tenants receive very different compensation from their work. Although the land reform of the early fifties eliminated big landlords and decreased the proportion of tenants to about one-sixth of all farmers (computed from DGBAS 1981: Supplementary Table 5), there are still landless migrant workers who follow the harvests. Except for the large tracts owned by such state enterprises as the Taiwan Sugar Corporation, most farms are now run by owner-operator families whose adult men and younger members increasingly find nonagricultural work, leaving the farming to wives, children, the elderly, and hired labor.

Agriculture—even with Japanese innovations such as foot-pedal rice threshers, new irrigation systems, and narrow gauge railroads for sugar transport, and those that have been implemented since the 1970s, especially motorized plows, threshers, and vehicles—remains a physically taxing undertaking. Even with the Nationalists' improvements—land reform, wider rural electrification, some farm mechanization—life for most farmers has fallen behind that of nonagricultural households in standard of living and difficulty of work. Most rural young people seek opportunities to leave farming for easier and better-paid jobs in livelier town or city settings.

Because of the island's small size and good communications and its people's entrepreneurial skills, rural Taiwanese have founded multitudes of small new businesses in the countryside—frame knitting, tile manufacturing, plastics injection (Harrell 1982; Niehoff 1987; Stites 1982)—while larger enterprises have been encouraged by the availability of cheap rural labor to set up factories there as well. Although the gap between cosmopolitan Taibei and a rice-growing village seems great to their respective inhabitants, virtually the same working-class jobs have been accessible to rural as to urban folk since the mid-1960s. A job almost anywhere in the island's more densely settled western half can be combined with at least part-time residence in the worker's family home base, wherever that might be; by express train, the island's two biggest cities, Taibei and Gaoxiong, are only four hours apart. Farm families, then, are no longer sharply distinguishable from urban ones, while at the same time agricultural work is easier to escape from than it was when our subjects were young.

None of the subjects of these life histories is a farmer, though many, like Miss Guo and Mrs. Lo have done farm labor, and most can trace their families back to agriculture. In this, they represent the general experience of Taiwan's people today—connected to farming life by memories and relatives, but personally free of its drudgery, and glad to be so. Instead, they engage in such typically working-class occupations as manual labor, factory work, service work, military service, and small-scale manufacture, commerce, and house renting.

At the bottom of this occupational scale is the hard manual work, such as digging building foundations with shovels or carrying concrete in buckets, which the Chinese describe as *ku gong*, "bitter labor." Such work, more common in the past, is today being replaced more and more by mechanical methods. Because most households in Taiwan now have some form of piped running water, water carrying, a common occupation of poor men in the past, is no longer necessary. Large modern buildings in Taiwan are now built with complex cranes and cement mixers; but on small ones, women like Mrs. Lo still carry buckets of concrete up shaky ramps all day long for the price of a few meals. Though there is far less of it now, unskilled construction work, stevedoring, street cleaning, the emptying of privies, and agricultural migrant labor still employ perhaps 10 percent of the labor force in "bitter labor."

Service work is another area of occupation: about 15 percent of Taiwan's work force is employed this way (estimated from 1981 DGBAS data). Service workers include domestic servants; restaurant, hotel, retail, and similar personnel; and entertainers, including the large number of bar girls and prostitutes Taiwan's militarized economy has encouraged. Like "bitter labor," service work is disliked because the hours are long, it pays poorly— usually less than factory work—and it requires so much deference to the employer or customer. Chinese servants are usually on call twenty-four hours a day, with only one or two days off a month, and often they must tolerate considerable abuse. Service employees such as the young sales-women in large department stores are also kept on long shifts and low wages, and are required to perform much "emotional labor" (Hochschild 1983), flattering and cajoling customers to buy. Older women frequently must depend on service work if they want to earn an income but have no capital to begin a business of their own.

Modern industrialization has created a wide range of manufacturing jobs in which human effort has been largely replaced by machines, employing people who in the past either found no income-producing work or who worked on farms and in small handicraft workshops. Jobs in big, export-oriented factories are eagerly sought, especially by young women and men in their teens. Easier than "bitter labor" because it is indoors and phys-ically lighter, factory work also pays better, as machine-assisted productiv-ity is so much greater than that of hand labor.

Because about half of all factory workers are between the ages of fifteen and twenty-four, with few in the older ages (Gates 1979:395), our subjects, nearly all of whom are older people, mention factory work only in passing or as an occupation of their youth—like Miss Guo—or of young relatives. In today's economy, however, they are an extremely important group, for it is with their labor that Taiwan's "economic miracle" has been built.

The young women who make up one-third of this important work force (Taiwan Provincial Labor Force Survey and Research Institute 1971:50) have been described by Linda Gail Arrigo (1980, 1984), Norma Diamond (1979), and Lydia Kung (1983, 1984). Kung especially gives us a very full picture of the lives of women industrial workers in the mid 1970s. For rural youth, who make up a large proportion of factory workers, these jobs at first also have a certain glamor because of the independence they appear to offer (Kung 1983:72–73).

Such factories actively recruit young women from the countryside, providing them with inexpensive barrackslike housing, canteens, limited medical services, and some recreational activities (Kung 1983:109). Others live with relatives or in cheap rented rooms in the poorer neighborhoods and suburbs (Arrigo 1984). While some young people appear to enjoy the opportunity to leave home and escape parental restraint on their daily activities, others become homesick or disillusioned with the dull work routines, the limited opportunities for advancement, and the unpleasantness resulting from dishonesty, sexual exploitation, and insincerity. Young women especially complain that these factors add up to a new understanding that life "out in society" is unpleasantly "complicated," *fuza*, a term that people often contrast with the simplicity or straightforwardness of family, school, and village life (Kung 1983:159–64).

The dangers of factory life are not merely social, however. Some work—such as assembling microchips—is widely believed to result in rapid deterioration of eyesight, while many factory hands are exposed to unguarded machinery and toxic substances. In 1975 a worker in an asbestos-weaving factory told Linda Arrigo (1980:31): "Your whole body gets covered with asbestos fluff. . . . There is no air-conditioning, and in the summer you are sweaty and sticky over your whole body. The company says they can't put in air-conditioning because the fiber is too damp and the air-conditioners would get clogged." Asbestos, of course, causes both asbestosis and cancer.

Factory work offers young people from poor families an opportunity to earn money for various purposes, including their own educations. The goal of completing high school at night while working to pay the fees their families cannot afford is common especially among woman workers. While some succeed in this attempt, many find the pressures of work, study, and dormitory life too much, and give it up before graduation (Kung 1983:155). Many parents of unmarried factory workers expect their children to remit all their wages but pocket money to pay family expenses, including school fees for brothers of working daughters (Kung 1984:112). Some are less likely to comply with these demands, but daughters often feel they have no choice, for they and their families believe girls should repay the costs of rearing them before they marry (Greenhalgh 1985c). As one of Kung's (1983:119) informants exclaimed: "What's the good of having a daughter if she doesn't bring any money home?" A recent study shows that girls in one factory-oriented rural community are receiving fewer years of education, as they begin outside work at younger and younger ages (Niehoff 1987). Wages are low—U.S.$25 a month was a common wage in the late sixties, and in the early eighties, the going wage had reached only about U.S.$150. Such an income provides only a meager living for a single person—not enough to give the sense of freedom that many young people hope to find outside the family.

The women Kung describes belong to a company union that collects dues but provides almost no services in return. As one remarked, "The way I see it, the managers of the company are the ones who run the union, and they have the final say. Their interests and ours are different, and naturally they'd look after their own concerns and not give much attention to what we want" (1983:108; see also Stites 1985:227–46).

Since the industrial boom of the late 1960s—although about one-fifth of the work force works in large industrial enterprises (estimated from DGBAS 1981 data)—factory work is rarely a lifelong occupation. Factories generally discourage the employment of married women, as does the typical Taiwan pattern of rapid childbearing right after marriage. Men withdraw from factory employment as they mature because factory wages are rarely adequate for a growing family and because the discipline and routine become increasingly hard to bear (Stites 1982). As many as can, find other kinds of work—very often as small, independent businessmen (Stites 1982; Harrell 1985). As women round out their families and consider returning to income-producing work, they too look for opportunities outside the factory system. Many start small shops or restaurants, work parttime as servants or service personnel, or finish products at home for larger industries.

Factories, then, are operated by a part-time proletariat of young people, soon replaced by another generation of docile teenagers who will work for little more than it takes to support one person. In recessions, these young people are easily laid off, and return to work in their families' farms and small businesses. Their rapid movement into and out of factory work has been a great advantage to factory owners, Chinese and foreign: this cheap and flexible labor supply does not bargain, strike, bring political pressure to bear, or even settle down in working-class neighborhoods near the factories. Such a group does not directly reproduce the next generation's industrial workforce, but depends on the existence of a large small-farm, small-business sector whose sons and daughters "enter society" temporarily during their youth to work in factories. They then return to found or continue family enterprises whose sacrifices of time, energy, equality for women, and heavy discipline of the young benefit not only themselves, but also the big industrial sector (Gates 1979).

An unusually large working-class occupation in Taiwan is military service.

Under Nationalist rule the island has for many years supported one of the largest standing armies in the world. Most of its enlisted men were young draftees, serving three (or since 1973, two) years, beginning at age eighteen. This prevents working-class young men from taking up training or permanent employment until their enlistment is over, which delays marriages and encourages some to become the temporary factory labor on which industry relies.

The regular army, however (as well as the air force, navy, and marines) is staffed with a very high proportion of older men who came from the mainland with Jiang Jieshi. Many, now retired, receive pensions and other benefits from the central government. The wages of even the regular and retired military personnel, if they are of low rank, are below those of factory workers and insufficient to support and educate a family. But they receive other benefits: free medical care for themselves and their families at veterans' hospitals and—like all government employees—monthly rations of rice, salt, oil, and fuel. Some receive housing and additional benefits for dependents; sons are often given unofficial preference in military advancement, and many who have retired since the mid-1960s, like Mrs. Lo's husband, have been employed in government organizations and enterprises. Those who retired or were demobilized in the fifties, however, often received no help at all from the government in making a new life in Taiwan. Some old Mainlander retirees have nothing to rely on except the rather grim veterans' homes. But, while even low-ranking Mainlander servicemen have had certain advantages, they increasingly find themselves competing on disadvantageous terms in an economy for which their lives in the service have not prepared them well. They and their families depend more and more on working-class jobs to survive.

It is unusual to refer to soldiers as members of the working class. Except for occasional emergencies, for example, after typhoons and floods when soldiers are brought in to repair roads and irrigation systems or to save crops, they are not part of society's productive labor force. By now, however, most of the original mainland soldiery has retired into typical working-class jobs, and many of their children have entered the working class as well. Career military service at the enlisted level is often seen as a Mainlander occupational specialization; it produces a level of living comparable to that gained in factory work.

Except for a career in the military, in which some Mainlanders take considerable pride, the working-class jobs discussed so far are not generally seen as very desirable except as an escape from the even greater drudgery of farm labor. A great many working-class people, however, hope to achieve a more valued occupational goal: to become the owner of a small business.

It is hard to exaggerate just how small these enterprises can be. A Chinese folk story tells of a rich man who began his career by buying five peanuts for a single small coin, and selling them for two. While I never saw quite such commercial miniaturization in Taiwan, there were, and still are, many businesses that start with a minimum of capital. The sellers of "shoulder pole noodles," well known in Tainan City, carry an entire restaurant—stove, cookpot, ingredients, dishes, and a stool for the customer—in two boxes slung on a shoulder pole, from which they produce bowls of delicious noodle soup for the comfortably waiting buyer. The late evening streets of all of Taiwan's cities swarm with slightly larger versions of these portable restaurants, usually mounted on bicycle-powered carts. For a small fee, they plug into an electrical outlet in a nearby house, turn on the bulb, and set up shop for the strollers who emerge in the cool evening to enjoy cheap snacks and the gaiety of the promenading crowd. A former army man in Prosperity Settlement makes his small family's living with a grindstone and emery paper, polishing the rough edges from newly moulded U.S. Army good-conduct medals. In 1968 a common sight at the entrances to city markets was a young girl with a magnifying glass, mending runs in nylon stockings.

Many small businesses are more substantial: rice-milling shops are ubiquitous in Taiwan, as are tailoring establishments, barber shops and beauty parlors, grocery stores, photographers' studios, and a multitude of tiny factories that produce everything from bean curd and incense sticks to electronic subassemblies for bigger factories. In the late sixties I lived near a household whose members bought used light bulbs door-to-door, smashed out the glass and inner works, dipped the brass bases in acid baths to repolish them, and sold them back, in great, glittering festoons, to a light bulb factory.

Many of the more complex traditional handicraft industries, such as those where the craftspeople make elegant hardwood altar tables, carve images of gods, and tailor are learned first by apprentices who later become skilled journeymen working under master craftsmen with their own shops. These independent-minded workers travel from shop to shop, rebellious against discipline and willing to forgo high earnings for plenty of leisure and a good time. Eventually, however, most hope to set up their own shops as masters (de Glopper 1979).

Most small businesses are run by families using family labor, young apprentices from related or neighboring households, and sometimes a few hired hands. The businesses occupy the front of the house in which the family lives, and are attended to by family members in between other activities such as housework and baby care, school attendance and homework, watching television and entertaining visitors, shopping for stock or selling products. People in such businesses work hard, but they can also take a day off for illness or a funeral, rest or nap when the heat is unbearable, go to the bathroom without having to ask permission, and have the kinds of control over their own actions which factory conditions are designed to prevent. Such reasons are often cited for the popularity of small businesses.

The economic basis of small business is different from factory work as well. In a family enterprise, as in a farm household, the family, not the individual, is the significant unit. Family members do not receive wages but draw on household funds, usually managed by the wife or mother-in-law, when they need money. She may also regularly distribute a little pocket money for cigarettes, snacks, or movies. Household members work at jobs for which their talents and other commitments suit them, not for the short-run reward of wages but for the long-term good of the family. If jobs are plentiful "outside" and pay better than the value a member can contribute at home, the family urges her or him to look for work and mobilizes its network of contacts to help find it. When a family member working "outside" is laid off, she or he returns home and expects to be reabsorbed into the family economic unit.

Such small businesses are well suited to Taiwan's expanding economy; in 1973 enterprises with fewer than ten workers made up 90 percent of all businesses (DGBAS 1974: Table 230), though this percentage has been diminishing in recent years.[1] Such enterprises are rational and positive adaptations to Taiwan's economy because they use labor in a flexible and inexpensive way—people in them work hard and long, sometimes only in return for simple shelter, food, and clothing. In prospering households, they will receive a more comfortable standard of living—even luxuries such as a higher education—and sons will receive shares in a growing investment of capital in the house and business.

The experience of Mr. Kho, whose life history is detailed in Chapter 7, tells us what can happen when a small-scale family business expands and becomes successful. He was able to educate one son, now a professional in a related field and living elsewhere, while the other son, still living with his father, continues as a small contractor. Mr. Kho's general-goods store is managed by his daughter-in-law, and the whole family has gained financial advantage from the rents that come from his final large investment, the

1. Because of changes in government statistical categories, it is not possible to calculate the 1980 figure for these very small businesses.

apartment building he built and retired to. This family is not rich, but their daughter-in-law can afford a trip to Southeast Asia.

By contrast, the family of Mrs. Lim, whom we will meet in Chapter 9, runs a house-front shop that was only very modestly successful for years as an electrical repair business and that now does a little better as a fruit-and-ice shop. They hope that training a son to bake bread will improve business enough through diversification, provide work at home for one of the under-employed daughters, and enable one of the sons to support a wife. Miss Ong's picture-copying business (see Chapter 6), for which no one else in her family is trained, struggles along, dependent on the suitability of her home as a business location.

Through education, some working-class young people escape the neces-sity of manual labor or shopkeeping by finding white-collar jobs as office workers for the government or large private businesses (I will discuss this much desired occupational shift in Chapter 9). Very few people can achieve such education by their own efforts. An economically stable family that is willing to pay the student's expenses and forgo the labor he could contrib-ute or the income he would otherwise earn is behind most successful white-collar workers. This pattern has existed for a long time: Mrs. Lim's backing from her educated and prosperous families enabled her to become a schoolteacher; Mr. Kho's respectable farm family encouraged his rise to the position of tea agronomist. The poorest person among our subjects, Mr. Kang (Chapter 6), has no relatives at all in Taiwan to help him. In general, the relatives of people who have been laborers all their lives, like Mrs. Lo, have had little to help them with.

When we examine working-class occupations, we see that the most desirable of them, small business, promises a decent living, often actually provides it, and offers hope that with careful management and the right kind of family a really substantial enterprise, or professional career for the children, can be attained. The values of small-business families permeate the rest of the working class, whose members, despite severe odds, are sometimes able to escape from bitter labor by good luck and adherence to those values. The desire for the independence and social mobility that small businesses make possible motivates the traditionally frugal, savings-conscious, hard-working life style of traditional Chinese families, and ex-plains the deep distress felt by some of our older subjects at what they see as the free-spending, pleasure-loving younger generation. A family whose younger members fail to learn the tough lessons of their parents may indeed cut themselves off from many opportunities. As long as the expan-sion of the economy continues, however, even the slackers will find jobs to

[77]

support themselves. Prolonged economic stagnation or depression would very likely bring rebellious younger folks to a new appreciation of the importance, for working-class people, of the family as a safety net, a critical human resource.

The special place of small business even in the spirit world is symbolized for Taiwanese by a shrine in most places of business to either the Earth God, seen as a god of wealth, or Guan Gong, a god of war among other things. ("Why war?" I asked a shopkeeper. "Because being a merchant is a struggle—it is kill or be killed in business," he replied.) The Earth God is a benevolent-looking, white-bearded old gentleman seated on an imperial magistrate's throne, while Guan Gong, with the brilliant red face of a rough fellow, brandishes both his battle sword and a writing brush for keeping accounts. A foot-high wooden image of one of them, illuminated by red electric lamps, surveys most Taiwanese shops from a rear wall, cajoled by daily sticks of incense and twice-monthly food offerings to bring prosperity to the enterprise.

Working-class families often have several members who work, and consider it ideal that a family's occupations should be varied. A small business managed by the mother and her daughter-in-law, construction work for the husband and eldest son, a job as a clerk in a bank for the better-educated younger son, and a factory place for an unmarried daughter make a nice mix: stability, though low incomes, from shop and clerking, bigger wages, if intermittently, from skilled house building, and a little extra cash from the daughter's paycheck. Many parents deliberately steer offspring into such combinations and readily shift work to seize new opportunities. Although some working-class Mainlanders form small business partnerships for lack of kinfolk with whom to cooperate, the Chinese prefer the family as the basic economic unit. Whether success in life is to be achieved through business or some other route, it is achieved more readily by "pooling and sharing" group resources than by individual effort alone (Wang Sung-hsing 1971).

Even when they do not establish their own businesses, people like to find work near home. If they must go far afield for employment, rather than move their residence, many prefer long commutes or even periods of separation from their families, so that on holidays at least they can return to their "old home." The frequent moves from one city to another that Americans endure for the sake of steady work and career advancement would strike most Chinese as terribly disruptive to the network of human relations that everyone wants to develop. Fortunately for them, Taiwan is a rather small place with good transportation. When the economy is thriving, people can usually follow the employment frontiers while at the same time keeping very close ties with a permanent home. Though Taiwanese people have far deeper roots in island communities, even many Mainlanders have by now established such home bases in their adopted province. Military encampments, squatters' areas, and blocks of public housing originally filled with strangers have become neighborhoods, developing gossip grapevines and sometimes holding folk celebrations together. These new communities re-create, often with very heterogeneous populations, the villagelike places where characteristic patterns of social and family relations can thrive.

Rural villages and working-class city neighborhoods contain many workplaces, which are the result of innumerable choices made by people who trust personal over impersonal social relations, prefer self-employment to occupational subordination to others, and, probably quite accurately, suspect "society" of having very little concern for their well-being. Working for a living is risky business.

Guo A Gui: "People Have to Have Fun, Too!"

Guo A Gui is a native Taiwanese woman in her late fifties whose life has been spent in "bitter labor." Nonetheless, she has managed, through hard work and poor living, to accumulate a little property and become a landlord on a very small scale. Her life story reveals much about working-class Taiwanese life under both Japanese and Nationalist rule. For her, the change of government and the improved economy have not meant a great deal, although some of her misfortunes are the result of accidents that might have happened anywhere. Having entered into a union with a Mainlander who has no relatives or useful contacts, and having failed to produce a filial son of her own, Miss Guo has been unable to build the kind of patrilineal family that would have contributed to her income and given her an easier life. Like many of the women in this study, she has had to depend largely on her own exertions in a society where a woman's efforts do not receive many economic rewards. Despite what she sees as a hard, unfortunate life, Guo A Gui—Cassia Guo—remains cheerful, optimistic, and energetic.

When Miss Guo and I met in the cafeteria where she washes dishes and prepares vegetables, she set out to charm me, making the most of her limited Mandarin and my limited Taiwanese. Flattery, teasing, lessons in Japanese: soon she was interviewing *me*. When I told her about my collections of life histories, she not only volunteered but promised expansively to help me find many "sufferers" who would tell me how poor people *really*

[79]

lived. She did, too, introducing me into many houses in the squatter settlement in which she lived and inviting friends over to reminisce into my tape recorder. Lo A Lan, whose life story follows this one, was our most frequent visitor and interviewee.

Cassia Guo, Orchid Lo, one of my field assistants, and I sat together in Miss Guo's living room many afternoons, with Mrs. Lo interjecting an occasional episode of her hard history, the assistant and I giggling and taking notes, and Miss Guo getting uproariously, gloriously drunk. Sometimes she insisted that we all go out to meet people under her loud patronage. These outings were awkward for Mrs. Lo, humiliating for my assistant, and immensely revealing for me, as I was literally dragged behind the veil of courtesy and privacy that most Chinese draw around their families in the presence of an outsider.

I reluctantly discouraged these uninvited forays, pointing out that planned visits in which people could comfortably tell their stories were better for making the careful record my work required. Miss Guo acquiesced but reminded me repeatedly thereafter to be less serious about life: "People have to have fun, too!" She seemed to enjoy thoroughly the taping, the questions, the opportunity to expand on subjects of interest to her. While the alcohol she drank—a nasty-smelling medicinal liquor with genuinely unpleasant aftereffects—made for much repetition and sententiousness, it also created the extraordinarily relaxed atmosphere in which these near-strangers recalled their pasts.

Although she was willing to reveal herself in this way in her own house and neighborhood, Miss Guo presented herself much differently when she left the squatter settlement. At work, she dressed neatly, if ungracefully, in loose pants, blouses, and long knit vests; her hair was always tidily crimped; her words were deferential, even if her eyes were often ironic in her dealings with the blustering and nearly incomprehensible Hunan cook she worked under. Walking in the settlement, she would seize my hand as if to stress our friendship to her neighbors, dropping it as we left the area's boundaries where only strangers would observe us. While it was necessary to appear respectable in public, among people who, like herself, had few claims to respectability she could enjoy the undisciplined, emotional side of life.

Old ladies who drink heavily, talk openly about sex, and are bold in their relations with others are by no means uncommon in Taiwan. The older a woman is, and the poorer and more rural her background, the more likely she is to conduct herself in this way, at least in private. Miss Guo did not live in a village or even a large slum, but in a shrinking enclave of poverty set in what had come to be a fairly fashionable neighborhood. Comfortable upper-middle-class condos, superb little restaurants specializing in mainland cuisines, glittering boutiques, and one of the city's newest department stores were only steps away, making her poverty, her thoroughly unbourgeois style, conspicuous.

The squatter neighborhood where Miss Guo, her common-law husband, and about five thousand others live has no name. Land belonging to a wealthy Taiwanese family—their once-elegant ancestral hall still stands, surrounded by the hundreds of tiny make-shift houses—was confiscated for a barracks by the Ministry of National Defense after the Mainlanders arrived in Taiwan. Because the military compound occupied only a part of the land, the remainder soon began to attract squatter residents, at first the households of men stationed at the barracks, and then demobilized men and their families. In recent years, poorer migrants to the city from Taiwan's mountains and countryside have joined the mix. Though the houses have improved over the years in sturdiness and amenities, the density of population may be even greater than in the past. Miss Guo, for example, owns and rents out, to six people, a house with four 5-foot by 5-foot bedrooms, an 8-foot by 6-foot shared dining room and tiny cooking, bathing, and toilet facilities.

Accepting the inevitability of such squatments, Taibei City authorities over the years have provided some water and sewerage to this and the many other slum neighborhoods of the growing city. Each house is marked by the small blue plaque bearing its official address as listed on household registration forms and personal identity cards, slotting it in through bureaucratic procedures as a legitimate residence.

The area is now less noisome and dangerous to health than in 1968, when a large open canal carrying raw sewage and a local commercial specialization in caged watchdogs and dog meat filled the air with stench, mosquitoes, and perpetual, insane barking. The canal is covered, much of the housing has been removed to widen major roads, and the rest will soon disappear under urban renewal.

For the present, it affords Miss Guo a comfortable haven for her eccentricities—a handy base from which to find yet another in her lifelong series of low-paid service jobs, and a network of contacts among those who, like herself, often need a day's work, or a week's loan, or an hour's conviviality.

Guo A Gui told me her life story in the following words.

Look at me, an old bag of fifty-nine who can hardly read a word, telling my life to a scholar. That's a laugh! My whole life I've suffered because I didn't study, and because I'm too fast with my mouth. Being too quick to answer back is something that is just part of my character, I guess. Can't be helped. But not studying really wasn't my fault. When I was little, I was too lively. Then, in my teens, there was no money for it. At the end of the Japanese period, I was going to get the chance for night school—and the war ended. I lost that opportunity, too, so I'm still a dunce. Even so, maybe my life can be a lesson to young people to study hard, or they will have to live with the bitterness I eat every day.

My father was born in the Dalongdong section of the city, my mother in Sancheng, across the river. Father and Mother opened up rice fields in Dalongdong, farmed them, and sold rice, very respectable sort of work, because everyone depends on farmers. At first, they were quite prosperous, but about the time I was born, they started to lose their business and land. By the time father was dead and buried, when I was six, there was nothing left. Mother had a primary-school education, so she was able to get a job in the Japanese soy-sauce factory that my elder sister and I later worked in. She didn't want to marry again because she was afraid people would laugh at us children for having two fathers. No one with any face likes that idea.

I had an elder brother, who died serving in the Japanese Army in the war, and two elder sisters. Have they been lucky! The older was able to study and get a primary-school graduation certificate, even though she didn't complete all the courses. She married a man with a good job and land, although they lost almost all of it in land reform! Her and her husband's business has prospered so that she's been on a trip around the world. They are respected people. Their neighbors have elected him Neighborhood Head[2] many times. Second Elder Sister also married well, and has six sons. Their fortunes have been entirely different from mine.

Even when I was little, I was a mischievous child, always running away. Mother punished me, so I'd run away from her, too. "The farther you run, the more I'll beat you!" she'd say. I can remember running from her, watching her, not daring to go back until she went back in the house, afraid of being beaten. We country kids weren't very well behaved—running away, then sneaking home like thieves.

School was no good for me. I hardly went at all. It was more use to my family, and more interesting for me, to get little jobs harvesting, looking after people's water buffalo, doing things around farms that I could get paid for.

When I was thirteen, and my oldest sister married, our whole household moved with her husband to downtown Taibei. He was an official in the

---

2. The second lowest-ranked elective office in Taiwan, responsible for liaison between the government and about one hundred neighboring families.

electric-light bureau, rich enough to take care of us. I found some odd jobs, moving stone or coal for people. It was about that time that elder sister adopted a baby daughter-in-law to marry her son.

When I was fourteen, my second older sister used her influence to get me a job in the soy-sauce factory. Even though I had no primary school certificate—and that factory required education of all its employees—they took me on because she spoke for me. She was a diligent worker for them, very obedient. They even let her live in their dormitory. I worked there till I was nineteen, when the factory closed because of the war.

The factory was a really big one, with each of their sauce vats as big as this room.[3] There'd be a half-a-year's sauce in there. Above the vats was a mess of piping and gauges. It was awfully dangerous to go up there, because everything was so slippery; if you fell, you'd be dead for sure. No one else dared go up but me—I was young and foolish and had lots of nerve, so I went up to look at temperatures and see how much was left in each vat. Maybe that's why they kept me on as long as they did, because I sure was no model worker!

The place was run in a very orderly way. The couple of hundred people employed—Japanese managers and Japanese and Taiwanese workers— were all expected to arrive promptly at seven, when the bell rang. Anyone who came late was not allowed in, but had to wait till the one o'clock afternoon period began. I'd be scurrying along, barefoot, to get to work on time, jumping into my shoes at the door. (We had to wear shoes to work, but they were so expensive I wore mine only when it was required.) At twelve, when the bell rang, everyone stopped work for an hour's lunch and rest. The factory was very strict, regular, and better-run than factories are now, when people drift in late, goof off during working hours, and have to stay late to finish up. Sundays and holidays we had off.

I earned fifteen sen[4] a day, while my sister got twenty. We also got a New

---

3. About 8 feet by 10 feet.

4. Units of currency used in these life histories vary considerably in value over time; for a complete discussion, see Riggs 1952:103–107. In the 1930s the Taiwanese used the Japanese yen and sen (100 sen to the yen), which began to suffer from inflation after the Pacific War began in 1937. The yen, which had been a fairly stable currency during the earlier decades of the century, rapidly lost value as Japan's production was channeled into the destructiveness of war. When Nationalist authorities arrived to take control of the island after the war, they changed the currency to what soon was to be known as the Old Taiwan dollar, roughly equivalent to the inflated yen of the time. In June 1949, to cope with the rampant inflation brought from the mainland, OT dollars were withdrawn and replaced with New Taiwan dollars, each worth OT$40,000. The NT lost value consistently during the 1950s, although ever more slowly, so inflation of a serious nature persisted over a period of more than twenty years, most of it under Nationalist leadership.

Year's bonus of one month's wages—about five yen. If we were absent for a funeral or for illness, we got half our wages. For absence caused by a work-related injury, we were paid our usual wage and given money for medical expenses, too. A woman having a baby could have forty days' leave, although she didn't get paid.

I was a playful kid, and found some of their rules hard to obey. Though the factory forbade workers to go around and socialize during working hours, I was alone in that upstairs area, so I got bored. I'd buy cakes and candies from an old Japanese priest who lived near our house to give to friends at work. Once the head of the factory caught me, and he docked me five sen for that day. Worse yet, when the New Year's bonus was distributed, I only got half my bonus. If my sister hadn't pleaded for me, I'd have lost the job. Sister was furious: "How can you mess up right before New Year! Don't you see we're going to be short of money at home because of you, fool!" I think they kept me because I was willing to do the dangerous jobs.

One of the Japanese workers liked to lord it over us. He made only seven yen a month, but he thought he was a big shot, always trying to manage other people's business. When he told me I couldn't rest a moment, even though my work was done, I started to beat him up. We were taken before the special-affairs department of the factory where the dispute was settled in my favor. Even though I was a young girl and a Taiwanese, I had the right of it. The Japanese were reasonable people.

The Japanese were reasonable about most things, but they were fanatics on cleanliness. They wanted the environment kept really clean. For example, vegetable selling on the street was prohibited—it had to be in a market, and the market had to be swept and washed. Streets, privies—they inspected everything. I think they went too far, though, in pushing their way right into people's houses. These were regular inspections where they'd check windows for dirt, and so on, and they'd fine people ten to thirty yen if the house wasn't clean enough!

The Japanese were strict and punished people. They took money from us during the war, because they needed it. Otherwise, they weren't bad. They didn't beat us, or misbehave. They caught criminals effectively, so that

---

There is no simple way to convert these numbers to current U.S. dollars, and the problem is made yet more difficult because of the drastic difference in living standards and expectations between the present-day United States and the Taiwan of those years. The best measure of change is what a day's manual labor was worth: presumably a small family could survive for a day at least on such wages. Finally, because NT dollars are unofficially tied to the U.S. dollar, Taiwan and the United States have experienced about the same inflation since the 1960s—over 50 percent.

there were far fewer thieves and ruffians than there are now. But those house inspections were too much!

The Japanese had their own sections of town, housing clusters for factories and soldiers, and their own markets. They never mixed with us much, and they rarely took Taiwanese women as wives or girlfriends, except for a few waitresses. Taiwanese men didn't marry them either. We all know the reason for this; there's no reason to discuss unpleasant matters.[5]

When the war started, so did the bombing. At the soy-sauce factory, we'd stop work and take cover, then start again. It was very scary. As Taibei's factories were the focus of the bombing, some of them began to move to southern Taiwan, taking their workers with them. My brother-in-law's electricity bureau sent our whole family to Xingang City. Others were sent to Jiayi City. The Japanese took good care of us, providing us with transportation and necessities. We took all our relatives and some of our neighbors. For ordinary Taiwanese who did not work for the Japanese, things were much tougher. Only rich people could afford to flee south.

The Xingang people were good to us. Farmers sent us sweet potatoes, which we boiled and lived on while we were there, for about two months. For those who went to Jiayi, there was a terrible surprise—instead of bombing Taibei, the Americans bombed Jiayi, for two days. They just flattened it, destroying the airport and all factories and institutions. The third day was the day the Japanese surrendered.

We thought we were going to die in Xingang, but through Mazu's[6] protection, we were saved. Later, Japanese soldiers said that Mazu redirected the bombs that should have fallen on the town so that they fell instead into the harbor. The bottom of the sea exploded, and the fish died, but no people of Xingang, or nearby Beigang, were killed. That is why so many of us Taiwanese worship Mazu since Retrocession.

That is one example of how reasonable religious customs really are; here's another. There is a village in Hong Kong where the people don't eat pork. The reason for that is that long ago, all the adults died, and only one pig was left alive, which nursed all the babies with its milk. Afterward, their descendants wouldn't eat pork out of gratitude to the mother pig. We Taiwanese don't eat beef because cattle work for us so hard and so patiently. So we have our hands behind our backs as far as cattle go. Everything has its explanation.

When we returned home, our house had been burned in the bombing.

---

5. Chinese often describe Japanese practices in Taiwan as racist.

6. Mazu, the Taiwanese goddess of the sea, has a famous temple in Xingang, and is much revered in that region.

Some paper money we had hidden in the walls was lost, but it didn't really matter. The inflation had begun, and it took a lot of cash to buy just a package of cigarettes. I saved some Japanese coins as souvenirs.

After we returned to Taibei, a friend recommended me for a job in a cake shop, where I stayed a year. I can still make cake, too. My lack of education was no problem there. I was paid according to the number of pastries I made, but I worked so fast that the boss switched me to a harder kind. I was able to make about two hundred yen a day, worth about NT$2 (U.S.$0.05) now.

I was still a wild sort of kid. People differ so much—some are reasonable while they're still very young, others don't get sense till they're adults. Take my sister, always so obedient. But me . . . ! Mother was always dissatisfied with me, scolding me for going out to watch Taiwanese opera in the street: "Don't you have to go to work tomorrow? What are you doing, running around so late!" Sometimes when I came in very late, she'd have locked up the house, leaving me outside. Where could I sleep? At last, she'd let me in. My sister didn't go to see opera so often, because she was better educated. That's why I was so wild—no education. When I quarreled with people, they would taunt me, saying, "What kind of education have you had? It was wasted on you!" So some of us end up worse than the rest, and even cleverness is useless. If you lose out on education, you lose everything.

During and after the war, things were very chaotic in Taiwan. There was a period of about a year when the Japanese soldiers fell short of food because the bombing was preventing farmers from growing crops and bringing them to market. The Japanese couldn't help the people, and they couldn't help themselves. The whole island lacked rice, clothes, and medicine. If you got sick, you died.

Right after Retrocession, a lot of Japanese property was claimed by Taiwanese. Some Taiwanese robbed the Japanese, who couldn't put up any resistance—they were the losers. They were insulted and threatened by Taiwanese, too. When we came back to Taibei from Xingang, I was only a young person, but I stopped people from insulting some Japanese, who, after all, were just soldiers sent here by the government. *They* weren't to blame. In fact, they should be pitied. I gave one soldier a bowl of sweet-potato soup, and, for taking it, his platoon leader beat him up. I felt awful that that terrible beating came from something I had done. I was glad to see the Japanese soldiers being sent back to Japan. If they'd stayed here, they've have died, because there was no food on the island.

After the soldiers from the mainland came, things were very bad; everyone was afraid after Retrocession. Everywhere, their soldiers were out attacking Taiwanese women. Girls didn't dare walk on darkened streets or go to work. Things happened to many women. Some died, some got pregnant. Taiwanese men didn't dare resist when Mainlanders insulted Taiwanese women, just as nowadays the Mainlanders still take advantage of us in business. The Japanese were reasonable, and never let that kind of thing go on when they were in power, but now the Mainlanders oppress people and lie to us. When Mainlander soldiers got Taiwanese girls pregnant, their officers didn't order them to marry them.

At that time there were very few Taiwanese prostitutes, because in the Japanese period the government provided soldiers' clubs with Japanese and Korean women for the troops. Taiwanese women were forbidden to be in such places, because the Japanese despised us and would beat up Taiwanese women. The Japanese were very strict—if they wanted you to die, you obeyed. So there weren't many Taiwanese prostitutes. When all those Mainland soldiers came, they just acted as if we were all prostitutes. That's what happened to me, when I was twenty-four. I was too wild, and I became pregnant. At first, I didn't want to marry the man. There was always the chance that the army would counterattack against the Communist bandits, and he'd be sent back to the mainland. But our lives are arranged by fate. My father was dead, my mother said I needed protection. The soldiers had their rice every month, and we had almost nothing.

Then it turned out that he couldn't marry me after all! He was ten years older than I, and already married in his home in Sichuan Province. Lots of mainland soldiers were already married, and married again in Taiwan anyway, but this man's marriage was registered on his military identity card. So we couldn't be formally married. I suppose you could say he's just my boy friend! He had a seventy-seven-year-old mother, a wife, and three sons all left behind. It was a mistake that he was in the army in the first place. His brother was supposed to be taken, but since the brother wasn't home, the recruiters just took him. They put a rope around his neck, dragged him away, and sent him straight to Taiwan.

I'll say this for him, though. He stuck by me after I told him I had his child in my belly. He sent us food and a little money when he could during the years he stayed in the army, when he often had to move to new places.

He never learned Taiwanese, so I talk to him in a kind of Taiwanese Mandarin, and we can communicate. When I speak Taiwanese to him, he listens, and can get the outline of my meaning. He's always been a good cook, preferring his own cooking to mine. The kids used to say, "What Father cooks tastes good, what you cook doesn't." So I've always let him cook.

I continued to live with Mother till she died, about six years after

Retrocession, and with my first elder sister's children whom Mother was taking care of. Sister had eleven children, all brought up by Mother. As each got old enough for school, it would go home to Sister. The last was three when Mother died. Mother took care of my two girls while I worked too. I had to be out by six every morning to reach my job in a cafeteria by seven. It was too far to go home in the hour we had for lunch. Work ended at five, I was home by six, so Mother really had all the responsibility for my two, and several of Sister's, all those years. After Mother died, I still didn't have a son, so I decided to adopt a son from one of my relatives.

In those days, women had their babies at home. When I gave birth the first time, I sent for a midwife. The second time, just a neighbor and Mother helped me—we relied on each other and on experienced people. I didn't have any trouble giving birth, just rested a month before starting work again.

I nursed my babies—everyone did, then. We didn't have powdered cow's milk as today's lucky mothers do. While I was at work, Mother fed the babies rice water with a spoon—no baby bottles with rubber nipples then, either!

I didn't pay any special attention to bringing my children up. Those who are born obedient and reasonable will be obedient and reasonable. It's important to teach them some manners, of course. For example, when a guest comes, I taught them to serve a cup of tea or, if there's no tea, a cup of boiled water, so they'd become accustomed to proper behavior.

There's not so much emphasis on obedience to adults for today's children. Kids used to learn to *move* when their parents told them to do something. Nowadays, children just go on studying if you tell them to do something, or run off and play. People don't beat their kids anymore, or even dare scold them much.

In 1955 the government made a lot of soldiers who had served for ten years retire, so the five of us moved into this squatter settlement with a lot of other retired mainland soldiers and their wives. Some of the wives were Mainlanders, some Taiwanese, and some even mountain Aborigine women. The land was the government's, no one was living on it, so homeless people came here. The area used to be much bigger—there were a lot of squatters. We built a little house of whatever we could find, carried water from some taps that were put in, and managed as best we could.

It was hard for the children's father to find work in those days. He used to tell me he had been healthy and strong in his youth, but the army life killed his strength. Not enough food, too many diseases. Finally, he got a job cleaning up in the market up the street, the kind of work a lot of old Mainlanders get—cleaning toilets, sweeping up. He and I are pretty well matched, born into respectable farm families, but later becoming poor. Couples who differ too much can't be together.

We could have married, in later years, but we never did. Many men who had registered dependents back home arranged to have somebody in Hong Kong mail a letter saying the first wife had died. If we'd done that, we could have married. We wanted to, and I really wanted a husband. But in our hearts, we felt wrong about it. I took off my clothes for him, and had his babies. What was there to fear, really? Just other people's bad mouths. People despise me, but I can still live, talk with friends, have a few laughs. Me and my old lover!

After he retired, he got a few hundred a month from the army—not enough to eat on. He rarely had work, but I've always been willing to work. I worked in restaurants and in people's houses, mostly. Once, I cleaned and washed clothes for a judge's wife. They had a car—really rich people. Mainlanders. I was supposed to get NT$2,000 a month for two hours' work every day, but that woman was always cheating me. She'd always want me to stay more than two hours, and though I worked for her for two years, she never raised my wage. At midautumn festival and New Year, she only gave me five hundred, though it is customary to give a month's pay. She picked and complained and found fault. I had to take it—I needed the job. I was born to work all my life. Finally, I quit because she was taking advantage of me. In another job I had with a Mainlander lady, I was paid only thirteen hundred a month, always paid late, and had to listen to the boss talk constantly. I quit her, too, after a while. In a Taiwanese family who ran a wood business I washed and cooked for NT$1,800 a month. They were too harsh.

I still have two jobs, getting up at five to sweep streets till nine. I'm considered "needy" by the government, so I was able to get that work. It pays a couple of thousand a month. In the cafeteria, I peel vegetables for two hours every day—that brings in six to seven thousand. I got that through my neighbor, Orchid, who worked there before. Sometimes I substitute for this short-faced kid who works in a restaurant.

Neighbors around here help each other—it's not a bad place to live because of that. People help me get jobs, I help them when they need someone to work for them. We watch each other's houses, take in the laundry if it rains, that kind of thing. One of my neighbors is registered as "poor," a welfare case. She's had a terrible time, so when I have leftover food, I take it over to her. She got used to eating people's leftovers, though these days people are usually too proud to do that. Everybody helps her. After all, it's awful to waste food. We help each other with money, too. I'll pop in on Orchid, and say "Hey, Orchid! Hurry up and lend me three hundred for a few days" and she does. I'd only do that with a good friend; other people would laugh at me. We don't charge each other interest or anything. Poor people don't do that. It's just for friendship. I run a tab with the little shops in the neighborhood, too, paying when I get paid.

I wouldn't dare borrow from a moneylender who charges interest. The poor, if they want to borrow from the rich, have to persuade them with a lot of ass-kissing talk. If they're flattered, they'll lend—otherwise, not. People like me don't form rotating credit clubs,[7] either. In those things, you can go broke if the person organizing it gets overextended, or if somebody runs out on his debt. I work myself to death for my money, and can't take the risk. Besides, rich people wouldn't ask us to join their rotating clubs, not if we live in a squatter settlement! And if I had savings—which I don't—I'd put it in the post office or a bank. It's safer.

There are quite a few pawnshops around here, but it's mostly young toughs who go there. I'm bold, but I wouldn't want to be seen going into one—too shameful. Once, when I was so broke there was no money for food, I pawned a coat. I asked someone else to go to the pawnshop for me, though. It was so embarrassing.

People pawn all kinds of things. Motorcycles are always being pawned, though you have to have the owner's registration to prove the bike is your own, not a stolen one. Interest is heavy, about 5 percent a month, in advance, for three months. After that, the pawnbroker gets to keep it if the debt hasn't been paid. Pawnbrokers offer less than the thing is worth, then sell it at a high price, so it's a hard way to get money. Better to go to friends.

There are some rough characters living in this area, especially young ones. Some of them organize gangs, drink, smoke, and get in fights. Occasionally one of them knifes somebody, or one of them gets beaten to death. They seem to go bad during junior high school. If they go bad then, they go bad all the way. The best that can be hoped is that they stay out of jail. They don't bother me, though. I've got nothing to steal, and everyone around here knows me.

Up to five years ago, I had a lot of friends in this neighborhood—nice people, well-off. One lady's husband was a gold jeweler; others had other kinds of shops. They could afford to take trips, go to entertainments, ride on motorcycles. They used to invite me to come along because I made them laugh and have a good time, even if I was poor. They're all gone, now, though, leaving me a lonely old woman.

What happened was that there was a big fire that burned up a lot of the squatters' houses. A lot of my friends moved away. My house was burned,

7. Groups that pool small sums to make unsecured loans to each member in turn.

too. I dug through the ashes afterward, and found only a few coins I'd saved. I had some gold jewelry, my radio, a lighter, a tape recorder—everything went. I had worked so hard to buy that house about a year before. A lot of people were burned out, right in the area where the Taibei City government wanted to build the overpass Orchid's husband is working on. Strange, eh?

I got some disaster relief—a thousand (U.S.$25) from the local Ward Office, five hundred (U.S.$12.50) and a piece of clothing for each person from the Guanyin temple by the market, and a hundred and fifty *jin*[8] of rice from the government.

Two months later, I scraped together eighty thousand (U.S.$2,000) and bought this house. Owning your own is better than renting. There are always squabbles about how to divide up the electric and water charges when you're a renter. It pays me fifteen hundred (U.S.$37.50) a month—NT$500 for each room. A couple of years later, I bought another place behind this one for a hundred thousand (U.S.$2,500). It has several rooms that I rent out for five thousand (U.S.$125) a month. These houses are all built on government land, and the whole area is going to be cleared out for modernization in two or three years. I'll get thirty thousand (U.S.$750) and a small moving fee when it happens, but that's laughable. I guess the best thing for us to do is to move in with my relatives back in Dalongdong—that's where my kids are—and get all the rent I can until I lose my investment here. I've had such terrible luck! Whenever I make any money, fire or the government takes it away!

If my husband had stayed in the army till he was sixty, he would have retired with a good pension and a high rank, like Orchid's. We'd be rich. As it is, he only gets nine hundred a month.

My daughters complain anyway about me living here and working at my age. They're like all my female relatives—good fates, every one of them! My elder brother died in the Japanese Army, and of course my husband has no relatives here, so my sisters' families are all I've got. I've never wanted to let them see how poor I've been, never liked asking them to help me. My daughters didn't work and earn money for me—they just wanted to get married. Their husbands didn't give me bride-price, either. They weren't rich, so I was ashamed to ask for it. My adopted son is not so close to me. There is just me and my old man.

I think my fate was a bad one: born to be a laborer, not getting a bit of the good things of life. I wish there were someone to pity me, but there's not, so I just live like this, keeping independent so others won't despise me. My

8. A *jin* is approximately one and one-third pounds.

sisters are rich, but I don't eat their food. I'd lose face. No matter what kind of work I do, I am criticized. Time makes people see clearly, though. After a long time, they will know I've been a good person.

Lo A Lan: The One Who Was Sold

Mrs. Lo, now in her early sixties, is descended from the Mountain People who inhabited Taiwan before the Chinese came. While there are now perhaps a quarter of a million Mountain People in Taiwan who are recognized as such, many more have, over the centuries, become sinified by learning Chinese languages and customs. Some have melted into the Taiwanese population, which itself is well mixed with mainland minority peoples. Chinese people generally see sinification as a process of cultural betterment, or progress; an Aboriginal background is something to be overcome and to conceal. Mrs. Lo does not think of herself as a Mountain Person, though the Chinese around her do, partly because of her round-eyed appearance, and partly because her original surname, Pan, was taken by many Aborigines as they "became Chinese." She accounts for the differences between her mountain home and the cities of the lowlands in terms of poverty and wealth, insisting she is Chinese.

In a country where most people are relatively short by American standards, Lo A Lan is exceptionally small, a smallness that comes, almost certainly, from childhood starvation. Orphaned, sold, widowed, and left destitute with her children by the time she was thirty, it is no wonder that much of her conversation revolves around food and that her eyes follow automatically when others eat. Her face and hands are calloused, her scarred feet give evidence of the hardness of her life, and she makes no attempt to prettify them. Her early life of "bitter labor" reveals the kind of poverty that many islanders and Mainlanders alike suffered in the early decades of this century. It shows too the special hardness of life for girls and women in rural areas. Lo A Lan's introduction to Taiwan's new Nationalist rulers was the best thing that ever happened to her; she was amused when I suggested that many Taiwanese remembered the prewar days warmly. "Rich people, maybe," she wryly agreed.

It is difficult to believe now that this tiny, aging woman ever had the strength to earn her living as a construction worker and to struggle successfully through to what will probably be a fairly comfortable old age. She seems to have run out of life. Even in lively company, after a drink or two, she looks quiet and tired, though she says her health is good. Although at times she cries over her memories, she shows no anger—and only traces of other emotions—at the events of her harsh life. It may be that anxiety will never let her go now, after such long association. Her automatic precautions against want are at once visible in her living room, which is neatly crowded with careful savings: stacks of newspapers, folded paper and plastic bags, hanks of string and rope, sacks of rags, empty glass bottles. When I brought cakes and pastries for her and a friend to eat during our meetings, she would accept nothing, or at most a half piece, though the rest of us nibbled greedily enough. She was too used to bad food, she said, to really enjoy good; it made her uneasy. Perhaps she feared to acquire a taste for things beyond her expectations; perhaps she took more satisfaction in controlling her appetites than she could feel in indulging them.

The house where I sometimes visited her told other things about her. It was built of random pieces of scrap lumber, painted and unpainted, old and new, neatly and securely fashioned into a residence with a small bedroom, a living room, and a tiny, tidy kitchen and bathing room. The separate toilet was shared with the thirty-odd other households that lived in similar motley cottages, laid out in two neat rows, in a field of rubble. They had been built from the fragments of other demolished houses by her husband and the other men of the crew who were constructing an overpass for a major freeway crossing the city.

In front of her house, in the barren subsoil, grew a few undernourished cabbages and leafy greens, and several feeble clumps of flowers. She grew them to make the place look better, she said, but mostly to have something to keep her busy. When she popped in on her friend, Guo A Gui, her conversation was often about work: finding it, losing it, how much she could do, why her husband wouldn't let her take this job or that. Becoming too anxious to sit still, she would pop out again, birdlike, to find some occupation. In moments of quiet, she told me her story.

When I was young, down in the south of Taiwan, there weren't as many people as there are now, and life was very hard. We southerners were worked to death, just to get enough for three meals a day. We were paid so little for our work—just enough to keep alive. People today are much better off. Then, only if we had work that day could we eat that day. In my mother's time, it was bad too. But children now have even become fussy about what they eat: if it's not good-tasting, they won't eat it! Food today's children won't eat was food we never even saw on our table. When I was small, when there was any food at all, I was glad to see it.

We southerners ate mostly sweet potatoes and salt fish. We bought the cheapest little salt fish, boiled them, and drank the soup to give some flavor to boiled sweet potatoes. There are lots of bamboo shoots in the mountains

[93]

to gather. We ate those fresh in season, and preserved some in Japanese sauce and salt for later. Ginger grows well there too. We didn't grow leafy vegetables, and as it took half a day to go down the mountain to market, we never bought any. Very rarely, we would buy ten sen worth of peanuts or bean curd as side dishes. When I was attending school, I ate gruel with a little salt. The other children called me to sit with them, but I would go off by myself to eat, because I was ashamed of what was in my lunchbox. I'd come home and say, "Mother! The other children's food is good. Why is ours so bad?!" She could not answer me. I don't find fault with food now. I'm used to bad food. I can eath both good and bad food.

I am sixty-three now. I was born in the countryside of Tainan county, in the foothills of the mountains in south Taiwan. People planted patches of sweet potatoes in the valleys and collected wood and mountain products for sale. Growing the sweet potatoes was difficult. Farming is always hard, but in the mountains wild pigs come at night and root up the potatoes. Some are bigger than domestic pigs, with sharp tusks—really dangerous. A wild pig was eating our crop one year and ate up a whole field. We predicted that it would move next to another nearby plot, so Father, Uncle, and I dug a deep pit for it. We covered it with bamboo and then with earth. The pig fell right into it. A bunch of us stabbed it with sharpened bamboos to kill it, although it tried to get out and gore us. Its meat was very good, with no fat on it, just real meat. Everyone who had helped kill it got a share of that pig.

In the inner mountains are tigers. We lived in the outer foothills, so we never saw tigers. There was lots of game though—deer, rabbits, and birds. They are all hard to catch, but some men from our mountains were expert hunters.

There were only four families on the mountain we lived on—our family, my uncle's family, and two neighbors. It wasn't like big lowland villages. We had to walk about as far as from here to Taibei Railroad Station[9] before we came to another little hamlet of three or four families. With the mountains all around, we had to know how to get places, as it was easy to get lost. I was careful to remember that this path went home, that went to a friend's, and so on. Father always went first, and we followed him, learning the way. We didn't dare go out alone when we were little, for fear of not being able to get back. If we had to go by ourselves, we made signs of grasses to point out the road for ourselves.

The land up there belongs to the government, but we really own it. If the government wants it, they must pay for it. We farmed it, but it didn't produce much. Nowadays people even have machines to plow with, but we

9. About three miles.

pulled the plow ourselves. People left farming whenever they could get work in the lowlands, because it was so unrewarding. Even collecting rubbish or selling tea door to door is better.

My father and all our neighbors were laborers, cutting firewood and bamboo in the mountains, carrying it down on a shoulder pole, and selling it in the plains. There's hardly a flat place to stop to take a breath in, and there are no smooth paths. Every step is hard, and the loads were heavy.

When I was about eight years old, I went to school for a year. The school was a long way from home, down the mountain: if we started at six in the morning, we could reach school by 8:30. But I and the other children really wanted an education. We went every day, even in the rain, and studied diligently. Everything I learned was Japanese, though, so it became useless later.

Our clothes were patched and mended, but that's all right. It was enough that they were clean. Our teachers checked our collars, made sure our hair was neatly cut, and really insisted on good hygiene. Mother's nephew came home from school one day, boasting "The teacher said I was clean, just like rich people!"

Students were required to wear white blouses, but white cloth was not as easy to get as it is now. We used flour sacks, which we had to buy—two for each blouse. We made them ourselves, at night, as there were no ready-made clothes then, and we never dreamed of paying a seamstress. We were just glad to get enough cloth.

When I was nine, my mother died, leaving me the eldest of three girls. The others were six and three years old. Without Mother to grow food and care for my sisters, I had to stop studying—I couldn't even afford food, let alone books and tuition! How could I study?

Father left us up on the mountain while he continued as a wood chopper. He'd go and collect a load, carry it slowly down the mountain, sell it, and come back. He'd come home every two or three days. He sold units of one hundred kilos of wood to buyers who came to the foot of the mountain with ox carts. There were different grades of wood, some more expensive, some less. The profit went to the carters, who resold it in town. They paid my father almost nothing. Sometimes Father came back, sometimes he didn't. I had to manage somehow to take care of my sisters. My uncle's family was up there, but they were poor, too. They couldn't help us much. I sighed over my hardships. I washed clothes and cooked; Father kept on chopping on the mountain. Having a strong body is really important in life.

Not long after Mother's death, Father decided to sell us. He sold my six-year-old sister first, then the three-year-old, then me. They were bought by families who wanted brides for their sons. My first younger sister went to one of our neighbor families, and remains there to this day. I visit her sometimes, though it's a terribly long journey. The littlest sister is in Tainan.

When I was ten, he sold me, too, to be an adopted daughter-in-law. This is a terrible thing to be, and a pitiful, hard fate to have. My adopted mother was fond of me, so there was some good in it. My husband was about eighteen when I went to live with his family. It was eight years before we began to sleep together. We didn't have a real marriage ceremony, just bowed to Heaven and Earth and to his ancestors, and ate a chicken that my husband brought from down on the plains. He never liked me very much, I don't know why. He didn't beat me, though, because my mother-in-law liked me.

He made our living chopping wood. Sometimes he gambled his money away, sometimes he drank up his earnings. We were always poor. I thought about leaving him and finding a better husband. But how did I know whether another husband would be any better? He might be good, or bad. What would happen to my children if I remarried? The best thing is to be patient and face facts. Young people these days are more willing to divorce. In my time, we just went on and accepted what fate determined for us.

I had three daughters by my husband. Nowadays people think it's necessary to eat fish, rice, and meat after giving birth. When I gave birth to my second daughter, I could only ask my six-year-old to go out to dig some wild vegetables for me. I cleaned them, salted and boiled them, and ate that. People say nowadays that after giving birth a woman should not eat this and that, and should rest. We didn't have such habits. Farmers can't pay attention to all that—there is always work to do. I was out of bed after two or three days, not a month as rich women do. I've known women who had to return to tea picking with newborns on their backs. If you talk about suffering, though, none can compare with mine. I can stand anything.

When my daughters were nine, just under three, and three months old, my husband had been sick for two years, and my mother-in-law had died. I had no money, no one to help me, so I paid my sister to take care of the children and signed onto a labor gang going to Hainan Island. I told her to keep it a secret where I was going, because I thought my husband and my father would stop me.

The Japanese wanted to build new concrete housing for their troops from Taiwan who were stationed on Hainan, because the Communists had blown up the barracks there. The soldiers were all living in tents. Laborers were recruited in the south for this work by a labor contractor who offered us a thousand yen for the trip, twenty yen a day, and money for three meals a day. That was a *lot* in the Japanese period. The contractor took care of all the red tape for us—bought our tickets and arranged for somewhere for us to sleep. There were seven women in our group, but there were men in our labor gang too. Men slept in one room, women in another. I was just over thirty then.

The trip over was frightening. Air raids were beginning in Taiwan, and on the sea we were afraid of being bombed or of hitting a mine. The trip took ten days, with all of us seasick most of the time. It was interesting to arrive in Hainan, though. I had never been anywhere away from our mountains. There were a lot of new things to see. The food was very good in Hainan. We ate rice every day, and good fish. Although carrying concrete was bitter labor, I felt better than I felt at home. My strength improved.

Suddenly, though, I felt unwell. I decided to go home for a visit, and asked the labor chief for permission. He reminded me that my contract was for a year, but he was kind and gave me and another woman tickets to go back. I promised I would come back in a few days, leaving without even taking my clothes.

After I got home, though, my sister asked me to delay a while so we could both make offerings to Mother's spirit on the anniversary of her death. I waited. When I tried to return to Hainan, I learned that the Communist bandits had captured Hainan, so I couldn't go there and the others couldn't come back! We two were fortunate to have come back, as otherwise we would have died. But it was impossible to get my thousand yen.

I stayed on the mountain with my children until after the Retrocession. In about 1947 my uncle took two bamboo baskets and went to Tainan City to collect rubbish and scrap iron to sell. As he found he could earn enough to buy food, he came back and suggested that we leave the mountain. I was very doubtful. I knew nothing of Tainan. What if we starved to death? But he said we could collect scrap and live! Father wouldn't leave the mountain, but my sisters and I came down.

We worked for a boss, who rented us a three-wheeled cart for the scrap and a room to live in. We gave what we collected to him, and he paid us, deducting rent for the room and the cart. We built a stove by ourselves in our room with concrete.

In the morning, Uncle and I started collecting about dawn. When we started, the boss gave us three yen for breakfast, which was plenty. We worked till eleven, and he gave me forty or fifty sen for lunch. After lunch, I went out again until six o'clock, when the boss gave me another two yen. We ate rice and fish and vegetables, and I even had money left over.

This work wasn't hard. We were eating, and one of my sisters stayed home with all the children. But this work is only for the most useless, lowest kind of people. I had to go through garbage, even through the contents of privies. People despised us.

My husband joined us in Tainan, but he was still too sick to work. He was with us a few months before he died. We borrowed money and buried him.

I got a job as a construction laborer, earning ten yen a day for carrying baskets of earth, concrete, and sand on a shoulder pole. When men laborers dug out the foundations, I carried the earth to carts. When they mixed concrete, I brought them sand. When the concrete was ready, I carried it to the forms and poured it in. *That* was hard work. I still have trouble with my legs and back from it. My sister took care of the children, and I paid her so we could all live.

Then things became really bad for me. In 1947 there was a lot of trouble between us Taiwanese and the soldiers. It was bad for business. I worked less. When the 2:28 troubles were over, it was harder for me to get a job because there were more men looking for work. I have a small body, and though I am strong for my size, I can't compete with men in carrying things. My sister was afraid of starvation, so she took her children and went back to the mountain. There was no one to care for my children, no work, and no food. My children cried for sweet potatoes, remembering how in the mountains we could just go to the fields and dig them. Here, though, I thought of going out into the countryside at night to steal food. I was afraid, but sometimes I had to do it anyway. There are people who don't mind telling the world they're without food, begging for it. I wouldn't do that. I kept my problems to myself, giving everything I could get to the children. The one thing I was determined not to do was to sell my girls, or even put them out to work in labor gangs. If only I could get enough food for us!

We had no place to live, so we moved into an unused air-raid shelter. The people in charge were not supposed to let vagrants live there, but they took pity on me, and turned a blind eye. Some days I got work. When I had more money, I bought more; with less money, I bought less. I bought the smallest, cheapest sweet potatoes, and the smallest, oldest fish. The children ate the fish, and sometimes I ate nothing. I had only one pot to cook in, and it was so thin and cheap that the salt from cooking corroded through it. How ashamed I felt to live like this, to try to raise my kids in such a makeshift way! But I told myself to be patient and to accept that this was my bad fate. I wouldn't let myself be angry with the children. It was not their fault. If I had been angry with them, I would have sold them long ago. It was my responsibility to bring them up into adults. My own mother and my adopted mother had died, leaving me to grow up by myself. I would not leave my daughters.

In 1948 I found work washing clothes at a military camp outside Tainan. I worked there, doing all kinds of odd jobs for the soldiers for five years. When I first went to work there, the soldiers were the "62" troops—young boys, fifteen or sixteen years old, who had been shanghaied into the army when they were caught on the road somewhere. They weren't proper soldiers, just kids, really. They got two meals a day at our camp, at ten for breakfast, and five for dinner, usually getting coarse rice, bean waste, and peanuts. There wasn't much leftover food at that camp! These troops stayed in Taiwan for a year, then they were discarded, sent back to fight on the Mainland. They were replaced by the Youth Army, all junior and senior high school graduates, officers, and good soldiers. Things improved. Three days after they arrived, one of their cooks gave me the head and tail of a pig! It was a real feast for my children.

The Youth Army was divided into nine groups. I lived in the third, working for them and groups one and two for four years. Everyone treated me kindly, and called me "Goodlooking." "Hey, Goodlooking! Come! Here's some food for you." They gave me all the heads and internal organs of the pigs they ate. Having been so poor, I was glad just for ordinary food, but this was something special. The men ate rice and were given clothes, and I got these too.

The officers were always calling me "Hey! Goodlooking! I want to give you some food. You can't eat it all? Take it home to your kids." "Goodlooking! Come! My shirt needs mending. Would you do me a favor and sew it up? You have no thread? Take this money to buy some." We laughed and joked during those years. That's how I learned Mandarin. Otherwise, where would I go to study how to speak it?

When visiting big brass came to give out gift packages of clothes and canned goods, the officers told me to stand in rank with the short soldiers, so I got some too. After we were dismissed, a couple of the soldiers asked me for the clothing—it was for men, of course. I gave them the puttees but kept the rest of the uniform to make over for myself and my family. I got a share in the regular army distribution of rice, salt, oil, and fuel which all soldiers get. When they killed pigs to celebrate midautumn festival and lunar New Year, I got that too. That was the first time in a long time my family had celebrated the holidays. Although the troops were always good to me, I had to be a bit careful with the officers, try to figure out their moods. Sometimes the officers got all worked up and yelled at me; sometimes they were kind. The higher officers were gentlemen—they knew how to behave. It was the lower ones who were trouble. They would try to bother us women sometimes. I was always careful not to be alone with them.

Once, when the troops were preparing for a combat mission, an officer announced that everyone must get his photo for his identity badge renewed. He told me to get a new one, too, saying, "Your picture isn't very attractive. Get dressed up tomorrow, and go take a better picture." I said, "I've got no money for that. What does it matter to me if my picture is good-looking or not?"

He insisted on giving me money for a dress, even though I refused several times. When I got my new picture, he asked me for a copy, and wanted to give me one of his. I asked him why he wanted *my* picture. At that time, he was to be sent somewhere to fight—maybe back to the mainland, maybe to somewhere in Taiwan—I can't remember now. He said that when he looked at my picture, he would remember our acquaintanceship here in Tainan, and hoped I would remember him, too. Maybe he was afraid he might die in the fighting.

Anyway, the troops came back the next night, all but two who were killed. They were all so happy to be safe they got some liquor and called me to drink with them. "Old woman, Good-looking, bottoms up! I toast you! Everybody's back safe!" We drank one cup after another, toasting all around.

The arrival of the Youth Army from China was a really good thing for me, much better than the "62" troops. Some of them were from families that were well-to-do on the mainland. They were deceived into thinking they would be allowed to study if they came here, but they became soldiers instead. The training was tough, and they considered the food very coarse. Really, their situation wasn't so bad, I thought. It was just like ordinary people's lives. When some of them cried over their fate, others comforted them, saying, "It's not so bad. You'll get used to it." Even if they didn't get used to it, they had no choice, because they could never go back home. Things turned out pretty well for most of them. They nearly all married women here and have families. At that time, considering how poor everyone was, women were glad to marry them.

My present husband, Old Lo, is a retired soldier, though not from that group of educated youth. We were introduced by a soldier in the camp I worked in after I had been washing clothes for the army for nearly five years. He wanted to marry because he had been fighting for many years and he missed home life. Now that there was peace in Taiwan, he wanted to start a family. My friends told him I was hard-working and did not complain about difficulties.

I thought hard about marrying him, trying to decide if it would be good for me and my daughters. At that time, many soldiers were being retired against their will. Some were too old, or too young, or too sick, or too stupid. The country didn't want to pay them. So many men looking for work! But my husband was still in the army. He was a war hero who had been shot in the fighting. They had operated on him to remove the bullets, and he recovered, as good as new. He was considered to have made real contributions to the country. I thought, "Maybe it will be bad to marry this man, as it was with my first husband. Maybe not. If I stay single, I cannot improve life for my children. If I marry and he is bad to us, I can leave him and support myself again. The children are mine. He cannot take them."

Also, I liked his appearance. He is a strong man and very capable. He can speak Cantonese, Shandongnese, some other dialects, even Japanese. He learned Taiwanese, too. So I agreed to marry him, and I became "Mrs. Lo."

For the next few years, my husband was transferred a lot from place to place. I followed him, with my children, staying wherever the army arranged—in railroad stations, in schools, in temples, sometimes in little lean-tos beside buildings. We carried cooking pots and bedding and managed the best we could. We wives helped each other, because the men were in their camps most of the time. I worked whenever I could, to earn money for my children. The army gave us rice, salt, oil, and fuel, but almost no money. Though I tried to send them to school, we were rarely in the same place very long. They couldn't study well. Then they sent him to Pingdong, where we stayed for ten years. He sometimes went away for several months, because his work then was building the government's roads in the mountains. But we had a house in an army "new village." Things were better. My two oldest daughters married soldiers, too, men much older than themselves, and my youngest was able to complete elementary school. The schools for army children are not so good, but at least she learned to read.

In 1967, when my husband was fifty-five, he was permitted to retire from the army and join the government's engineering company that employs only veterans. He has done this ever since. His job requires him to live near the roads he is helping to build. Right now, we have lived for a year beside this squatter settlement where the Taibei City government is building an overpass. From the materials from the houses torn down for the right-of-way, the construction crew built our houses. There are about forty families living here, all older retired soldiers. Most have wives, some Taiwanese, some mainland women. My husband knows the other men because they work together, but I only know a few women. So I work to keep busy, doing washing and growing vegetables in our yard. We'll be here another year or so. Who knows where we'll go next?

When my husband is sixty-five, he will retire again, and we will get a lump sum to live on. We get paid enough to live on every month—

NT$9,000.00 (U.S.$225). Depending on length of service, people get three or four hundred thousand, or a million. My husband has a long period of service, about fourteen years. The office of the president sent him a plate of green marble on a recent anniversary of Retrocession to honor his contributions, and he gets a platinum ring every year as a gift. Our rent is only NT$500 (U.S.$12.50) a month, very low these days.

We probably have enough money, but I am used to working. I've worked in families as a servant, in restaurants, and most recently I do laundry wherever we go, because my husband gets angry when I work outside. I feel anxious when I don't have work.

My daughters and youngest sister are in the south, my other sister in the mountains. I see them occasionally. For next month's national election, our company has given both my husband and me railroad tickets back to Pingdong, where we are registered, so we can vote to support the party. At that time, I will visit my relatives and see my grandchildren.

My husband wanted to have children of his own, but I never became pregnant with his child. I know there is nothing wrong with my body, because I had five children altogether—two died after my first daughter. He raised my daughters like his own children, always treating them well. They call him "Father." I am grateful to him.

[6]

Home and Family

In Taiwan, people often speak of the differences between life at home and life "outside, in society," where social relations are often described as *fuza*, "complicated." The family is the most private circle, but because long-term residents in a village or working-class neighborhood know most of each other's doings, the local community may become an extension of the home. In the working-class neighborhood in Taibei that I call Prosperity Settlement, during the unsophisticated late sixties men could appear at home or anywhere within the Settlement's boundaries in sleeping pajamas or underwear without anyone taking special notice. But they put on more formal clothing to go out into the wider world, or when representatives of that world came visiting. Most ordinary folk prefer the warmth and familiarity of home and family to the impersonality and possible dangers of "society," although there are always adventurous exceptions who seek out anonymity under the bright lights.

The coincidence of kinship ties, economic advantage, and the Chinese state's age-old tendency to treat families as primary social units makes families central to Taiwan's culture. Few extrafamilial sources of support or charity exist in Taiwan: government welfare services are extremely meager, and religious and other private charities are stretched thin, though the local temple procured fire relief for Miss Guo and her neighbors. For these reasons, as well as for the emotional ties they provide, Chinese strongly value, idealize, and identify with their families.

More than Americans, Chinese are conscious of the lifelong nature of family commitments, and are given to thinking of long-term effects on the whole unit of the actions of its members. Parents and grandparents plan for the education, occupations, and marriages of the young, basing their decisions in large part on the effect the choice will have on the whole family. When Mrs. and Mr. Lim (introduced in Chapter 9) decide the family can afford a daughter-in-law and the children she will bear or adopt, they will urge their son to find a suitable girl and help him do so. His occupation as a future baker is being chosen for him—though in these enlightened times, he can veto the idea—to fit in with the realities of the family's good business location and none-too-productive fruit-and-ice shop. In contrast, the Zhangs, whom we will meet later in this chapter, failed to influence their sons, Bright Reputation and Bright Nation, to work in their dumpling restaurant, while Miss Guo's adopted son doesn't even visit her regularly. Family economic planning does not always work. But when it does, it contributes greatly to both stability and prosperity.

The smooth cooperation of family members is often disrupted by a determined individualism that, although not a part of the American stereotype of Chinese character, is encountered constantly in Taiwan's working class. Miss Guo's unconventional life and refusal to take help from her better-off sisters, Mrs. Lo's determination to keep her daughters and her willingness to leave her mountain for far-off Hainan Island, and Mrs. Zhang's Shandong outspokenness are the acts of tough people who know their own minds. They often find it hard to conform to the family-based decisions of others, as Mrs. Lim did so painfully in marrying her "brother." Being part of a family is not easy, but it is deeply valued, it brings practical rewards, and it is enshrined in an elaborate code of correct kinship behavior that is known to everyone.

The ideal Chinese family—promoted by the state, applauded in folklore, and put into practice most visibly by the elite of imperial days—is as perfect an example of patrilineal patriarchy as has been envisioned anywhere on earth. A man and his sons and grandsons, forming a property-owning corporation, ideally lived together in a continuously expanding household that might, in time, encompass a proverbial "five generations under one roof." These men and boys worked together under the control and authority of the eldest living male member of the senior generation, hierarchically ranked according to generation and birth order. All significant decisions were ideally made by the "family head," and were obeyed respectfully by his juniors. When this arrangement broke down and segments of the original household wished to go their own ways, the property was divided equally in shares among the senior men. Once the decision to divide the property had been made, the new segments became economically independent, each segment accepting the authority of its own family head. Under some circumstances—for example, when the need for large work groups or for defense against outsiders was especially strong—families organized themselves for work, war, and ritual as lineages, maintaining written records of their relationships over several generations. Some of these grew to thousands of members, controlling whole regions with many villages, especially in southern China (Freedman 1958 and 1966; Pasternak 1972).

Whether in families or lineages, men regularly worshiped the spirits of the men and women ancestral to them on domestic altars or in lineage temples. These rituals reminded the members of the debt they owed to senior generations in giving them life and the property on which they lived, reinforced the age hierarchy among living fathers and sons, and emphasized the centrality of men in kinship matters (Ahern 1973).

In this ideal version of kinship relations, women took a distinctly and overtly inferior place. Because she was considered less valuable than a son, almost not a member of the family, a daughter's only legitimate destiny was to marry and become a mother in some other family. Then, as a mother (especially of sons), her spirit would deserve a place on that family's altar as an ancestor after she died. Contemporary Taiwanese make such comments as, "She is only a useless daughter; we will have to feed her for years until she can do things, and then some other family will get the advantage." A woman had no right to the family property except for a dowry of clothes, furniture, and jewelry. When she married, she left her father's home forever; he had no obligation to take her back if she were divorced or widowed. In many societies, the marriage of a son and daughter is often seen as an opportunity to bind two previously unrelated families together in ties of in-lawship. In China, affinal relationships were often weakly developed, especially among agriculturalists, although they expanded to fill social vacuums when necessary (Gallin 1960; Gallin and Gallin 1985:101; Harrell 1982, chap. 4). While lineage "brothers" of a woman from an elite family might intervene to protect her from mistreatment in her marital home in order to maintain their own prestige (Freedman 1966:58–59), relatives of ordinary women were much less likely to take action against the man to whom they had given power over their sister or daughter (Pruitt 1945:30–32, 42). A married woman was transferred completely from her father's authority to her husband's (or husband's parents' while they lived); when widowed, she came under the legal guardianship of her son.

It was considered shameful and disgusting for a married woman, or even an engaged one, however young, to remarry should her spouse die. Families with "a chaste widow" of many years' standing could petition the imperial court for a grant to erect an archway over a road to commemorate her chastity. Women could not divorce except under extraordinary circumstances, and, since they could not return to their fathers' homes or easily

[105]

earn their own living except by prostitution, many unhappy wives preferred suicide to separation (M. Wolf 1975). A woman's children belonged solely and exclusively to her husband's family, whatever became of her. She was expected to act as a humble, servantlike daughter to her parents-in-law and to obey her mother-in-law in everything. Warm and affectionate relations between wife and husband were to be concealed, if they developed, for fear of the mother-in-law's jealous disapproval.

To assure that women would accept these tight constraints, a girl-child was raised very differently from a boy. Girls began to work at chores, tend babies, or do elaborate needlework while boys were still playing freely or in school. Because "stupidity in a woman is a virtue," girls were rarely educated, and in an act that both symbolized and realized their inferiority, the feet of many little girls were crippled by the breaking of the foot bones and binding the toes to the heel—an act of "beautification" that sometimes resulted in death.

Parents had absolute rights over their children, as men had over their wives. Husbands and fathers were ultimately responsible for agreeing to marriages, though the negotiations were usually arranged by women; it was impossible, both economically and legally, to marry without the agreement of the bride's and groom's fathers. Weddings were elaborate affairs in which a red-costumed virgin bride, paid for by a substantial bride-price and accompanied by a large dowry, was carried in a red sedan chair surrounded by musicians from her father's to her husband's parents' house. Marriage ritual clearly indicated that the transfer was to be final. Men could give out or adopt both boy and girl children, though the transfer of boys might require permission from the lineage. Though it was shameful to do so, men could sell their wives and children.

Families—again, ideally—achieved acceptance of these rules of family life both through economic and legal power, and through socialization. In a largely agricultural and very slowly growing economy, people needed membership in a family corporation to gain access to resources from which to gain a living. Custom and law upheld the rights of men and fathers to control the family and its resources. The Qing dynasty punishment for a son who killed his father was the same as that for high treason—being slowly cut into pieces (van der Sprenkel 1962:62).

In the young, however, rebelliousness was more commonly controlled not by the legal violence of the state, but by the intense socialization of children, especially in the principles of *xiao*, commonly translated "filial piety." *Xiao*, meaning complete submission to parents, is reckoned as one of the highest of Chinese virtues and the key to the maintenance of the hierarchical family structure.

Even in the preindustrial past, the reality of the Chinese family was considerably more complex than the simple model just described, though that model was, and still is, constantly present as a guide to conduct. Differences in families' economic bases varied the degree of adherence to the model. Sons of a rich father with much property had more to lose through disobedience or independence than sons of a man with nothing to give them; brothers who inherited agricultural land might find it easier to continue a cooperative family corporation than men who worked for wages (Freedman 1966:47). Among the very poor, marrying even one son might exhaust the family's resources, so second and later sons were often unable to marry and expand the household. Here and there, when the penetration of industrialization made women's labor especially valuable, as in the silk-spinning areas of Guangzhou, women sometimes rebelled at their subordinate roles in the patrilineal system by refusing to marry and setting up cooperative living arrangements with other women (Sankar 1984; Stockard 1985; Topley 1975). Even where families took on a form close to the ideal, women created informal "uterine" families made up of themselves and their children within the patrilineal households, using the intimacy of mother and child to bind sons more closely to themselves than to the authoritarian fathers (M. Wolf 1972). These segments of larger families struggled for autonomy, often prompting the division of brothers' families or the separation of sons from fathers. Regional differences further complicated the variations in agricultural labor needs, population, fertility, and the degree of control over families exercised by lineages and the state.

Taiwan in this century has displayed considerable variation in family patterns, particularly as these are affected by marriages and adoptions, two of the primary institutions for controlling family form. Certain departures from the simple patrilineal model of family relations result from the natural uncertainty of reproduction. In Taiwan, as in other parts of China, families who produced no adult sons needed to supply this deficiency to meet their family's requirements for labor, care for the aged, and ancestral worship. A family could adopt a son from a poor household with surplus boys; this usually required a substantial payment to the boy's natal parents. The adoption of a son from outside the family's agnatic kin was and is considered a risky business: adopted sons, such as Miss Guo's, are notoriously unfilial in adulthood. Families that could not afford to buy a son would try to persuade a man whose own family had nothing to leave him to marry their daughter, live in their home, and take their surname in an uxorilocal marriage. It was shameful for a man to abandon the responsibilities and ties to his own parents, as symbolized by his surname, and in doing so, he gave up all claim to his patrilineal relatives' property (Ahern 1973:121–25). An uxorilocally married man could try to negotiate to keep his own name, and perhaps one or more of the children he fathered, to carry on his own line of descent.

North Taiwan has been the locus of kinship patterns that simultaneously display a particularly strong male bias in form while giving considerable decision-making power over adoption to women. Arthur Wolf and Huang Chieh-shan (1980) have analyzed this system, whereby, throughout much of the nineteenth century and the first third of the twentieth century, rural families gave or sold out to adoption up to 70 percent of girl babies within their first few months or years of life. These babies were usually adopted and nursed by women who had just given birth to girls of their own, who in turn were given away to other families. Such a girl, called a *simpua,* or "little daughter-in-law," was destined after puberty to become the wife of a son of her adoptive family in a simple ceremony. By bringing up a daughter-in-law (a "minor marriage," in Wolf's term) instead of looking for an adult bride when the son was grown, Taiwanese parents spared themselves not only the expense of a traditional wedding, but the difficulty of training a grown woman in the ways of her mother-in-law. This arrangement also limited the degree of interest a girl's natal relatives would express in her welfare, giving her husband's family a completely free hand with her. Because the young couple, raised as brother and sister, usually found the relationship sexually "uninteresting," *simpua* marriages had the additional effect of undermining any potential for the "disloyal" affection between a son and his wife that mothers especially feared. All in all, it was an extraordinarily neat solution to one of the greatest problems of the ideal family, as seen from the parents' point of view.

Wolf and Huang argue that, in north Taiwan at least, the only reason there were *any* "major marriages" (those between adult women and men) was that some families raised their own daughters as insurance against having no sons. As a result, there were never enough girl children put up for adoption to meet the demand for *simpua* and minor marriages (1980:251–60, 272–81).

As the Japanese brought greater prosperity and diversified occupations to Taiwan, work opportunities that gave young people the option of rebelling a little against parental authority opened up. By the 1930s, so many young men were refusing to marry the *simpua* they had grown up with that the system broke down. Fewer girls were adopted,[1] and of those who were, most married outsiders when they grew up. Mrs. Lim (Chapter 9), coming

---

1. Adopted daughters in their teens and twenties were still common before 1980; both Arrigo (1984:125–32) and Kung (1983:97, 119, 142) encountered them among factory workers.

of age at about this time, accepted her families' arrangements for her as a filial daughter was trained to do. Her husband/brother, himself adopted and not much trusted by his suspicious foster mother, was not secure enough in the Lim family to object either. They are an unusual couple, because despite their dislike for the marriage, it has endured and produced a large number of children, uncommon in *simpua* marriages (Wolf and Huang 1980:161–77).

Marriages of young adults in Taiwan slowly ceased to be arranged entirely without the bride's and groom's knowledge or consent early in this century. It became customary for parents, having located and investigated a suitable prospect, to arrange for the young people to meet, well chaperoned, to look each other over. As more young people attended schools, groups of class-mates helped each other find partners, providing respectable opportunities for acquaintanceship before the young couple turned the formalities over to their parents. Occasionally today, one hears of a couple who has married without involving their parents—it can be done in a simple civil cere-mony—but this is still considered shocking and ill bred. At present, young working-class women and men seem more likely simply to live together without any form of marriage than to attempt the formalities without parental backing. Parental control over young people's marriage plans is therefore still strong among working-class Taiwanese, where both bride-price and dowry continue to accompany most marriages. For these, and for the lavish feasts that make a wedding joyful and legitimate rather than a shady private transaction, young people still need their family's assistance and consent.

Expanding economies on China's mainland coasts similarly affected the control of parents over children in the first half of this century. Married Mainlander immigrants had often known and courted their spouses before marriage, like the reluctant Mr. Zhang—though Mr. Kang's marriage was arranged for him by his parents (Chapter 6). Many Mainlanders' expecta-tions about marriage were not, perhaps, very different from those of more urban Taiwanese when they arrived in the forties. But their arrival strongly influenced Taiwanese marriage patterns.

Wolf and Huang have calculated that it cost as much to raise a *simpua* as to pay for a son's wedding, but that for most people, it was more convenient to spend the money in small sums over the years (and also have the *simpua's* help around the house) than save it up and spend it all at once: "A *simpua* was a kind of savings account" (1980:271). The cost of a major marriage lay primarily in the brideprice negotiated for the bride's parents by a matchmaker. During the Japanese period, the necessary sum, along with the other wedding expenses, could take a farm family ten or fifteen years to accumulate (Wolf and Huang 1980:269). Traditionally, the bride's family spent far more than they received in brideprice for an elaborate dowry with which she furnished the room in her parents-in-law's house, where she and her husband would live. The gold jewelry that was always included, along with some other gifts of money, remained the private property of the bride (M. Cohen 1976:178–91). Grooms' families, then, received most of the brideprice back as dowry, and brides' families were out of pocket for raising the girl and for certain engagement and wedding expenses (see Harrell and Dickey 1985).

When the Mainlanders, predominantly men who had come to Taiwan without families, began to seek wives in the fifties, they created a strong upward pressure on brideprices. As brideprices rose, the value of daughters was enhanced; some parents became eager to profit from marrying off their daughters. Taiwanese men, undercut in the marriage market by the Mainlanders' advantages, resented the newcomers more than ever.

The postwar reemphasis on brideprice may have slightly reversed the earlier tendency for the greater independence of young people: daughters, as they became valuable resources to manipulate in the marriage market, and sons, as they needed greater family assistance to amass higher brideprices in the more competitive market, came back under strong parental authority. Also, the generation that came of age in the bad economic years from the late thirties to the late fifties had fewer work opportunities to give them a degree of independence. But families responded differently to these pressures. Today, parents vary widely in how much independence they will accept in marriage decisions from their children, and in the degree to which a large brideprice is seen as essential to a working-class marriage. Miss Guo was "embarrassed" to ask for money for her daughters—her sons-in-law were poor men. Mrs. Zhang's in-laws asked for a brideprice of NT$40,000 (U.S.$1,000) but returned all but a token NT$4,000 (U.S.$100). Although a return of some of the negotiated price is customary, this was a generous return.

Changes in marriage practices reflect relatively slow responses to changing economic and population circumstances, but the change in the acceptance of divorce amounts to almost a revolution in Taiwan in recent years. Divorces are vanishingly few among the thousands of marriages recorded in the household registries for Prosperity Settlement from 1905 to 1970, although informal separations and the setting up of secondary, nonlegalized unions certainly occurred. Several of my older women acquaintances, whose husbands have long since left home to live with other women and the children these "little wives" have borne them, refuse legal divorce, even where the husband makes no contribution to their households. "I'm just an old-fashioned Shandong woman," said one of them, "and I couldn't stand to lose that much face."

In 1980 government figures quote the divorce rate as eight-tenths per thousand (DGBAS 1981: Table 18)—twice what it was from 1959 to 1974 (compared with thirty-eight per thousand in the United States [Population Reference Bureau 1977]). While divorce is still uncommon by Western standards, its increasing frequency shocks Taiwan's Chinese. During my 1980 visit, friends often mentioned the growth in divorce and the new attitudes people were beginning to express toward it. The Zhangs' discussion of their sons' marital careers in this chapter shows both the parents' distress and their resignation over their inability to control the shape of their families through settling their children in permanent marriages.

Although parents in Taiwan now deviate from the ideal that they alone should decide about the marriages, adoptions, and divorces that shape the family, family form has not changed as radically as one might imagine. For working-class people (and for other classes as well), membership in a large family with several occupations and a wide social network is still very useful. Family backing for education, job hunting, marriage, access to capital, and many other goals still makes their achievement easier than individual effort alone. Poorer, wage-earning working-class households seem a little more likely to separate into nuclear families than do better-off business households; but as the latter educate their children for white-collar and technical professions, they, too, often fragment into smaller units.

Economic advantage or its absence shapes families, as does the culturally sanctioned ideal of a large, multigeneration family. This concept seems to appeal more to people as they grow older and hold more authority in such households. The struggle that many Chinese families endure between the older generation that wishes to keep the family together and the younger generation that prefers some independence and privacy does not mean that ideal family of old will soon disappear; many of today's "conservative" parents wanted and even achieved greater independence when they were young. In Taiwan, 75 per cent of couples live part of their lives in multigeneration families (Chu 1969:163–65). A domestic cycle of expansion, breakup, and rebuilding remains the norm for working-class families now as it has in the past. In 1970 in Prosperity Settlement, of a total of 109 families, 58.8 percent of the families but only 36.7 percent of individuals lived in fragmentary or nuclear families, while 42.2 percent of families and 63.3 percent of individuals lived in more complex families. In these households the average number of members of the more complex families was 10.59 (Rohsenow 1973:59), with one family numbering 27 persons. In a somewhat similar neighborhood on the far side of Taipei City in the same year, Tang Mei-chun (1978:66) counted 75 percent nuclear and fragmentary families and 25 percent more complex units; he omits information on the numbers of individuals who live in these settings.

Americans emphasize "love" as the cement of family relations. Especially within the nuclear family, love between husband and wife, parent and child, and sibling and sibling is held in very high regard. When "love" ceases, those who formerly loved each other are thought to be acting appropriately if they terminate or diminish the relationship. Divorce, leaving home, and ceasing to contact family members are common and, though perceived as regrettable, accepted ways of behaving. By contrast, "love" is rarely invoked in explaining or maintaining Chinese families. Instead, *xiao* (submission to parents), duty, and obligation are the feelings that people usually describe when speaking of families. Wives and husbands do not expect to love each other romantically—though young people hope they will and family happiness seems to be greater when they do—and they are not expected to show their affection publicly. Chinese fathers especially feel they will lose authority if they are less than stern (Diamond 1969:35; M. Wolf 1970:41), so children who love their fathers may find their feelings impossible to show in direct ways. A young teacher once shyly confessed to me that he voluntarily performed the extremely old fashioned *ketou* (from which we get the English word "kowtow"—kneeling and bowing his head to the floor) to his father at the New Year because it was the only way he could express his deep love and respect for his severe parent.

Love plays a more overt part in the relations between mothers and children. A woman belongs securely to her husband's family only through her children, especially her sons, who become her allies, if necessary, against the rest of the family (M. Wolf 1972:32–37). She may need her sons' love to assure her of kindly treatment in old age, and throughout her life her children may be the only people whom she can freely love. The self-sacrificing, all-forgiving, wise mother is a cultural stereotype of considerable power in Chinese culture, and many sentimental movies and stories resolve their plot problems through a heroic mother's love.

Mothers and married daughters may also retain close ties now that the strict rules about the separation of a bride from her family have grown looser. Many women informants have observed to me that in modern times, daughters are closer to mothers than are sons, who now become "too attached" to their wives and neglect their mothers. "If you see a grandmother taking care of a baby nowadays, it's a good guess the child is her daughter's, because a woman feels closer to her daughter's children through love for the daughter," a perceptive young woman with a new baby told me. Affection among siblings, and especially between sisters, can be an important source of emotional support as well, but ties between brothers, inhibited by tensions over property and family responsibility and by the emotional restraint expected of men, do not always offer much intimacy as the brothers mature.

As in other relationships, attachment between parent and child is expected to take a tangible form. Parents support and nurture children while they are too small to help themselves. As they grow up, children's earnings properly belong to their parents, especially the mother, who normally keeps the family purse. In old age, parents can properly claim the right of support from their sons. During the children's maturity, however, when they have young ones of their own to feed, daughters and sons show their love and sense of responsibility most directly through money presents, especially at lunar New Year. Parents who receive red envelopes of money at these times know they are respected and feel they have raised their children well.

Families symbolize their unity and continuity by regular rituals that focus on the deceased relatives who gave living members their lives and property. In the main room of a dwelling where visitors are entertained, most Taiwanese working-class people maintain a domestic altar on which they keep slips of wood with ancestors' names on them in decorated boxes. Mainlanders usually do not set up such altars, in part because most do not know whether their parents have died yet or not. As time passes and the certainty that their parents must by now be dead grows, some set up temporary altars at the New Year, where they make prayers and offerings. This is especially likely to occur when a Mainlander man has married a conscientious Taiwanese woman who wishes to do her filial duty by her husband's family, while at the same time setting a good example for her children. Christians and agnostics, who are fairly common among Mainlanders, omit these ceremonies.

In Taiwanese households, the more punctilious housewives offer the ancestors tea, incense, and prayers every day. They commemorate the death days of many patrilineal relatives each year by a small feast of the dead person's favorite foods, which the dead person's spirit is invited to attend, along with the living family. And they invite their ancestors as a group to join the family at especially good dinners on the first and fifteenth of every lunar month (in business families, on the second and sixteenth), at the New Year, on other major ritual holidays, and at special family events like weddings. Hardly a week passes in a large and filial household when

[113]

ancestors are not called to be present among the living. This creates constant reminders of the duties the juniors owe their seniors, and of the unrepayable debts of life and property owed to them.

Families celebrate engagements, weddings, and the successful completion of the first month of life of babies by inviting guests for a feast; but they reserve their most spectacular and public displays of household rituals for funerals, especially when an old person with many descendants dies. Such a ceremony, in which so many details of performance concretize and reinforce the sense of obligation owed by the younger to the older family members, is most instructive for the anthropologist as well as for the participants.

Town families usually celebrate wedding feasts privately in restaurants and hotels, but the Taiwanese conduct funerals at home. In the cities, because dwellings are small, this means that many essential parts of the ritual are quite public. Even Mainlanders, who often hold simplified services at funeral parlors, escort their dead to their graves in lengthy public processions that include bands playing surprisingly cheerful Western marches. The approach of cacophonous traditional funeral music is still one of Taibei's most characteristic sounds, drawing attention to the formal display of filiality that all families wish to make for their dead.

When death occurs in a working-class neighborhood, the family pastes a white sign on their house front. All nearby neighbors ward off the possible ill effects of contact with the dead by putting up red pieces of paper over *their* doors. Family members wash the body, dress it in clean clothing, and place it in a tightly sealed coffin. Because it is unseemly to rush a relative into the grave, and because there are expensive preparations to be made for the funeral, the coffin remains in the main living room for a few weeks or even months. During the time, the deceased's spirit is thought to hover near the body, very aware of how it is treated. It requires food offerings at a temporary, white-draped altar in the main room at mealtimes and is soothed by the regular and formalized wailing and prostrations (*ketou*) that its living relatives perform. When relatives are attending its needs, they don special burlap sack or white clothing—a special costume for each significant kinship category (A. Wolf 1970b).

For a few days before the funeral, on a horoscopically suitable date, the bereaved family hires a group of Buddhist nuns and monks to recite sutras for the spirit's well-being. These religious specialists, who live in temple convents or monasteries, arrive with a marquee and much ritual equipment, rented as part of the package. The marquee is raised, usually on the sidewalk and street in front of the house, and the monks and nuns busy themselves with reciting the number and kind of scriptural chants for which they have been paid. Sometimes Daoist ritual specialists are hired as well. One or another of these specialists usually hangs up gruesome paintings of the fearsome torments that souls being judged in the next world may undergo—being ground between millstones, sawed in half, or, for women, raped by animals.

On the day of the funeral itself, guests gather to pay their last respects to a small paper image or a large funeral portrait of the dead person on the temporary altar in the marquee. An arriving guest goes first to the record keeper, generally a friend of the family or distant relative, who lists the guest's name and condolence gift. This is usually money—at least enough to cover the cost of the feast the guest will later consume—in a white envelope. Sometimes the presents are dress lengths of cloth or, from important men who are invited to more funerals than they can attend, a white cloth banner with an appropriate message of respect for the dead and the giver's signature. These are hung throughout the marquee, evidence of the family's respectability and connections. The guests file slowly up to the altar, fold their hands in prayer, and bow deeply three times. Often, a dish of fragrant sandalwood powder stands by a little charcoal brazier, inviting each guest to burn a pinch—a means of warding off the contamination of death. As guests mill about, talking in subdued tones, the funeral musicians and trucks for the processions arrive. Some families hire out-of-work opera actors to appear in the costumes of Buddhist fables to accompany the procession. These brightly made-up street toughs drift around, waiting for the simple food the procession workers will receive before the coffin is taken away.

After all the guests and relatives have paid their respects, the coffin is given its final "closing" nails. Women in their childbearing years retreat into the houses at this powerful moment for fear of injuring their fertility. At this time, a father will beat the coffin of a son who has unfilially preceded him in death. Laborers hired for the day's heavy work heave the large, ornate coffin onto a truck decorated with white paper flowers, and the funeral procession of bands, loudspeaker vans full of chanting nuns, costumed figures, and jeeps or taxis carrying wreaths moves off toward a mountainside cemetery. The major mourners follow on foot for a few blocks, before climbing into the vehicles for a speedier trip. At the graveside, workers lower the coffin ceremoniously amid the relatives' loud weeping. The family makes offerings of incense and paper spirit money before hastening back for the funeral feast.

Late in the evening of the funeral, the family gathers to perform the rituals that will lead the new spirit into the other world and provide it with the money and clothing it will need there. Old-fashioned families hire

Daoists to perform acrobatic juggling acts with flaming torches to "entertain" the spirit one last time before it enters the hell of judgment. After this is done, the Daoists instruct the family to bring out several large cooking woks and fill them with a sum of folded spirit money, calculated on the basis of the person's birthdate. Some of this money will pay the deceased's mystical debts in the other world, freeing his spirit to be reincarnated after undergoing punishment in hell for his misdeeds. The spirit can use the rest of the money to buy what he needs, and, it is hoped, to bribe himself free of punishment (Gates, 1987).

As the money burns, the Daoists lead the mourners in a circle around the fire. The chief mourner carries the dead person's paper image, while another may carry the paper image of a wife who died before her husband, so that the two spirits may travel together. Others carry incense pots or bamboo branches that attract spirits. The long, imaginary journey to the dark and dangerous other world ends when the great heaps of spirit money finally burn down—the new spirit has "crossed the bridge" into hell. Finally, for his use in hell, the family brings out a colorful, completely furnished paper house, sometimes six feet high and costing two months' wages, installs the paper figure of the dead, and sets it all alight. For a moment, light glows out the windows, revealing paper pictures on the walls, a television set, and elegant furniture. Then, in a burst of flames, it is gone—transformed by fire into a real house in another world—a sad and lovely ending to a life.

The family will ask a Daoist to inscribe the dead person's name on a wooden tablet on the family altar. In a careful household, it will also write the name on a slip of paper pasted inconspicuously on the altar table with the names and death dates of all recent ancestors. The family will celebrate these death days yearly for generations to come, and someone will pray daily before the ancestral tablets. The real effect of all these rituals is, of course, on the living, who through their performance are taught the significance of the family, a respect for its continuity and the subordination of individuals to it.

We have seen that in Taiwan's working class there is a close connection between a family and its members' work lives. Do people make decisions about their occupations in order to keep their families together—as most Chinese would surely insist—or do they shape their families to fit their available (and prospective) resources? The first option seems the obvious choice. Throughout the life histories, we see parents using the labor, skills, talents, and property of the whole family for the maintenance and betterment of a unified family household. Families do divide, usually at times of marriage or death, but occupational plans are frequently made which will enable a household to expand by adding or retaining members. People choose occupations to realize the patrilineal coresident family whose image is the culture's ideal.

But the view that resources shape families is also tenable and may have been even more pertinent in the recent past. Families that own income-producing property such as farms and small businesses also need human labor if they are to support themselves from that property. Chinese farmers have always been acutely aware of the need for enough labor, especially male labor, to till their fields without recourse to hiring workers. Carpenters, miners, tailors, and many others often prefer to work in teams of two or several men, ideally a father and his sons, and some of the homemaking, artisan, and shopkeeping activities of women are more efficient, too, if a mother-in-law and daughter-in-law or daughter can take turns or assist each other. Under some circumstances, especially in the years since 1960, children who could not be usefully employed at home could easily find work elsewhere, so family labor resources could be allowed to outstrip family labor requirements in following the patrilineal ideal. In the past, when such work was not so available, children were more frequently sold, adopted, or married out, often shortly after birth.

But even the family ideal has changed over time: now, daughters *should* work and *may* choose their own husbands; divorce is thinkable, if still a tragedy; a few well-educated children moving into the white-collar world may represent a better family investment than a lot of sons doing manual labor. More than ever, a complex calculus among factors of capital and labor, and economic necessity and desire to approximate kinship ideals governs the composition of families, the success of businesses, and the evolving shape of the working class.

Mrs. and Mr. Zhang, introduced in the next section, tried hard to model their family after the ideal, although they realize that in modern times the ideal has changed. Because they themselves chose their marriage partner, they do not expect to choose their sons' wives, though they are not sparing of their opinions on the subject. Because they left their parents behind on the Mainland and have thus done nothing to fulfill their filial duty of support, they expect only limited aid from their sons in the future. The external circumstances of the Nationalist retreat to Taiwan have left them with an atypically minimal family, while the expanding economy has given their sons room to maneuver economically in ways that move them away from the kinship ideal. The Zhang family shows clearly the changes that, often more subtly, continue to reshape Chinese families in Taiwan.

[117]

Zhang Xiuzhen: Immigrant Cook

Like many of her fellow post-1949 migrants to Taiwan, Mrs. Zhang has always expected that she and her family would one day return to the Mainland—by choice, to the northern home in Shandong province where she was born over fifty years ago. Living with other Mainlanders in military enclaves, she has not bothered to learn the Taiwanese language and still finds the southern climate and surroundings alien. She is uneasy at the way her sons have adapted themselves to local life, and at the way that life has drawn them away from the tightly ordered family created for them through much sacrifice. Like many Mainlanders, she believes that if only she and her husband had been able to return to the Mainland under a triumphant Nationalist government, their loyalty would have been rewarded by high position, and her sons would have remained filial, as she remembers men to be "back home."

But Mrs. Zhang is practical. She has worked hard as a servant and plans to take advantage of the expanding economy of the 1980s while she has her good health. Her life shows us something of the advantages and the disadvantages of being a small part of the state-employed sector in Taiwan, and of the determination with which Chinese parents pursue traditional goals for their families.

Zhang Xiuzhen's vitality lights up her plain, round face. Her dark eyes snap and sparkle as she talks, and she talks a great deal. Plain-spoken, in the tradition of her earthy, downright Shandong forebears, she always has her say. Entering her fifties has not slowed her down, nor has her appearance changed much in the last twenty years. Only a little gray shows in the thick black hair she wears cropped near her head. It is hard to recognize on this broad, unlined brown face the pale, fragile-looking features of the seventeen-year old bride in her wedding picture.

Her liveliness of speech is broken, sometimes, by an almost-conquered stutter that seems to result from an excess of energy that is unable to escape through mere words. Mrs. Zhang has worked hard all her adult life, and by nature remains in motion. She knits—sweaters for friends and relatives, warm bed socks for herself, toys as gifts for children—or sews—traditional handmade Chinese rag dolls, curtains, clothing. Wherever she is, she dusts, cleans, airs, scrubs, scalds, whitens—always efficiently and with good cheer.

Her real vocation, though, is cooking. In a society where food preparation is a grand art and discriminating eating is a sign of personal cultivation, Mrs. Zhang's food is adjudged superb: northern dishes from her own background, southern-style learned from her Guangxi husband, Cantonese and Sichuanese food from and for old friends from these provinces, apple pie and turkey with sage and onion stuffing learned to please American visitors—all are perfect of their kind. Pickles? Pickles indeed. She is constantly making them, drawing on peasant food preservation methods from all over China, preferring, herself, the fiery, sour, fermented cabbage of Sichuan. "Once you get a crock of that started, you can keep the liquid going for years," she told me, and she was right. Steamed breads, dumplings, homemade noodles? There is always dough being kneaded or slapped or rolled out in her kitchen. A trip with her to one of Taibei's big city markets is an education in the art of purchasing the absolute best for the absolute least.

With these skills, Mrs. Zhang has earned money for her children's education and supplemented her ailing husband's small income. Her abilities have given her the chance to see much more of life than she would have had she remained just a housewife in a rural military town. In 1982 her talent brought her to the United States for a year, a pleasure that proved to be greater in the anticipation than in the reality. She is proud of these accomplishments, but their costs have been high. For twenty years, she has lived in other people's houses, often able to return to her own only once every two months.

In one of these employers' homes she paused long enough to give me this account of her life. It was one of her better jobs—cooking only, no housework—for a rich military family from her own province. Like all the houses in which she has worked, the contrast with her own is great. The general's house and garden might be anywhere in southern California, despite its large domestic staff and numerous Chinese art objects. It contains imported American furniture, appliances, plumbing and security systems, space and luxury within; fresh air, tranquil suburban sounds and privacy without. It is as different as possible from the crowded, noisy, and often malodorous military village where the Zhangs live.

These residences are not home. She is a servant in them, no matter how kindly she is treated. But they are comfortable and interesting. She sees, hears, tastes, and experiences things "outside" that she never would have had she stayed at home. Her shuttling back and forth was at first suffered only for the children's sake; later she grew to like the comforts and the stimulation. But the gains from this life, though real enough, conform to no cultural pattern of aspirations. They are pleasant, but ephemeral and frivolous. What she believes she has lost—a strong, responsible, and supportive family—is the classic Chinese goal. When she weighs her life, as she often does in brief allusions or through comments on the lives of others, the failures seem clear-cut, the achievements blurry. Perhaps her American adventure will shift the emphasis somewhat. Her plans for the future hint of this.

Ren qing, "human feelings" or "human-heartedness," is a Chinese ideal that requires that people recognize and act on each other's essential humanity, regardless of externals. The flavor of Mrs. Zhang's *ren qing* influences all her dealings with people and, on one occasion at least, with other creatures as well. Although my voracious, flea-ridden cat was the bane of her frugal and cleanly existence while she lived in our house, the morning the cat had kittens found Mrs. Zhang busy preparing chicken and ginger soup—the traditional Chinese broth for new mothers.

My ancestors are from a village in Shandong province in Yantai City, but I was born in 1930 in Qingdao City, where father worked as a builder. I had an older brother, an older sister, a younger sister, and a younger brother. Mother was a beautiful woman, very capable and very strict with us children. She was well educated, too. My older sister was very like her— taller and fairer-skinned than I, and both docile and good at her studies. Mother's brothers disciplined my older brother in the old-fashioned way. They'd slap his face if they caught him outside the house smoking or looking untidy. My mother's family was very well organized and upright.

Father was not that way. He drank a lot and did not have a strong character, so we lived with Mother's brothers in Qingdao, with occasional visits to Father's village home.

I took care of my little sister and brother more than anyone else because Older Sister only like to study and didn't like to look after them. Playing, I sometimes lost my little sister, who was only three years younger, so I was scolded a lot. By the time my little brother was born, I understood things better and took good care of him. Once, when I was ten, Little Brother had some kind of infection and couldn't urinate properly, but neither Mother nor Older Sister seemed to pay much attention. I walked a very long way to pick some leaves to make a tea to cure him—I had learned some medicine from Mother. Nobody told me to go, I just decided to do it.

I went to school for about six years—one or two at Protestant missionary schools, the rest of the time at Chinese schools. I didn't like it much. The rooms were cold, the lessons dull, and my mother didn't tell me I had to go, so I skipped a lot.

When I was nearly twelve, Father became ill. We went home to his village to wait for him to die, living there for about a year. In Father's village, my father's sister told me many things about country life that I did not know. She was a very devout Buddhist and liked to go on pilgrimages. Lao Shan, the mountain with the famous mineral-water springs and temples, was a few days' walk away. She would have taken me there, but because I had not completed my twelfth year, she was afraid that the gods would covet or injure me. One of the things I remember about her descriptions of the temple there was that a famous goddess was worshipped there who helped women bear children. A woman who wanted a child came to the temple and prayed. The temple keepers gave her medicine to eat, incense ash to carry home, and a small image of a baby boy or girl made of earth to take away with her. These earth babies were to be buried in the thick adobe house wall over the earthen sleeping platform, sealed in. You could paste a picture over it so no one would know it was there. After you had a child, you made a pilgrimage to return the earth baby, and made a thank-offering of oil or money to the goddess. My aunt knew a lot of things like that, so I learned something about country life.

I also remember that while we were living there my younger sister and I decided we wanted to have our feet bound. Auntie helped us to do it. Oh! Did that hurt! We tried for two days, and then we were glad to give up that foolish idea.

My sister was seventeen, and very pretty, so she was asked for in marriage by the son of a rich landlord, the local *baozhang*.[2] The parents talked it over and agreed to something very modern: they allowed the young couple to meet at our house to have a look at each other. It was very embarrassing for both of them, because young people were very innocent in those days. "His eyes are too small," my sister said, but she didn't seem to really object to him, so they were married in the country fashion, with the bride carried to the groom's house in a closed sedan chair followed by the groom in another. This was before my father died.

The family she married was rural and old-fashioned, but at least they were rich. They owned a lot of land, had many tenants, lived in a big courtyard-style house with many rooms, and kept cattle, horses, and donkeys. Also, there was no mother-in-law, and only one unmarried sister-in-law was still at home. Her father-in-law and husband's brother's family were good to her. She seemed happy, and in a year had a little boy.

A year later, in 1947, the Communists came, and killed her husband because of the family's wealth and Nationalist connections. The older brother was killed too, and the old man was paraded before the villagers to punish and humiliate him.

One night, Sister heard someone on the roof, spying on the family—a Communist agent. But he was also an old family friend, who had not known who she was. When he found out she was to be arrested, he came secretly

---

2. A low-level Nationalist official.

at night to escort her and the baby on a six-hour walk to the nearest railway, from which she returned to us in Qingdao.

Mother urged her to remarry for safety's sake, although normally a widow should wait three years to mourn her husband. Since all his family was dead and their name was dangerous, my sister married. Later, she became pregnant again, and was unlucky enough to be giving birth when her husband was sent to Taiwan in 1949. The second husband sent someone to get her, but the messenger could not find her because she had come to Mother's to have the baby. She is still there, as far as I know. I sometimes hear from her husband here in Taiwan; he married a Taiwanese woman after it became clear that we could not go home to Shandong.

We had stayed in the village for a year after Father's death, but returned after that to the city because Mother couldn't get used to country life. My father's brother farmed our village land, and every year sent half the proceeds to us, which we lived on. Two or three years later I decided to go to work in a clothing factory. My girlfriends were going, and I thought it would be fun, though we didn't really need the money. They paid very little, and it wasn't fun at all. I couldn't stand it after the first day, so I quit.

In about 1947, young men from an air force regiment from the south just then stationed in Qingdao began to meet sweethearts. My girlfriend's future husband brought Zhang Zhengming for me to meet, thinking he needed a wife. He was twelve years older than I—I was seventeen then—and he was around thirty, so I felt very shy of him, considering him just another boring adult. He wasn't especially handsome, either, because his teeth stuck out so.

He began to come to our house to chat with the older people and occasionally to take me and my younger sister and brother to the movies. After a couple of months, he began to ask me if I liked him, and he spoke to my mother about our marrying. Mother asked me if I wanted to marry him. I was too embarrassed to say half a sentence! "Whatever you want me to do is all right with me. It's not *my* concern!" I answered. My girlfriend, already married, said that marriage was fun, because I could have my own house and no one would order me around. So I agreed.

Mother liked my husband and thought it was a good thing for me to be married to someone with his kind of special training. It was awkward arranging the marriage because he had no relatives in Qingdao to do things for him. Mother treated him like a son,[3] and made a wedding feast for us. She sent cakes to our relatives to announce the wedding and helped us find

3. That is, took on the financial responsibilities appropriate for a son's wedding.

a small house to live in near home. I wore a Western-style white wedding dress, like the women in the American movies.

When I was married, I was seventeen by our count, sixteen by Western reckoning.[4] I was really a child, knowing absolutely nothing about adult things. And of course, I was completely innocent about the relations between men and women. I couldn't cook, so every day I'd go home while my husband was at work and eat my mother's food. He would come to fetch me, and we would all eat there. He could cook, because of his early life as a peddler and because you have to take care of yourself in the service. Sometimes he would cook for me. But often he went out to drink and gamble with his air force buddies, leaving me alone, so naturally I often went home to Mother.

After a year of marriage, when I was pregnant, the order came to fly to Taiwan. Mechanics like my husband and his friends could take their wives because we had lots of airplanes. There were so many rumors then.

My family was afraid Mr. Zhang would simply go and abandon me. I was furious that they had not warned me of this before the marriage! They wondered if he had another wife who would be taken instead of me, and I was more and more miserable. Also, I had a lot of morning sickness at that time. When the time came, though, he got me on a plane to Nanjing with a lot of other Qingdao girls, and from there we went to Taiwan.

Everyone said we would be back soon. How were we to guess we would stay so long? Several of my girlfriends were going, and one unmarried girlfriend came to say good-bye at the airport. We all coaxed her, "You come too, to Taiwan. It will be fun, and we will come home soon and go to apologize to your mother for going without permission." She came with us, without saying good-bye. None of us have ever seen our parents or heard from them again. I don't know if my mother is alive or dead, though I suppose she must be dead by now. It's been so many years.

When we arrived in Taiwan, we were stationed in Taoyuan. At first we slept in temples, and they cooked rice in a big pot for all the dependents. It was crowded and frightening, but we helped each other. Our husbands got paid most of the time but everything was very expensive and hard to buy. After half a year, we moved to another post, where we stayed for about three years in married barracks.

Just after we moved, I had my oldest son, Bright Reputation. A year

4. Chinese people count every calendar year in which they have lived. A baby born one day before new year's counts as one *sui*, and the next day, in the new year, becomes two *sui* old.

later, I had a daughter, who lived only fifteen days. The older child injured the baby while playing, and she died. I often wish now I had a daughter; they are closer to their mothers than sons. A year later I had another boy, Bright Light.

Two years later, in 1954, my husband was transferred to where we live now in the south. It was really a little country town then. The air force built housing that we were later allowed to buy, where my family and many others from that group still live. The houses were quite small at first: two rooms about three meters by three meters each. We cooked outside and used public toilets at the end of each row of houses. Each house had a small front yard, the same size as the house, so we have built another room on the front and a kitchen on the back. Some people make a flower garden in their yard. We still use the public toilets, the biggest shortcoming of our housing. Some people are not very clean.

After we settled there, I had my sons Bright Virtue and Bright Nation. We were going to call the fourth son a more refined name, but my illiterate old man got it mixed up, and the registry official put down "Nation" because it sounds so patriotic. In those years, I just bore children and took care of them. It was very hard, but sometimes it was fun. There was so much to do to take care of them, and I was young. I had no mother or mother-in-law to help me or tell me what to do. It was hard to get good food and medicine, too.

The fourth boy was very sick when he was small, sick for more than a year. He had a terrible ear infection—his ears ran and he cried all the time. I was afraid he would be deafened. Because he had fever, I fed him only rice gruel for a long time, so as not to cause more heating of his body's humors. He cried for food, but I would only let him eat gruel. That year his hair fell out and got a reddish color and his stomach swelled. I thought he would die and kept trying to get medicine for him. The military hospital would treat him after a long wait, but it didn't help. Finally, I borrowed money and went to a private doctor. He gave him pencillin and the ear infection cleared up. Medical care was very hard to get for us lower-level military people then.

At about that time, I became a Catholic. I had heard about Catholic missionaries in Shandong who gave free food to poor people and helped them with medicine, so I was not surprised when I saw nuns in their black clothes. Some nuns began to come to our married barracks to preach their faith. They spoke about doing good, not doing evil, and abandoning superstition, saying it was not necessary to believe in gods and spirits. They came often, and some of us younger women brought our stools and listened to them. After a while, they gave us an examination. Those who passed could be baptized and enter the church. I went to church fairly often, when I had time, bringing the little boys sometimes. The Catholics did many good deeds in those days, giving powdered milk and medicine free to people who needed it. They often helped me out.

When my first boys began to attend elementary school, the teaching was very poor. I knew they would need a lot of help, but we couldn't pay to send them to cram school. So I decided to learn to read again to help them. We studied their lessons together, and I made them do all their homework. That's how I really learned to read.

When my biggest passed the examination to enter junior middle school, Old Four[5] began primary school. Junior middle school required school fees in those days, and all the boys needed uniforms and supplies for school. We didn't have the money for all that, so I had to go to work outside our home. For a while, I bought vegetables from the wholesale market to resell in our neighborhood, but the profits were too small. Taiwanese farm women could always undersell me, which meant that sometimes I lost money.

However, because by now my husband had taught me to cook, I began to go into other people's houses to earn money. At first, I found a job with a Chinese professor's family in Taibei. Later, I began to work for American graduate students. I am a Shandong person, very outspoken, like you Americans, and I speak the national language with a standard accent, and only a little bit of a Shandong accent. American students liked that and they liked my cooking. I worked for a different student couple every year after that until 1974. Then the students stopped hiring people, because our wages in Taiwan were getting bigger as their scholarships were getting smaller. Working for them was interesting. They were learning Chinese, so we could have fun talking. They were more democratic than Chinese people, so when I spoke my mind, they were not angry.

Living away from home was really worrying for me, though. The boys were growing up, and I could only come home once in every month or two. My husband was away working during the day, and he didn't supervise their studies at night because he can't read. Also, my working away from home caused gossip. Other children sometimes said bad things about me, so my sons would fight them. It was very bad for them to have such rough habits.

My wages were no more than NT$1,000 each month. Of course, I ate my employers' food. So sometimes, even though I worked, there was not enough money for school fees. Sometimes I had to borrow from my employers, sometimes I formed a rotating credit club with my friends. We kept

5. Children in Chinese families are often referred to by the number of their birth order.

them in school, telling them it was important for the family's future that they study. In spite of all that, not one was a good student. Not one graduated from a good senior middle school. The oldest did his military service for three years, then became a laborer.

The second joined the air force to become a mechanic. Because he really knew how to talk, people liked him. He had a lot of Taiwanese friends, spoke Taiwanese, and wanted to marry a Taiwanese girl. Then he died. While he was repairing a jet engine, the pilot started the plane. He was crushed. That was in 1975. The country gave us NT$300,000 (U.S.$7,500) in compensation when he died, and NT$130,000 (U.S.$3,250) every year for ten years afterward. The country was going to bury him in a small military cemetery, but his father said he had died for his country and should be buried in the national heroes' cemetery. He and my oldest son went again and again to argue for this. Finally, the authorities permitted it. Now his grave is with all the other air force heroes who have died in Taiwan for their country. Every year there is a big ceremony, with high dignitaries to honor them.

My son died only a few weeks after he had become engaged to a very nice Taiwanese girl. She had loved him for a long time, and really suffered sometimes from his bad behavior. She was very loyal. After he died, I treated her as a daughter. When she finally married, five years later, I went to her wedding and quietly gave her NT$500,000 (U.S.$12,500). This was just for her; her husband's family didn't need to know about our real relationship. Now she has two children and I think she is happy.

My third son was too stupid to finish school. He had a tumor on his vocal chords while he was in high school and needed an operation. We had to take him to the air force hospital to be treated, which really worried me in case they cut him carelessly and he became a mute. Fortunately, that didn't happen. After serving in the army, he went to Taipei to work in a restaurant. He has a girlfriend, one of the mountain Aborigine women, but won't get married. I hardly ever see him.

Number Four was always a happy, joking boy. I feel I was unfair to him more than all the others because I left home to work when he was so young. He did pretty well in school, served three years in the army, and took lessons to learn to drive a truck. Now he is married and lives near us. I told him not to get married—his eldest brother's marriage should have been an example to him—but he got married anyway. We had to help him. Now I tell them to wait to have children. After they earn some money they can still have them.

My oldest son was married in 1975 to a very pretty Taiwanese girl from a big family near a fishing town in the south. I rented a small bus to drive me and about ten friends to go to their house for the engagement, so I met the people in her family and saw how they lived. They are country people, with customs different from ours. Neither I nor any of our friends could speak Taiwanese to them, and only the children could speak Mandarin to us. I can say one or two things in Taiwanese, but mostly we talked to ourselves and they talked to themselves at the engagement party. They served us a big meal—they had invited more than twelve tables of guests, close to two hundred people—including the raw fish that Japanese people eat. My daughter-in-law's father had bicycled into town at four o'clock in the morning for the fish, so it was very fresh. But we mainland people don't eat such things. The father and mother announced the engagement to Heaven and Earth and their ancestors, and my son gave my daughter-in-law an engagement ring. We gave them NT$40,000 (U.S.$1,000) as a bride-price, and her mother gave it all back except a few thousand. I was glad of that, because it showed they were not the kind of family that sells their daughters, like some Taiwanese. We took a lot of photographs of the two families, and then we went home, taking our guests to a few scenic spots on the way home. It seemed like a good beginning for my son's marriage.

A few months later, it was our turn to take responsibility. We held the wedding feast in a restaurant in our town. A few people, including her parents, came from her side, but mostly the guests were our friends. We invited four tables. It was quite simple, really. The new bride was not coming to live with us, so there were no gifts coming to our house. Each guest gave one or two hundred New Taiwan dollars (U.S.$2.50–$5.00) in a red envelope at the dinner, which paid for the food and liquor.

The new couple went to live near my son's work in Gaoxiong, where my daughter-in-law found work as a hostess in a restaurant, because she is so pretty. We hoped they would work for a while and save money, but no. They had three children—a boy, a girl, and a boy—one after another. I kept telling them to stop, and finally my son had an operation so they wouldn't have any more.

In the early years of their marriage, I went back to work to help them out with money. I found a job with an American missionary family, working for them about two years.

After two years, I got very tired and upset because of my eldest son's marriage troubles, so I went home to rest for a few months. The missionary family was a good family, but they didn't understand our Chinese ways very well. They understood how to give orders, but not how to show real humanity. Anyway, I needed to help my son and my daughter-in-law run their family better. They had three children so quickly, even though I told them to wait. Then they didn't want to work hard to support them, especially my daughter-in-law. She only wanted to wear pretty clothes and go out to be entertained every night. My son, who gets dirty from manual work, wasn't good enough for her any more. She didn't seem to care about the children. Sometimes she left them in the country with her parents for a long time where they got sick, and their legs were all scabby from mosquito bites. For a while I tried to tell them how to behave properly, so they could establish their family solidly.

Because everything costs money, after a while I looked for work again. A friend told me that a high air force officer from my home province wanted someone to cook for his household, someone who could cook the wheat-based foods we Shandong people like. I went to see them and saw they were a very rich family. There was only the general, his wife, and his old mother at home. They had a gardener and a Taiwanese woman to clean the house, do the wash, and wash the dishes, so all I had to do was shop for food and cook. They lived in a pleasant, mountainside suburb with fresh air and good surroundings. So I decided to stay. That is when I took up jogging. They paid me not too much in salary, but they gave me presents, and when guests came they left very large tips for my cooking. When their old mother died after a year or two, the family gave me a large gold ring in her memory, for helping nurse her at the end. In this way, they behaved toward me in the old-fashioned Chinese way. My position in the house was so good that the Taiwanese help were jealous—the only bad thing about the job. I cooked for them for three years.

During that time, my son's marriage broke up and he and his wife got divorced. That was a terrible time. I was furious, and sometimes I thought I would just go to the sea and throw myself in. Oh, I was angry! I *told* them what they had to do, but they wouldn't do it. I gave them money. I brought them to live in a little house just across from us, where my husband could look after the children and cook for them while our daughter-in-law worked. We treated her like an empress, with her father-in-law waiting on her, and me working to support her children! Oh, I was angry! But there was nothing for it—they divorced. She took the two older children and left the youngest for my husband to care for. My son moved back to Gaoxiong, where he seems to drink up all his money. I hardly hear from him, and don't want to. The little boy is company for my husband, who is very good to him. The mother will want him when he is older though. It's right for the brothers and sister to grow up together, and to be with their mother. My husband has old-fashioned Chinese ideas, and thinks we should keep the children, or at least one of the boys, because they bear our name, and because his son will not be able to have any more children. What can you do with a situation like that?

After they were divorced, I thought I could teach my eldest son a business so he could stop being a laborer and have a better life. I quit my cooking job and went home to make and sell meat dumplings and little meat-stuffed buns. I am a good cook, if I do say so myself. Besides, in Taiwan now anyone can make money selling food. So many people are working, so they have money and don't want to cook. We freeze dumplings—I can make three hundred a day by myself—that they can take home and boil or steam themselves. It's very convenient, so many people come to buy them. At first, we didn't know how much to charge. Others who sell meat buns told us we were selling too cheaply. We thought if half our selling price was profit, that was fine. But three-fifths of the selling price should be profit. After all, we work all day, almost every day, and don't count the cost of our labor. If we had to pay anyone to do it, there'd be very little left.

It's not easy to calculate all the costs, either. We learned some tips from an old friend who makes buns in Taibei. He advised us to sell by weight, not by number. When you sell by number, it makes it hard to tell how much the cost is. We got a scale, and sold by weight, we raised our prices a little, and soon we were grossing NT$15,000 (U.S.$375) a week. So the money wasn't bad. We really worked, though.

I took some savings, rented an empty house near ours, bought some second-hand chairs and tables, and opened a restaurant. I tried to teach my son how to choose the best meat and vegetables, how to make dumplings, and how to treat customers. My husband helped a little, but his manner is very rough. When you run a restaurant, you have to talk nicely to customers and treat them right. My husband just says, "Take it or leave it," and walks away. He's no help. My son is too much like his father. Besides, he doesn't want to learn anything from me. He worked for a few months, then said he wouldn't work any more. When he left town, my blood pressure was so high I nearly died from anger.

My fourth son married a little while after that. He and his wife were having a hard time making ends meet, so I asked that son to help me sell dumplings and buns. I found them a very cheap rental near us, moved them down there, and started to teach him the business. Things went all right for a while, till they decided to take over themselves. I told my son that I had had an offer of NT$25,000 (U.S.$625) for the furniture and equipment. They could give me NT$15,000 (U.S.$375) for it over time, out of their earnings. They talked about it, and told me they thought that was too much, that I was trying to make money off them! I nearly died of anger. My husband I are getting old and I am still working to help these sons. I need my money for my old age—these sons don't give me anything! How can I afford to give them everything? I told them I wouldn't sell the things to them. They will have to look after themselves.

My son got back his old job driving a truck, but they still live nearby.

[129]

They come over all the time to ask my husband to cook for them, and he does. I tell him they need to learn to be independent, but I know he doesn't listen when I'm not there. He feeds them anyway.

All this really made me angry for a long time. As luck would have it, the general's family contacted me about then, wanting me to work for them again. Their daughter in America needed someone to help with her new baby, so they wanted to send me to her for a year. The general would pay for my travel there and back, and for a visit to Taiwan after six months. His daughter would pay me U.S.$300 each month, as well as my food and housing in their house. I was glad to get away from all the family troubles, and I have always wanted to travel. I said I would go.

I'm glad I went. It was interesting to see how Americans live in their own country. I have known a lot of Americans, and understand some of their customs, but to see them in their own country is different. There are both good people and bad people there, just like in Taiwan. I could have stayed, for the general's family could have helped me emigrate, but decided not to. I was really lonely there, with no one to talk to. Getting used to the food was really hard, for while some American food is good, to my taste a lot of it is bland and uninteresting. There are too many frightening and unfamiliar things in your country, and it's not safe to walk alone in cities there. Being away gave me time to think about my and my husband's future, though.

What I think is this. We live in different times now. It is useless to try to have an old-fashioned Chinese family passed on from generation to generation. Even I didn't take care of my parents and parents-in-law, because my husband and I came to Taiwan. How, then, can I expect our sons to care for us? I don't want to use up all my money on them and then, when I am old, have to go begging to this one and that one for food. Two of my women friends and I are going to reopen the restaurant, work hard, and make lots of money. I'm going to save everything I can from that and from my husband's pension.

He gets NT$60,000 (U.S.$1,500) each year now. His pension was raised recently because of the rising cost of living. We get rations of oil, salt, fuel, and rice which are more than we need, so we sell some. But it is not much these days. My husband is too old, his health is too bad, and he is too illiterate to find work, especially in our town where most businesses are Taiwanese. My sons give me nothing. I have to work to earn money.

If I can save NT$100,000 (U.S.$2,500) more for each of us, we can buy places in an old folks' home where they will provide food and medical care for the rest of our lives. That's the way society is now, and that's what I'm going to do!

My, my, life is very complicated. We taste the sweet, the sour, the pungent, and the bitter in our lives. Sometimes when I think about how hard life is, I cry, but then, when old friends get together, I feel warm and happy. We just do the best we can.

Zhang Zhengming: Air Force Loyalist

Zhang Zhengming, Zhang Xiuzhen's husband, is a retired air force mechanic from south China. Now in his late sixties, he has served the Nationalist military since his youth and cannot even imagine another system of government or a Chinese who would want one. Anyone lacking in his kind of affectionate loyalty, he thinks, must be either wicked or absurdly ignorant. He points out that there are flaws in the operation of the sociopolitical system under which he has lived his life comfortably. Nothing is perfect. But with better education, the right men in charge—society would operate as well as anyone could wish. There are many men like Mr. Zhang who credit their rise from rural hardship to a modern occupation in a prosperous country to Jiang Jieshi and the Nationalists. What Mr. Zhang cannot understand is how, after all the social betterment he has seen during his life, young people can have degenerated so quickly. He represents a segment of Taiwan's population—Mainlander career enlisted servicemen— who have not needed a place in the rapidly industrializing economy, and who cannot understand the difficulty their children are having in finding theirs.

Zhang Zhengming and I talked about his life through several long afternoons at his home of twenty years, part of a large complex of quarters for married military in southern Taiwan. The house shares walls with neighbors on each side, and more neighbors live across the 5-foot alley that passes the front gate. In winter this sunny corridor serves as a meeting place for little knots of knitting women and card-playing men, seated on the tiniest of stools, chatting in dialects from everywhere in China. In summer the trees that families have planted in their yards help cool the breezes that pass from door to door, carrying the smells of cooking, of carefully tended flowers, of the community toilet at the end of the row.

Mr. Zhang lives now, as he has throughout his life, in unavoidable intimacy with many other people. Two doors away, a family struggles with the burden of a senile old mother who, having gone blind, cannot tell night from day and loudly demands meals at inconvenient hours. Family rows erupt occasionally; everyone's taste in television and radio programming is as public as their normally loud-voiced conversations.

[131]

His ties to many of these families come from the shared past, when the men traveled together on the China mainland, fighting the Nationalists' wars. They know each other well, though intimacy does not necessarily mean liking. Some people pass in the narrow alley, or at the nearby vegetable market, with the curtest of nods or with no greeting at all. The burden of a life lived so publicly is an accustomed one, but Mr. Zhang feels it as a burden nonetheless.

Mr. Zhang, perhaps more than most, finds his position an ambiguous one in the world and in his family. While Taiwan enjoys unprecedented prosperity and the changes of affluence come ever quicker, his life, his possessions, his salary, and his opportunities remain the same. With his wife working away from home to support the family, he, in poor health, remains behind to cook and care for children. He had four sons, an accomplishment many Chinese would envy, but his sons live apart from him and do nothing to lighten his old age.

It should surprise no one, then, that Mr. Zhang is often grumpy and does not take neighborly needling well. What stands out, though, is his gentleness in the care of his small grandson, the shining neatness of the house, the soldierly pride in his appearance. A short, slight man, he carries himself with dignity, eyebrows shooting out like a Chinese opera hero's over round, alert eyes. A set of ill-fitting false teeth makes his heavy provincial accent hard to follow, but he talks with verve and much gesticulation. Initially uncomfortable about the interview, he quickly relaxed, expanding enthusiastically on his earlier life, when as a young man he was one of Republican China's few modern warriors in one of this century's great conflicts.

I was born in Guangxi Province in 1922, near the Guangdong border, at a time when "the area of the two Guangs" was not yet controlled by the central government; each province was independent then. The Cantonese[6] are very regional-minded. Even now, when two of them are together they will speak their own language regardless of whether others can understand or not. I learned to speak Cantonese as well as my native Guangxi dialect while I was growing up in that area, learning our national language only when I entered the service. I grew up among many relatives, but my own father, mother, and brothers died when I was seven. My elder male cousin had married early at nineteen, but after many years his wife had no child. This made all the relatives angry, so in his forties he married a second wife. She had no children either. Our lives are determined by Heaven. We only

6. People from Guangdong province.

receive what we are given. This aunt raised me and my two sisters as adopted children, and was kind to me. I lived with them until I was seventeen.

Our lineage had three divisions: one, that of my cousin and his four brothers, had only two sons in the next generation; the second, where the only son died, had three daughters; and the third, through my father and me, is now here. I had four sons, three of them living, and my first son has two sons, so I can say that I have continued our family as well as anyone. Many of my older relatives back home must be dead now. Even my sisters, who were in their twenties when I was in my teens, must be old by now.

Where I grew up, most men farmed, if they had land, or carried goods from place to place as porters, or they operated some business. Before I left home, I helped my cousin peddle goods to the mountain villages. Guangxi is mountainous—real mountains, big, blue-green, with no grass on them, and lakes here and there. Many have big natural caves that the Communist bandits used as hideouts, living for decades and never getting caught. They could always retreat deeper into the mountains and find food there, though people who didn't know the mountains could easily get lost in them. I've walked up and down those mountains many times, going from my village to Liuzhou City and back. Also in the mountains, lived many Zhuang and Miao[7] people. Their clothes, languages, and customs are all different from each other and from ours. Sometimes the language changes from village to village. In the course of doing this kind of business, I learned Cantonese, which is how we communicated with these people. How can one province have so many different customs! Some Mountain People wore huge ear-rings. Some didn't bathe themselves in their whole lives; in other places, the people were neat and clean. In many villages, we couldn't understand anything that they said. When I got to Taiwan, I realized that the Mountain People here are very much like them, even in the way they tie bands around their heads.

In their mountains, even if we were empty-handed, we could not out-pace them; when they were on our flat ground, they could not outpace us, even if we were hoisting heavy loads, because, they said, their feet felt floating, unstable, down on the plains.

The mountain girls were pretty, but the men were too dark to be called good-looking. The girls stayed at home, and didn't work outside, so they remained fair. As long as we behaved ourselves politely and did nothing improper, the people entertained us well, and we were safe. But their men each carried a long knife just in case. Some mountain paths led to just one

7. Non-Chinese ethnic minorities; Mountain People of south China.

house, but if you asked people the way, they told you honestly which were the main paths. Some villages took two or three days' walk to reach. Peddlers like us usually hired a guide who knew all the routes from long experience.

We used to start into the mountains between the second and fourth lunar month. We just kept walking, doing business along the way, till the end of the lunar year, when we'd reach home again. We sold cotton cloth sometimes, but mostly needles, thread, cosmetics—light goods. We'd walk a long way for only one household sometimes, and even then might sell only two or three little things. It was hard work. They didn't use paper money, only silver coins.

Within the mountains was an inner plain, a hilly area. Rivers ran through, so with transportation better, people were able to buy goods from other sources. They were richer, too, planting corn, sweet potatoes, and taro, but no rice. We'd visit them too, and they fed and housed us free because they said we only came once a year, and they didn't need our money.

We didn't earn much from this kind of business, but still the girls criticized our high prices. What we bought was not cheap, and we couldn't sell very dear in remote areas. We had to make a profit over what we spent on keeping ourselves. Except for what we spent at inns, we kept every coin. Nowadays, children spend what they earn pretty freely, but we sweated so for our profits that we didn't want to spend them unless there was some real need. The bundles we carried on our backs were very big, and coming home at the end of the year we always ran into snow. We couldn't see the roads and nearly froze our feet, though we wrapped them up in whatever was left of the cloth. It wasn't easy to earn that money. Working out there for half a year, we earned between half a year and a year's food as profit. It was better than farming.

At home in the village, my family members farmed our land. In those days, villages were very large, with thousands of people. They grew wet rice and some vegetables. When it wasn't too dry and the harvest was good, one year's harvest would provide three years' food. Then we were rich. But rural life is hard; it takes time to get used to it. Even women were expected to do some outdoor work, the way a bride must carry water to the household the day after the wedding. But most outdoor work was done by men, with women permitted to help only with planting and harvesting. Their usual job was to carry water and feed the cows and pigs. Rich families kept many cows and pigs, which required a lot of water carrying. Even one pail is heavy. In the countryside, though women didn't go to school, boys could, depending on their interest. I went for two years, but I didn't learn much and am now nearly illiterate. I can remember playing on the way to school and the beatings I got better than any of the books! The children of the rich were sent to town for junior school, and a few to senior school. Girls stayed at home, and most boys worked on the farm.

In those days, lunar New Year was our gayest time. We got a set of new clothes (which we wore till they were worn out), and people killed the chickens, ducks, and pigs they had raised. Chickens were dried so that they kept till the seventh month; fish were smoked. Before New Year's, we put away enough salt, oil, and special foods to last the year, so we didn't have to buy them frequently, for rural markets met only every three days. One of our local customs was for married sisters to come home around New Year. We made special glutinous rice cakes for them—so many that we were still eating them in the third month. We'd fry a couple for breakfast before work every day. Ordinary people didn't have fish or duck to preserve, but they salted, dried, or stored their vegetables. Common people were very frugal then, depending on rice for most of their food. Lard was a treat, and we didn't eat fowl unless we had guests visiting us. Ordinary food consisted of rice with a sauce of chiles, soy sauce, and salt. Families with young boys sent them to the canals to catch fish, which counted as little feasts. It wasn't like it is now, with people eating oil all day, eating this good thing and that.

During the year, we could rest only between the last harvest in the eleventh month until the end of the New Year celebrations in the first month. Then the farmers ploughed again like mules, never stopping. Men worked like this till they were my age now, when they had accumulated something, and had grown sons and daughters-in-law. Then they could retire, have fewer burdens, play cards. If they had no sons, though, only daughters, they would have to keep on through their sixties. If the fields weren't tilled every year, they were ruined as big weeds got into them.

Farming is hard, so I gave it up after one year. Every day, hauling things. In dry weather like this, the crops would wither in the field and there'd be no harvest at all. At harvest, it was a rush. Everything had to be brought in at once, or crops would be lost. You needed additional workers, but they were hard to hire. You had to give them a variety of foods to eat, pay them, and treat them well, or they wouldn't stay. It was like a military campaign, when all the rice turned yellow and had to be harvested at once. Americans use machines, but we did it all with big knives and our backs, with no rest for anyone. To thresh the rice, a man stood at each corner of the threshing floor, each striking alternately with a big flail. Women cut the grain, men carried and threshed it. The baskets of rice weighing about one hundred kilos were carried by men in their twenties. It was best to have lots of brothers.

[135]

Our village had one rich family that owned thousands of *mu*[8] of land. They sent one of their sons to middle school in Liuzhou City. This was during the warlord period, and the son got a position supplying foodstuffs and horses to the warlord. He came back once, riding a horse very arrogantly, like a god. I wonder what happened to them when the Communists came!

After I was seventeen, I was considered an adult. Before that, boys and girls could play together, but afterwards, it was not permitted. We could just smile in passing. In our area, people married at nineteen or twenty. My relatives told me in three or four years I should marry and build a house, but I would have to wait till then. I wanted to save money for my marriage, not wanting to be a burden to my relatives, so I left home and went to work as a porter for three or four years at the harbor in Liuzhou.

Except for children in rich families who had daughters-in-law and servants, boys learned how to carry goods with a shoulder pole. There is always lots to carry on a farm, especially in Guangxi, where we didn't have ox carts or horse carts. We didn't even have roads, except for the little paths on the dikes between paddy fields, so men carried everything. Down in the city they needed porters, too. There were few water sources, so rich families, barbershops, and restaurants all needed to have water carried.

After working a few years at this, I began my military service. Most families didn't send their sons into the military. Boys who had no parents, or who wouldn't obey their parents but just followed their own inclinations, were the only ones who became soldiers. Good men did not become soldiers in those days; now, of course, it is different. The best go into service.

What I entered was a warlord's local militia. There was no fighting, and those soldiers ate well and had good clothing. There was nothing to do all day, yet we got a salary. The men weren't like real military men, as we came to be later, but more like common people. There was no draft then—that didn't begin for years.

In 1936 we began to hear of incursions by the Japanese in Guangdong and Guangxi. The Guangdong region still wasn't controlled by the national government, because warlords controlled some areas, and there were Communist bandits in the hills. By 1938, though, the whole country was united under our present government, except for a few small nests of Communist bandits. Military troops were few then—only 600,000 men and women in Guangxi under General Bai Chongxi. The draft began. Ordinary people didn't know what was happening, but we knew the Japanese wanted to fight

---

8. A *mu* is approximately one-sixth of an acre in Taiwan.

us. There was no television, and few newspapers, so some universities sent students to inform the people that the Japanese were attacking us here and in other parts of China. I decided to join the army, spending 1938 to 1939 in Sichuan with that service. I was stationed with an air force unit, and was able to gain an apprenticeship with them.

There was no exam at first for entering the air force, though when the war with Japan started they began to examine applicants. When I joined, they were glad just to have volunteers. At that time, there were about 300,000 men in the air force; if they all had to pass an exam, there wouldn't have been enough people. It wasn't necessary to have any book learning to do the routine work we were trained in, like removing screws. At some levels, of course, specialists had to be able to read technical materials.

My training as a mechanic was easy. I worked in a group where each person learned a certain part of the aircraft and was responsible for replacing it if there were defects. Each person did his own part and didn't learn about anyone else's. We didn't have to make any judgments. "If something is worn out, take it out and replace it," they told us. One plane was maintained jointly by a team in this way. Engineers from companies that built the planes were responsible for supervision and for solving problems we couldn't handle. We needed to learn from them what was standard or normal, and what counted as defective, what we should do if a part sat too high or low. If anything was abnormal, we told our group head. The condition of each part was recorded in a book. When everything checked out, we could send the plane on as available for flight. The flight-availability group then signed off each plane, took responsibility for it. If anything went wrong with a plane, and they had signed it off as ready for use, the responsibility was theirs. The whole system worked like this, with equipment carefully checked and responsibility divided in an orderly way.

We usually spent the morning inspecting planes, though during the war Japanese bombers might come at any time and disrupt everything. Sometimes the sirens blew ten times a day, and we'd spend the whole day running for cover.

During the war, life was good for me. Food was ample, the conditions of life were orderly. I went to the airport to work every day as dawn broke, and came back to barracks every evening at eight or nine o'clock. It was physically much easier then peddling or farming, and I liked to work with airplanes and machines. There was no place to spend money, so I saved some. I was single and young and had no responsibilities or duties, outside my work. I traveled with my unit, spending time in Sichuan, Xian, Nanjing, and Qingdao. There was nothing else I really wanted to do, just fight the Japanese.

[137]

During the war it was better to be in the air force than in the army, though even in the air force it was hard sometimes. The army had so many soldiers that they sometimes didn't get their food on time, and often didn't get paid. Sometimes in the army, troops were surrounded, so there was no way to supply them. Even if they were flown in, their provisions might be dropped at the wrong place, and taken by the enemy. In the air force, it was all right after you got used to it. Though things were always in short supply, our officers took care of us, getting us food no matter what it took.

Life is full of bitterness, sweetness, and sourness. Each generation's situation is different. Children born today in peacetime enjoy real plenty. After the war began, it was better for us. There were no places to go for entertainment or any kind of recreation. Those who were highly educated could get away from the war; the rest of us just had to follow the military troops.

If it hadn't been for the war, most people would have stayed at home in their own provinces, working on the farm or being laborers. They wouldn't have traveled far—certainly not to Taiwan! When I was small, I heard older people talk of Fujian and Taiwan as the frontiers of China, but I didn't know what direction or how far away they were. Even businessmen rarely traveled from this province to that province, just going from one city to another in the counties surrounding their hometown. Only the biggest merchants went from one province to another and knew about distant places. People who traveled out of their own province were called "outside provincers," exactly as the Taiwanese call us here, instead of calling us "Chinese."

Travel was very difficult during the war. The roads in Sichuan were especially twisty, with roads hairpinning up the mountains, very narrow and dangerous. Cars had to drive so slowly that it took less time to walk if you cut across the loops and just went straight up to the hills. The government built a lot of roads during the war. They were built without machines, all by human labor. In Sichuan I saw an airport being built where hundreds of thousands of people had been brought in to work. Stones were broken up with hammers to a standard size to pave it. America sent some good materials for that airport. The surface had to be strong enough to support the big planes safely. The construction lasted for a long time. People swarmed like ants—you couldn't see the ground for people. Marines, soldiers, air force men, and civilians all gathered there to collect stones. Each household had to collect so many kilos from the riverside. The food for all those people was brought in every day by ten big trucks full of rice baskets.

The mainland is so large that it took years to build just one railway. When I was in Guangxi, I didn't know how large it was, having never seen a map.

Even now, if you ask me how big Taiwan is, I couldn't tell you. I have a sense for which places are larger and which smaller, from things I've heard other people say, but I know our Mainland is one of the biggest countries on earth.

In 1945 the Japanese surrendered. Our capital returned to Nanjing, where I was sent for two years. We were still at war, this time with the Communists, so in 1948 I was sent to Qingdao to our biggest air base in the north.

After the victory over Japan, if a man had the chance he went home to see his wife, if he had one, or to get married. Everyone wanted to get married, but for some it was too far to go home. Then he would marry a local girl. Especially while we were stationed in Xian a lot of fellows married local girls. Sometimes their parents wrote and urged them to come home to find a wife because their own women spoke the right language. At that time, however, the women's families weren't so fussy about the men's backgrounds, about whether the two families were well matched. If a man earned a steady salary by serving the country, that was good enough, and the families didn't ask for brideprice. Some of us got good women, which was good for us. Others had bad luck.

The Communists had us pretty much cut off in Qingdao, so it wasn't easy to send mail home. Roads, waterways, airlines—all were cut off. The first two letters I sent home—I had them written for me by a letter writer—never arrived. I wanted to tell my relatives I would go home to get married and asked my cousin and his wife to help me find a girl. But I had to wait till the married men had returned from their home leave before I could take mine. I sent another letter, containing pictures and several thousand yuan, which they got. At the time, a thousand yuan would buy many hundred-kilo baskets of rice. If they wanted money, they should let me know, I told them. They wrote back, saying they didn't need money, but I should come home to get married. They wrote to say they would wait for my return to make marriage arrangements.

About sending mail on the mainland at the time: it was very difficult and slow. We wrote to our relatives in care of some person in the rural market nearest our home. There were no proper addresses. Then the letter waited till one of our friends or relatives came to the market, and asked about letters from us. If you were sending money, of course you needed trustworthy friends. From the time I sent a letter until the time I received their answer took half a year. The fastest time was about three months. During the Sino-Japanese war, sometimes you just couldn't get through, or the letters had to go by very indirect routes. Sometimes it caused a lot of worry. Money arrived even more slowly because we always sent it person-to-person. The post office placed a one-thousand-yuan limit on the amount sent, so you could not cash big postal orders easily. In 1949, after we arrived in Taiwan, I wrote back once. After that, all communications were stopped. I know nothing of them now.

In Qingdao my friends were trying to help me to marry. I had some Cantonese workmates who were really good to me. Several of us had rented a couple of rooms where we lived and ate together. We played mah-jongg and enjoyed each other's company. Two others were married to Qingdao girls. One of them said to me, "You're still not married! You'll be an old bachelor." I was twenty-seven, still young, and I knew my relatives wanted me to come home to marry. I said, "I have nothing. How can I marry? I don't care about all that!" I hadn't any savings, just depended for food and clothes on the government. Whether I married would be up to fate; I wasn't going to take any initiative.

Another friend introduced me to a girl, brought us over to her home for a visit. Another's wife promised to introduce me to yet another. The girls worked in the Qingdao textile factories as spinners. I got together with these girls often, after dinner, with our friends. But I had no money and no courage. I was afraid I wouldn't be able to support a wife. As a soldier, I had only what the government gave me and no other ways of getting money. As long as I was single, it didn't matter if I was transferred here and there. But if I had a home I would worry about it. So I delayed another half a year. Every day my friends nagged me about being single.

Finally, someone introduced me to this wife of mine. She was just a little girl, only seventeen, with a tiny face. I said to my friend, who had introduced us, "Don't you think her body's a little lacking?" "Fool," she said, "she's young yet. After she's married, her body will mature."

My friends' wives did all the worrying for me. They invited her to come over when I was back from work. Finally, I told her, "I don't have any money, or much of anything else. I left home when I was young. I can provide you with food, and I have a good character and temperament. These two ladies can vouch for me."

I was asked to go to her home the next day. She had an uncle, her mother's brother, a young brother, and an elder sister. I told her mother clearly, "My two friends can tell you that I have no wife in my home town. I have no money and can't provide your daughter with beautiful clothes, but I will feed her well." And so they agreed to our marriage.

In Qingdao we lived in a two-story house that the government had taken over from the Japanese. It was a very good house for that time. I could get it because there weren't very many of us air force people there then.

Not long after this, we retreated to Taiwan. That was late in 1949. Only about a dozen of the men in my group were still unmarried by then. We got some of them married off here, later. The unmarried men came by boat, while those with families were sent ahead by plane. Those who had registered their marriages first went first. The officials' arrangements for our families were good.

My wife became pregnant after only one month of marriage. Our eldest son was conceived on the Mainland. After that we had three other sons, one after another. Unfortunately there was no family planning in those days. Our failures in raising our family are due to this. There is no use in having many children if they are not filial. My wife has been very good, but I haven't given her much of a life. I'm indebted to her.

Raising our sons was not easy, especially after my wife went out to work. I tried to supervise their homework and encourage them to study, but I'm no good with ink and paper. It used to be that if a man worked hard and was loyal, that was enough. Of course, we have to look at today's society, too. Nowadays, young people are not like our generation. We really valued money, planned how to use it, and held on to as much as we could. They eat, drink, amuse themselves, spending without taking any thought for the future. We were always concerned about the future, both saving money for it and trying hard to have enough sons to take care of us when we get old. If a married woman didn't have children, all her in-laws would treat her badly. My wife and I had our children and tried to save money, but our future is still uncertain. Society has changed a great deal.

My wife has described our eldest son's family problems. There is nothing more to say about that. We must try to bring up our grandson, who has our family name and is registered as a Guangxi person, to have a good character.

When my second son died, I could not believe it. We had suffered a lot in earlier years, I had been through the war and was never wounded, and suddenly, he was dead. He gave us a lot of trouble to raise—skipping school, hanging around with Taiwanese hoodlums. He was even in military prison once for fighting with his messmates. He played around with women, gambled, and drank too much. But I kept telling him his future was in the air force, which is the best of the services, the most skilled. Our Mainland people have the say-so in the air force, and we keep the spirit of the nation alive. Finally, he was beginning to settle down, learning his job well and being responsible. Then this.

His death was bad for us all, but his elder brother and I had a further burden to bear. We had to arrange for his death benefits and for his burial in the official cemetery. At first, they wanted to say it was his fault, so there would be no death benefit, and we would have to bury him.

We knew what had happened! That pilot was careless and stupid. Bright Light was doing his job, with no way of knowing some fool would interfere. I am an old soldier. I have given the country my strength and my duty since I was a young man. In everything I have been loyal, so I have no fear. I went from office to office, insisting that my son died honorably. Some people said I should pay someone a little something to smooth the way, but I refused. A father and his four sons have all served this country; we have rights.

Finally, it was all agreed. They paid us NT300,000 (U.S.$7,500) and buried Bright Light in the highest air force cemetery as a national hero. I am still angry at the pettiness of those officials.

Life has not always been easy for us in the service in Taiwan. There have been good things about life here, but also bad things. When we arrived in 1949, the island was a mess. Americans had bombed the airports and factories and there wasn't much food. We always were fed, and I was paid regularly, but a lot of army people weren't so lucky. There was a lot of sickness in the military camps, with many of the oldest and weakest soldiers dying in the first few years. Many were forced to retire, too, after we had been in Taiwan a few years. Later, it became hard to retire, at least in the air force. If you wanted to get out of the service, you had to bribe someone high up; then you could be released.

All along, though, I was lucky. The air force gave me priority because they really needed us skilled men. Since I was married, I got more pay and rations and better housing. In the fifties, when Taiwan's economy was very backward, the government took care of us, and others envied us our steady salary and secure position. I continued to work at my various postings, just as before. We repaired aircraft for training missions and sometimes for secret reconnaissance flights to the mainland.

It was still wartime—we are at war with the Communist bandits even now—but it was also a kind of peace. Many of the men got slack, and our work was less good. While my wife was working in Taibei all those years, she could have flown free on military transport to come home on her days off, but I wouldn't let her. By then, it had got too dangerous. We had a lot of crashes. They don't always put them in the newspapers, but they were frequent. When we went to the air force cemetery to bury my son, I saw all the graves of our young Mainlander airmen who had died in the line of duty since we came to Taiwan. There are hundreds. It's terrible. That is partly the responsibility of the mechanics. That kind of thing made me feel less and less satisfied with being in our service.

Also, in the early sixties I was beginning to have back trouble. In the old American planes equipped for parachute drops, there's a spring mechanism for releasing the parachutes from the plane. Because we Chinese are shorter than Americans, we had to use our legs, lying on our backs, to retract the springs. This is really bad for the lower back; a lot of the men have been injured by doing it. My back got so bad, I had some X-rays, which showed some cracked vertebrae.

Consequently, they asked me to retire. I didn't want to, because I wasn't fifty-five yet, the earliest age at which I could get a pension. We argued it back and forth. They said also the newer equipment was all marked in English and more complicated, so we old soldiers weren't any use in fixing it. They let me stay till fifty-five, though, and then I retired.

The pension I got was very small—NT$40,000 (U.S.$1,000) a year. We could have lived on it but could not have helped our children. In those days, when our boys in Taiwan went into their compulsory three years of service, they earned practically nothing. If they wanted to come home for a visit, or buy an occasional good meal, or a piece of civilian clothing, they had to get money from home. We had sons studying and in the service, so we needed the money. My back was very bad, and I can't speak any Taiwanese, so in our small town I didn't see how I could find any work as a mechanic. If we moved to a bigger town, we could not live in our house, but would have to rent one, which would have been expensive. And anyway, I didn't want to be somebody's employee. I've been a soldier all my life, and I'm an old man. I'd lose face to bow and scrape for some boss. So I managed the boys and the house, and now I'm looking after our grandson!

Here in our air force neighborhood, there are men and women from all over China. Some are my old comrades-in-arms, some are fellow provincials of my wife or myself. I see my friends often—someone is always dropping in for a cigarette or a simple meal. I play cards or mah-jongg sometimes, or just chat. There's a lot of gossip in a place like this, though, and it makes me furious when I hear this one and that one talking about everyone's private business. My son's divorce was a real scandal around here at the time, because divorce almost never happened in the past. Now many families have such embarrassments.

When I think back about my career in our country's air force, I have mixed feelings. Some of our leaders were very great men. Our old president, Jiang Jieshi, was one of this century's greatest men. I was proud to follow him. But below him there are others—all divided into factions that don't always put the country first. Some are corrupt. I have never paid attention to politics because I'm just an ordinary soldier, doing my job. National affairs are none of my business. But I can say that since we have been in Taiwan, morale has been worse, our work is not done as well as before, and we old loyal families have fallen behind everyone else. Everyone is getting rich but us. I lost my own family because I followed our old president to Taiwan; but in Taiwan the family my wife and I founded is a modern family, all scattered and independent. We can never know what will become of us, only accept our fate.

[7]

Women and Men, Old and Young

An old gentleman well versed in religious lore once described the characters of the important local deities, the Earth God and his wife Madam Earth God, in a way that summed up much of what ordinary Taiwan people believe about masculinity and femininity. The Earth God, he told me, would like to give everyone who prays to him good fortune, for he is a benevolent being who fair-mindedly responds to the prayers and gifts of food, money, and incense made by sincere worshippers. Madam Earth God, however, blocks good fortune for some people. "If everyone got what they wanted," she argues with her husband, "who would come to worship us, carry our chairs in festival processions, and make us offerings?"

This, the old man told me, reflects Chinese men's and women's characters. Men strive for harmony, justice, and goodness, while women are "narrow-hearted" in outlook, selfish, and mercenary. Men value the spiritual, women the material. Mr. Gao might also have pointed out, though he did not, that these characterizations of the commonest of Taiwanese gods also suggest that while men are supposed to be responsible for important decisions, women have much actual control. Although women apparently have less prestige and power, they often get their way nonetheless.

Although ideas of "femininity" and "masculinity" are cultural constructs, Taiwan's working-class people believe women and men to be fundamentally very different because of differences in human biology. The biological behaviors specific to women—menstruation and childbirth—are seen as disgusting, unclean, and polluting both to the woman experiencing them and to anyone who might come in contact with the body fluids associated with these states (Ahern 1975:194–95). In a ritual performed by an especially filial son for the funeral of his dead mother, Daoists explain menstruation by reading the following texts to the participants:

> . . . a woman has within her the eighty thousand *yin* worms, which collect in her vagina. These worms have twelve heads and twelve mouths. When they feed, each sucks raw blood. Day and night they move about, wearying muscle and bone. Midway through the month, they slough unclean fluid. Each of these worms vomits pus and blood out of its mouths. Each exudes blood and pus that has a red color. These ulcerous worms: their mouths are like sharp needles, and they regularly afflict women, eating raw blood, irritating each other, ceaselessly crawling, disturbing a woman, making her body unable to calm itself. This is the result of karmic retribution, for which there is no surcease. (Seaman 1981:387)

Birth, too,

> . . . is an unclean thing: a woman's body is an unclean collection of worms' pus and blood, which comes together and collects. Ten months it ripens between the two viscera, entrapped, pressed into a female prison.
>
> . . . .
>
> There is only the stench of shit, where the fetus develops for so long.
>
> And this life can only enter and leave through a woman's vagina. (Seaman 1981:389)

These publicly declaimed texts "explain" and justify the distaste that men and women feel for women's genitals and the fluids they emit. This distaste is so strong that women themselvs are reluctant to discuss such matters, referring, if pushed, only to the "dirtiness" their bodies produce. While birth control is widely used, the diaphragm, which requires a woman to touch her own genitals, is not available. When I described it to close friends as superior in safety to birth control pills or the intra-uterine device (I. U. D.) they looked rather ill. Men, it would appear, are made extremely uneasy by the thought of contact with female "uncleanliness." Even intercourse is seen as polluting to men, who must abstain from it in preparation for certain ritual activities. Some gods, too, would be offended if a menstruating woman, or one who had given birth within the month, were to cross their temple's thresholds; domestic altars, with their collections of ancestor tablets and gods' images, should never face bedrooms where intercourse occurs. Mrs. Zhang, good Catholic though she is, reprimanded me sharply for hanging my just-washed underpants out of doors "where they would offend Heaven." She always hung such items under an awning.

While female body functions and fluids are seen as signs of weakness, male ones are signs of bodily and mental strength. Male sexual potency is generally taken as a sign of good health and well-being, and its loss or diminution creates considerable anxiety, at least if we are to judge by the extremely large numbers of medicines sold to "restore vigor"; drugstores are full of them. Foods, too, are eaten carefully for the effect they are thought to have on virility. In restaurants that specialize in freshly killed snake—for an American, one of the more unusual sights of a Taiwan city—male patrons dine amidst cages filled with squirming tangles of encouragingly lively reptiles.

Biological differences are believed to be responsible for the mental and emotional differences between women and men personified in the Earth God and Madam Earth God. Men are capable of higher virtues, finer feelings, closer friendships, and more filiality than women, but women corrupt them—partly through sexual enticement. Because of their "better natures" men should hold positions of responsibility and authority in the family and the wider society, while women should accept their leadership and stay close to home. This does not mean, however, that they should be ignorant of economic matters, for "home" has important economic functions. A woman's very "narrow-heartedness" may make her a sharp bargainer, a shrewd investor, and an astute businesswoman. Such qualities are admired in women, and in many households it is actually the wife/mother to whom the working husband and children give their wages, receiving pocket money in return.

The lives of our subjects show clearly how self-reliant in money matters many working-class women are. Mrs. Zhang and Miss Ong (this chapter) largely support their husbands and children, while the independent Miss Guo both earns income and has charge of the rental houses she and her "old lover" share; Mrs. Lo was the only support of her children for years.

Three factors inform the strong differences the Chinese believe to exist between men and women: the patrilineal structure of families, a pervasively dualistic world view, and the unequal treatment women receive. In their strongly patrilineally organized families, Chinese law and custom make men the main owners and transmitters of property and the most central family members. Women, necessary to reproduction and family continuity, must be taken into the family in marriage or given out to other families. While a man may live his entire life in the family of his birth where all his loyalties are focused, a woman's emotional attachments are divided among her family of origin, her husband's family as it exists when she marries into it, and the new family of origin she will create for herself, her children, and her husband. Adopted daughters-in-law, of course, are less torn between their family of birth and their husband's family if they are reared from infancy by their mothers-in-law, but most know their birth parents and feel ambivalent toward them (M. Wolf 1972:177). And all married women who become mothers confront the conflict between the primary loyalty their parents-in-law expect of them and the warmer affections they feel toward their children (and, possibly, their husbands). In complex families, where several married brothers share a household, conflicts often arise among the brothers' wives over treatment of their respective children, as each tries to secure the best for her own. Families are pressured to divide, often because in-marrying women cannot possibly acquire the simple, overriding loyalty to their husbands' patrilines that develops more straightforwardly in men. In short, women are believed to complicate and sometimes subvert patrilineal families. When, through extremes of self-sacrificial filiality, they do not actually do so, they nevertheless remain suspect. Because the patrilineal structure treats women as outsiders, they are naturally expected to be untrustworthy, even dangerous.

Following the lead of Mary Douglas (1966:174–75; see also Ahern 1975), we can argue that in such situations, the disruptive category—women—is likely to be seen as "out of place" and dangerously "polluting" to the "regular" category—men. Those aspects of physiology most characteristic of women—menstruation and childbirth—thus come to symbolize the lurking, hidden dangers of women.

We may also locate Chinese views of women and men within the wider context of a pervasive dualistic world view. All Chinese know at least superficially of the Chinese concepts of yin and yang. The Daoist version of this tradition (see Black, 1986 for others) teaches that the cosmos exists through the interaction of two great opposing forces: yin, which appears in the moon, darkness, death, women, and other "cold" things, and yang, which stands for the sun, light, life, and men. Out of their oppositions, the real world is made. Each needs the other, but the yin and yang are also antagonistic forces. While not everything that contemporary Taiwan people encounter can be classified as yin or yang—the dualism relates mostly to the natural world—people generally *assume* that most things must be either yin or yang. Things exist in dialectical relationships to their opposites. Cultural categories for "women" and "men" are almost automatically entangled in this world view, with women and men categorized as antagonistic opposites.[1] As men were the ritual specialists and the creators of their written tradition, it is mostly men who have defined the terms of the opposition—generally in their own favor.

---

1. Eugene N. Anderson, Jr., in his research on food and nutrition (see Anderson 1983), has written extensively on the Chinese tendency to overgeneralize intellectual paradigms.

Finally, Chinese people also see women as dangerous and unreliable because of the inferior treatment they receive. In many societies, people who are socially oppressed and therefore resentful are feared by others and believed to be witches (Gluckman 1955:94). Chinese women are not often cast as witches, but they are believed to be a source of danger to their families, endowed with the capacity to poison men through the secret introduction of menstrual blood into food (Ahern 1975:197; Harrell 1986). People cannot, I think, oppress those near them without being aware of the hostility that oppression generates and suspecting their victims of vengeful thoughts. If Chinese men are to control Chinese women, they need beliefs that can be used to convince both women and themselves of female inferiority. Uniquely female activities are therefore obvious symbols for such supposed inferiority.

Socially oppressed people may, to a degree, accept their lot and acquiesce in their own inferiority; but at the same time they may resent such treatment. Several Chinese women have told me of early childhood experiences of receiving less food or love or attention than their brothers, and of how it hurt to realize that they were less valued simply because of their sex. A Taiwanese woman, at her engagement celebration—a formal affair, conducted by her parents, and very binding—crooks the finger onto which her mother-in-law or husband tries to force an engagement ring. This is a struggle over the young woman's submissiveness—over whether she will allow herself to be completely dominated in her new family, as befits a woman. Though Chinese women often share the view that they are deficient, compared with men, they also harbor some hostility at the limits placed on them and, as the engaged woman's little struggle indicates, sometimes resist them.

While beliefs about men and women can in part be perpetuated through folklore, rituals, customs, and laws, Chinese women and men must also learn, as children, the behaviors that their culture considers appropriate for their gender. The socialization of girls and boys into gender roles begins early, continuing as people mature through various phases of life.

Boy babies are greeted in most families with far more joy than are girls. And if a girl baby comes at the end of an unbroken line of older sisters, she will be spoken of more as a nuisance than, as boys are, "your little precious one." Boy babies are often photographed by professional photographers in a favorite pose—seated with legs wide apart, so the little boy's genitals are prominently displayed through split-crotch trousers.

The greater value placed on boy children is not concealed as the child reaches the age when it begins to understand speech. I once asked a shopkeeper-father how many children he had.

[149]

"Three. Here are Number Two and Number Three. Old Number One is at school."

"And who are these two little girls?" (about three and five years old).

"Oh, they're my daughters. But we Chinese consider that girls aren't worth much, so we don't count them."

The little girls followed this conversation with bland faces. They had probably heard it before.

Many working-class families realize that a child who attends a preschool or kindergarten before enrolling in elementary school will find adjustment to school easier and may have a competitive advantage over other children. These cost money, however, and many families conclude that while the expense is worthwhile for a little boy, it cannot be considered for a girl. In 1974, for example, there were 60,314 boys enrolled in preschools and only 50,663 girls (DGBAS 1974:534–35). Preschool children who do not attend kindergartens play in or near home, especially if they live on a busy city street, but little girls especially are kept close by, often to help with the care of younger siblings. A five-or six-year-old with a year-old baby strapped to her back is a common sight. As they grow older, little girls help more, unless they seem to be exceptionally clever in school, in which case they are spared housework and urged to study extremely hard, as was Mrs. Lim. Boys roam farther, are more likely to have bicycles, and are rarely asked to help with housework or baby care.

Elementary school is coeducational in Taiwan, and most teachers, firm but kindly with their little charges, reinforce sex-role socialization. Children are taught a great many formal lessons that draw on relationships in idealized, elite families where Baba (father) goes out to work at the office, Mama stays home in a bungalow with a garden, keeping house, while Gege (elder brother) prepares for college and Jiejie (elder sister) arranges flowers. Songs and dances are an important part of training for social poise; children delightedly give performances in which boys are brave soldiers defending the island against Communist bandits, and girls are television stars, complete with plenty of makeup. An elementary school education of six years is all that many girls receive. While in 1974 about 98 percent of all children attended elementary school, only 76.7 percent of girl elementary-school graduates (as compared to 91.28 percent of boy graduates) went on to junior high (DGBAS 1974: Supplementary Table 6).[2] Many parents still argue that while a boy's education benefits his family, a girl's benefits only her hus-

2. More recent educational data from this source is compiled in ways that obscure the differences between girls' and boys' educational attainments by combining junior and senior high enrollment figures.

band's. Fewer children, especially girls, attended school under the Japanese, but their descriptions of that schooling are remarkably similar in respect to female/male socialization (see Tsurumi 1977:120–22, 219–20).

While boys have more worth and, often, enjoy greater privileges in their families, they also hold greater responsibilities. The first son, especially, grows up knowing he will have to lead his family, support his parents, and help his younger siblings get settled in life. He will inherit the primary duty of maintaining ancestral rites for a descent line that stretches back into the dim past. His family's future depends both on what he can accomplish himself and on how well he can hold them together. Until he is a mature man, however, he will have to consider his parents' wishes as to whom he should marry, what level of education to pursue, and what occupation to take up.

Since the 1950s young men have also come under the control of the state when, at eighteen, they are eligible for military service. The three years of service for draftees can be a real hardship, especially if they are sent to the heavily fortified islands of Quemoy or Matsu just off the mainland China coast, where discipline is tight, home is far away, and escape from the totally militarized environment is impossible. Even the prostitutes there, it is said, are government issue. Like young women, young men still have relatively few independent choices.

Some limitations on girls and women which at first appear to be gender-based are due instead to the strong age hierarchy in Chinese families, where generational seniority counts for a great deal. By the time women and men reach their forties, they have acquired maturity, social judgment, and control over the junior generation of young adults—their children. At the same time, the children's grandparents, now into their sixties, are beginning to turn over most family responsibilities to the parents. In the contemporary working class, older men seem eager to retire from their laborious jobs in favor of their juniors and are often willing, as well, to leave much of the family decision making to their sons. And, although Chinese like to brag about how authoritarian their fathers were, I suspect that many working-class men in the past were also glad to give up the back-breaking labor necessary to support a family as soon as their sons were old enough to replace them, even if this diluted their power in the family.

Older women, by contrast, are often far less willing to delegate real authority to daughters-in-law, holding on to the family purse sometimes well into senility. Mothers-in-law, however, can certainly transfer duties they do not care to perform to their juniors and indulge themselves a little in afternoon gambling sessions or week-long pilgrimages to distant temples with their women friends. I was often struck, especially in shopkeepers'

[151]

families, by the contrast between the sleek, plump mother-in-law, with her beauty-parlor hairdo, jade earrings, and clean attractive dress, and her harried, slatternly daughter-in-law, trying to cook, mind the shop, market for vegetables, and look after a couple of toddlers—all while burdened with a nursing child in her back sling and another baby on the way.

Young women, clearly, are in a doubly weak position at the bottom of both the age and the gender hierarchies. Taiwan's large industrialists, foreign and domestic, have capitalized extensively on the low status of young women by recruiting them as the cheapest labor. The docility and low expectations into which their families socialize women make them ideal candidates for the boring, low-paid, and even dangerous factory jobs on which Taiwan's economy has grown.

Even so, young people have more autonomy than in the past. In marked contrast with the lives of my subjects, who grew up prior to the industrial boom of the sixties, Taiwan's young people today, when they are not studying or working, have a relatively lively life. Movies are extremely popular: Taiwan has an enormous film output and imports many films from Hong Kong and the United States, as well. Theaters are always packed. Students and young workers gather in coffee shops, fruit-and-ice parlors, cheap restaurants, and the noisy, colorful night markets that offer food, drink, and the possibility of excitement until late in the evening. Since the midseventies the government has actively promoted recreational activities for young people, encouraging schools, churches, and the Nationalist Party Youth Corps to organize camping, mountain climbing, and seashore visits for their members. Senior-year school trips to the island's famous scenic places are high points in many lives. Dancing is very popular despite the fact that the Nationalists have banned it, in a haphazard sort of way, as inappropriate to the "wartime conditions" and a threat to the morals of the young. Consequently, "underground" dance studios and private dances in buildings under construction were common until restrictions loosened in the eighties. Young people, who are no longer forced into unwanted marriages and often have a little money to spend on fun, seem generally to feel rather satisfied with their freedom and opportunities. Many view American young people's sexual freedom, tendency to marry without parental consent, and political activism with the same disapproval as their elders.

Sex roles in Taiwan are profoundly paradoxical, as these life histories repeatedly hint. While society's ideals attribute power, responsibility, virtue, and strength to men and their opposites to women, in this collection of fairly typical people we see a number of strong, capable women and rather weak and limited men. Especially in the cities, in the real interactions of family life we can perceive the workings not only of the patrilineal, patripotent ideal, but also of a contradictory pattern.

Although most families hope their sons will be strong and responsible and their daughters timid and submissive, they often appear to raise children as though they aimed for the opposite result. Boys are given little responsibility at home compared to girls in their youngest years, so that girls receive considerably more practical training in useful tasks and in taking responsibility, within the limited sphere of the family itself. In more recent times, girls are often out earning income in factories, learning at least a little about adult life "out in society," while their brothers are still schoolboys. While teenaged girls go through a period of intense shyness in front of strangers, they quickly learn businesslike and even assertive behavior when given the responsibility of a job as a salesclerk, bus-ticket taker, or waitress. Many young married women live for a time in a household headed by an older couple. If that couple is over fifty, it is very likely that its balance of power will have shifted to the older woman, especially if her husband has retired from active work. A young wife learns her new role, then, from a mother-in-law who keeps the purse and may run a business, makes the ritual offerings, and often dominates not just her but the entire family. Men, conditioned from childhood to avoid closeness with their fathers but to rely heavily on their mothers for emotional support, guidance, and practical help, come to accept their wives in a similar role.

A Japanese psychiatrist has written of his own countrymen that the child's feeling of *amae*, "sweet dependency" on the mother, is a common, normal, and even desirable emotion that is often reexperienced with power figures in adulthood (Doi 1973). A kind of privileged childishness and rejection of responsibility similar to *amae* may exist between older men and their capable wives among Taiwan people. In a good relationship, such "sweet dependency" can be very positive; in a poor one, a woman's emotional strength is easily seen as threatening and even as sinister. There are, then, two sides to sex-role relationships in Taiwan's working class: the patriarchal ideology, constantly reinforced by messages from school, the economy, and the state, and the female-dominant behaviors that are so frequently acted out in parent-child and wife-husband interactions within families themselves.

In summary, the Chinese define masculinity and femininity as attributes of biological nature, but they also make efforts to socialize the young in patterns of behavior and response considered culturally appropriate for each sex. Definitions of gender roles change as adults perceive changes in the society around them: it is now believed, for example, that girls benefit from education, which enables them to get better jobs, rather than that their femininity will be harmed by learning, as Chinese of previous centuries have believed. But that women and men are both very different and unequal in intrinsic worth remains a constant in Chinese culture, which the increasing participation of women in the workforce has done little if anything to undermine (Diamond 1979; Kung 1983). Nonetheless, even in this patriarchal tradition, contradictions in behavior and belief point to the power that older women at least wield in their families.

The relationships between older and younger people are more consistently unequal than those between the sexes in present-day Taiwan. Here too, however, the economic changes of this century have widened the options of the young. Though young folks have more fun than they formerly did, filial obligation, *xiao*, still requires that a son—or an adopted daughter—must prepare to help support parents in their old age. Although Taiwan's recent history has brought fluctuations in the tendency for young people to exercise more control over their own lives, in practice the life choices of education, marriage, and occupation leading to the ability to do one's filial duty are increasingly made by the younger rather than the older generation.

In this sample of working-class people, we meet people of both sexes whose lives have centered around work and family. Four of the women have contributed as much as or more than their families' menfolk to the families' economic support, while the fifth (Mrs. Lim, Chapter 9) has also earned some income. All are outspoken women whose opinions carry weight at home; all have borne children and hence hold the honored position of mother. Today, all are linchpins in their households, and some are important members of much wider social networks. After a lifetime spent in low-paid, low-status, and often physically exhausting jobs, these women display the characteristics that so strongly shape Chinese working-class style: resilience, diligence, and practicality. Of the four men subjects, two have founded families, built businesses, and retired to secure old ages. The two others, largely for reasons outside their control, were less successful. Mr. Zhang's retirement future depends on his wife's earnings, and Mr. Kang (this chapter) is a "bare stick"—a man with no family, property, or prospects. Several of them seem lonely and discouraged.

Two of the men who told me their life histories are former military men who came from mainland China to Taiwan after the failure of the Nationalist cause, and two are native Taiwanese—both retired small-building contractors—who have lived all their lives within a few miles of Prosperity Settlement. But they are four very different men. Mr. Zhang (husband of the energetic cook) has rural roots in frontierlike southwestern China, which was then rather like Taiwan of the last century, while Mr. Kang, the other Mainlander, belonged to a shopkeeping family in one of China's most modern cities. Taiwanese Mr. Kho, beneficiary of a Japanese education and a convert to a Japanese religion, would have little to say to his fellow islander, Mr. Go, who has made use of the flashier elements of local folk religion to further his second career as a political bagman; but a frank political conversation between the more sophisticated Kho and Kang would reveal many ideas in common.

The men in this study, like the women, tell us of their families and work experiences, but they also speak more directly and at greater length than the women about wider issues: the war against the Communists, Japanese colonial policy, Taiwan politics, organized religion. These are matters on which men, who properly go "out in society," may have opinions. While it is a little unseemly for women to discuss politics—religion is an acceptable topic—men enjoy demonstrating their level of education by being conversant with current events and recent history.

People judge an older man's success in life partly by the size and efficaciousness of the network of contacts he has built outside his immediate circle of kin and neighbors. A man, telling his life history, will stress these ties, while a woman may ignore her network, useful though it may be, and emphasize family matters. In forming networks, gender is important, for though even a poor man may have some associates to claim, many women lead rather socially restricted lives within their families and neighborhoods. Working as a servant or dishwasher offers few more opportunities to meet and ally oneself with others than caring for a family as a wife/daughter-in-law. Men servants, of course, work under the same limitations.

Chinese men spoke to me through a filter of dignity that forbids expression of emotion. Even more than for women, opportunities to express feelings, and hence to analyze and elaborate on them, come rarely in their lives; their histories lack almost completely any references to emotion. Behind the composed faces, however, these men suffer deeply the loss of a young son, a beloved old wife, or a native homeland, and rejoice quietly in the birth of healthy grandchildren, or Taiwan's increasing international standing.

Although Chinese culture unquestionably gives higher status to men than to women, even in the family, it is hard to discern this from these lives where brothers, sons, and husbands are frequently depicted as weak, lazy, ailing, or irresponsible. This perception is partially true: families with ineffectual menfolk are likely to remain "ordinary," even poor, because Chinese society *is* structured to channel advantages to men rather than to women who find themselves supporting a family. But women, even in better-off families, often view themselves as having special strength to

[155]

endure suffering, work hard, sacrifice selflessly, and make family-oriented, practical decisions (like stealing to support one's children) that a "superior" man might have too much dignity to choose.

Miss Ong and Mr. Kang, whose life histories follow, are not "typical" people, if such people indeed exist. A young married woman who supports her husband and an old man without a family to give him status and support are anomalous in Chinese society, almost the antithesis of the cultural ideals. They thus remind us of the elusive quality of such ideals and how imperfectly reality exemplifies them. As a Chinese woman should, however, Miss Ong has fulfilled her cultural destiny through unhoped-for motherhood, and like the Confucian scholar who epitomized the past ideal of manhood, Mr. Kang braces himself against his inevitable and unenviable retirement with self-cultivation and a consideration of the wider sweep of history.

Kang Weiguo: Old Bachelor Soldier

Kang Weiguo, a Mainlander in his early sixties from Shandong province, is a retired soldier and the beneficiary of a low-paid government sinecure. He is loyal, like Mr. Zhang, but he is more skeptical than the air force mechanic of the ultimate rightness of his government's decisions. Nothing he has done on Taiwan has enabled him to found a family there, so he faces a lonely and rather uncertain future in a state-run old veterans' home. He accepts with good humor the narrowness of his daily activities and the rarity of any kind of pleasure or entertainment; he remembers living under far worse conditions. A whole generation of aging retired soldiers such as Mr. Kang will fade out of Taiwan's society in a few years, leaving no living representatives of the Nationalist era in continental China to insistently remind the young that their primary task is to "retake the Mainland."

Mr. Kang chatted with me nearly every day for several months while I visited in the government-run library where he works and lives. A pleasant-faced, balding man with a bumpy, broken nose and a cheerful disposition, he is both intelligent and well-informed, spending several hours each day reading the newspapers and magazines. He has the personality that Chinese describe as "round and slippery"—always on guard against intrusion, leaving no "handle" by which his inner nature can be apprehended. While he found out a great deal about me, he initially revealed very little about himself in these conversations, which he always pleasantly and humorously steered to impersonal topics.

I was astonished, then, when one morning he began to volunteer his life history as a contribution to my study. On three successive days, he told his tale, answered questions, and offered some of the frankest political commentary I had heard in Taiwan. Then he stopped. Having said what he had chosen to say, he returned to his pleasant, impenetrable pose. We never had another real conversation.

Many people in Taiwan hold jobs like Mr. Kang's, with its light work and ample leisure. Government bureaus, post offices, schools, railway stations, power plants, and so forth commonly employ former Mainland soldiers to sweep up a bit, to heat water for tea and to steam-warm metal lunch boxes, to fetch and distribute mail, to keep an eye open for crime or subversion, and to mention their suspicions to higher-ups. Such jobs are prized by men with no relatives and few friends in Taiwan, for they bring the dignity of association with a respected and powerful institution, as well as free shelter and a reliable, if low, wage. Better a cot in a railway station baggage room where one has a place and workmates than a solitary rented cubicle miles from work and from the chance of some daily sociability. The leisure such jobs afford is attractive as well, giving even the near-illiterate time to puzzle over the party's abundantly supplied copies of the *Central Daily News*, to gamble a little at cards, or to watch the world go by.

Many less well-off old soldiers, like those who still squat in an abandoned Japanese temple a few blocks from the library, live a quasi-military life of rustling up their own food, washing their own socks, and depending on odd jobs and what the government gives them for their livelihood. It is a way of life with all the discomforts of transient living but none of the excitement or novelty.

Mr. Kang is fortunate compared with many in this refugee fraternity. Unlike some quietly desperate men, whose simmering resentment boils over in perpetually angry voices and jumpy body movements, or whose cloak of depression is very nearly visible around them, he accepts his fate with dignity and courteous cheer. Too thoughtful to be a simple loyalist, he is also too wise to complain and too cultivated, in a way Chinese value deeply, to show feeling.

I was born in 1919 in the city of Qingdao, to a family that had land in the countryside and a peanut-oil business in town. We sold oil and other regional products on the national and international markets, so my family was an ordinary one, not poor but not really rich either.

I was the youngest of three brothers and also had two older sisters. When I was little, I studied for about two years at home, where in the evenings my brothers taught me what they knew of reading and writing from the classics. It wasn't easy to study, because then, of course, we had no electric lights, and ordinary people couldn't even afford candles. I used to sit at the table with my two sisters, reading while they mended and made the family's clothes. Studying that way was very slow, and I didn't learn much. As often as I could, I'd run away from the books and play.

Seeing I was no student, my father started me working in the business. He thought I should learn everything from the bottom up, because he feared I would become spoiled and wasteful of money. So I worked with the other two apprentices at the lowest work—sweeping up, running errands, moving stock—while my father, elder brothers, and two uncles managed the accounting and the customers. When things went wrong, if the other apprentices got beaten, I did too. I ate with them most of the time, but I slept inside with the family, not out front in the shop with the hired workers.

I never developed much of a taste for doing business, where a shopkeeper has to haggle back and forth with buyers constantly. It's not that it's dishonest—after all, everyone has to look out for his own interests—but it's not straightforward and clear. Also, the risks of loss are great, so each member of the family who works in the business has a big responsibility to bear for the family's future prosperity. I might have learned to like business, but I don't think so. I prefer to work for our country.

When I was eighteen, my family got a wife for me. We were together for only a few years and had three children. She was a pretty, quiet girl from the countryside, and we came to be quite happy together, although in those days it was very embarrassing for young married people to show their affection. We were teased a lot at first, and even scolded for being light-minded. My mother liked my wife because she was hard-working and dutiful and caused no trouble.

I suppose after I left she married someone else, because she would have thought I was dead. The children—who knows what happened to them? It's all so long ago now that I just feel that some must have lived, some must have died. I can't possibly influence them now, so it's better not to know about them. It would be possible, perhaps, to ask someone with contacts to find them for me. I've often thought of it. Such things are easier to arrange now than in former years. Anyway, if I contacted them, it would simply cause trouble for them.

I never married over here because I am too poor and useless for a woman to want me! And, so, of course, I'm alone, getting older all by myself.

During the war I had another chance to marry, though. When I was stationed somewhere in the south, I met an old lady who treated me extremely kindly and wanted me to marry into her family as an adopted son-in-law, taking her family's name. She gave me a lot of really good things to eat—chicken, eggs, everything—but I didn't dare marry her daughter. In the first place, they were farmers. I had never done any farm work, which is very hard work and a hard life. In the second place, the Communists at that time were only a little way to the north; I knew they'd be along soon and didn't want to be caught behind their lines. So I didn't marry that time. If I had done it, I suppose I'd be in some People's Commune now, going hungry.

The year I was eighteen—which was 1937—I entered the army. I was just an ordinary soldier, so life was hard. The food was not always adequate, especially for us hungry young soldiers. We weren't paid regularly, though I noticed the officers always had plenty of money, and the discipline was very harsh. While I was stationed in Shandong I could get home sometimes, but after a few years we were sent to the northeastern provinces—the Dongbei. There was very fierce fighting in the Dongbei—first against the Japanese, later against the Communists.

A lot of Shandong people had migrated back and forth between home and the Dongbei, so the foods and ways of life were somewhat similar, though of course the climate is very different. Our Qingdao is in a place where just 20 kilometers south it is warm enough to raise water buffalo, though up at Qingdao itself you can't, because they'd freeze. The winters are long and the summers short, so the peasants grow mostly wheat and millet. But the Dongbei is *really* cold: in the winter, your spit freezes before it hits the ground. Up there, we ate maize that was particularly good—I've never eaten such good maize anywhere else. They cracked the kernels to make gruel, and we ate that a lot, but we also ate *gaoliang*, soybeans, and millet—the coarser, mixed grains—which are very nutritious. I used to miss our good Shangdong sweet potatoes, which are especially tasty in late winter—very sweet. Sometimes the army gave us rice, and I would trade my rice ration for that good maize. It really had a fine flavor!

Up there in the Dongbei, there were some terrible battles after the Japanese surrendered and we were fighting the Communists. In one of the worst of them, we killed 300,000 Communists, and we lost only 100,000 men. It went on for days, the air was black with smoke; you couldn't see or hear for the guns, and people were dying on all sides of me—you can't imagine it. And *after* the battle, everywhere you saw the soldiers holding liquor-soaked handkerchiefs over their faces, because the smell was so dreadful. *Such* a stink—hundreds of thousands of dead men. You simply couldn't breathe in that stench.

I fought a lot in the Dongbei, often being the only survivor of a group that had been badly hit, but I was never even wounded. It was almost a miracle that I received no injury of any kind. While I was at war, I was always very

[159]

careful not to do any bad things—I didn't steal things from the people, or mess with their women, or hurt people. After a while, I began to be sort of superstitious about it, afraid that if I *did* do any of those things, Heaven would stop protecting me. I was careful, and I came through that whole dangerous time without any wounds. After the Dongbei, we went to Nanjing, Shanghai, Suzhou, back to Shanghai, and finally from there to Taiwan.

The war was so hard on the ordinary people! We went south and then north again, and on the way back, there was simply nothing left because so much had been looted or destroyed. We in the army had food, at least, and we would take things from farms to eat, killing the peasants' cows and pigs and chickens. If we ran into an enemy, well, he had a gun and I had a gun, so we were on equal terms. But the people—they just had nothing and no way to protect themselves. Soldiers would see a peasant, raise their guns, and knock him off—no one knew if it was an honest peasant, an enemy in disguise, a bandit, or what. So many people died.

Once, after the war against Japan was over, when I was near enough, I went home for a while. At that time, people would jokingly say that if the Communists caught one of our soldiers, they'd paste a stamp on him and mail him home. It was almost like that. If they caught you, they'd feed you, and ask you where your home was. Then they'd write it all down, and give you a paper telling exactly how to travel to go home. There were stopping places where you could rest and eat free. I had been told by someone I knew at home that if I went home, he absolutely guaranteed that the Communists, who controlled Qingdao at that time, would not hurt me. I thought I'd try it, so I went. After I arrived, I reported to my friend, who said all I had to do was to come to a meeting that was held for us government soldiers who had returned home. "Can I rest for a while first?" I asked. He said that I could take as long as I liked—seven or eight days— then come. At the meeting, we were all supposed to get up and *tanbai*— confess—the bad things we had done as soldiers. A lot of men talked about what they had done, but to tell you the truth, because of my superstition, I really hadn't done things like that. I stole a few chickens and some other small things, but nothing much, really. I told about those, and everyone said that was fine, now I had cleared my conscience. But soon, they asked me to go to another meeting and confess more. After that, there was a third meeting, and I began to worry about what would happen to me.

At that time, the Communists were getting things very organized. When our government conscripted troops in Shandong, it had taken only a few men from each place, but now the Communists got *all* the men between eighteen and fifty-five either to work in supply and transport units, or to go into their army. My two elder brothers were put into supply units and must have died, because a friend who visited Qingdao recently says he was told they never came back. I went south and rejoined our army instead.

When I left, though, I didn't just leave. I had brought a pistol back home with me, which I kept hidden in the house. One night there was some trouble, so I used the pistol to threaten some people. I told them to lie down on the floor for half an hour and not get up. While they were doing that, I slipped out and got away. So now you see why I don't want to contact my family back there. With that kind of personal history, there would be trouble for them. It's better that I leave them alone.

The Communists really used terrible methods when they got in power. With people who were loyal to our government, they hoisted them up on a high pole, hanging from their hands, which were tied behind them, and asked them if, from way up there, they could see the central government coming to rescue them. Everyone screamed at them to speak. After they said something, those holding the rope let go, and the person dropped to the ground and was crushed to death. In that and other ways, they killed hundreds of thousands of people after 1949.

In 1949 my unit was in Shanghai, so I was among the troops that came here. There must have been hundreds of thousands who were left behind because they were in the wrong place or in the wrong unit. That evacuation and the early years in Taiwan were real chaos. It was a continuation of the war. For a long time—years—we were always alert to the danger of Communist invasion. I see now that they were not strong enough to come over here, as they lacked ships and airplanes, but then, the threat was a real part of life. After all, there was nowhere else for us to retreat to. And, to be honest, we would not have received much help against them from the natives of Taiwan province then. It was the same as back on the mainland, where the local peasants didn't know anything about the great events of the nation but just feared and hated us soldiers because we disturbed their lives and took what we needed to survive from them.

Now, relations between Taiwanese people and us mainland people are much better. They understand they are Chinese and should support the central government. Taiwanese people have by now grown rich because the policies of the government were correct. Then, however, things were very different. These people were still very much influenced by the Japanese. To see a rich Taiwanese speaking Japanese, wearing some of their Japanese wooden shoes, and reading Japanese books made me furious! I had fought the Japanese in the Dongbei and had seen the damage they had done in our coastal cities. This hatred was very deep in my heart.

Dealing with natives was inconvenient, too. They couldn't speak the

[161]

national language at all when our troops first came. By the time I arrived in 1949, it was not much better. Even if they could understand, they sometimes pretended not to, just for spite. Once, when I lost my way in Xinzhu City where I was stationed for a while, I had to ask more than twenty people before someone clearly told me the right road to return on. Some refused to answer, others pretended not to know.

Taiwanese people are also very sharp in their business dealings. They sold things to us at high prices, but we had to pay them—there was no one else to buy from. Sometimes soldiers got so angry that they just took things without paying. Occasionally, one had to hit people. I was careful, myself, because I still had my superstitious feeling that my safety depended on being honest.

Anyway, most of our needs were supplied by the army. We got rice, though it was that short, nasty Japanese variety they eat here. I'll never really enjoy that. For a while, we lived in temporary shelters, but then there were barracks. For years, though the money they gave us was so little that you couldn't even get drunk properly very often, I always had enough to eat and wear. As life slowly got easier, I also stopped worrying about an invasion and began to feel more at ease here.

I went into the army originally because I was drafted, but also I felt it was right. We were fighting the Japanese; the country needed me. After I got to Taiwan, I served till I was forty-two years old. By then I didn't see any reason to go on serving, since there was no more war.

I retired and found a job at this government-run library through a Shandong officer's connections. I live here, sharing a room with the other men workers, and eat here. The wages aren't high, but the work isn't hard either. I keep the rooms clean and tidy, make sure there is boiled water in the vacuum bottles, take out yesterday's newspapers and put out today's. Sometimes I wash the floors and windows. I get every other Tuesday off, but I usually spend the time here anyway. I earn NT$6,000 (U.S.$150) a month, which is very little, but room and board are free, so I can save most of the wage. I also get a little over NT$1,000 (U.S.$25) in pension money from the army to save for my old age. It was raised to that level in 1975; before that it was only a few hundred.

While I was still in the army in Taiwan the government and army encouraged us old soldiers who were illiterate to learn to read. If you have books, a dictionary, and a little help, you can learn to read yourself. After all, it's my own language. Now at work I read the papers often and discuss events with my fellow workers, which passes the time. Of course I watch television here a lot too—the news is interesting, and I like some of the children's programs, like cartoons, because they're humorous.

It's always interesting to follow the news and try to figure out what is really going on behind the scenes. Things are not always exactly what they appear to be, you know. For example, what was the real meaning of the riot down in Gaoxiong last year?[3] Were those Taiwanese politicians really secretly supported by the Communists, or did they have some other motive? Most of them are businessmen, so how can they be Communists?

We know that the Taiwanese would like to form their own party and run candidates for election to national-level offices. But we can't allow that, because they would win the elections—there are so many Taiwanese—and then, what would happen to us? A Taiwanese president would see everything in favor of his people, and our Mainlanders would be in a very weak position. We might not be welcome to stay here. At the very least, many of us who have loyally served the central government would lose our jobs, maybe our pensions.

All the same, we also know there are Communists hiding among us. Every once in a while, I hear of Communist propaganda leaflets being put secretly at night into people's mailboxes. Sometimes this happens in the most expensive suburbs where lots of wealthy retired generals and other officials live. I don't think anybody pays much attention to such stuff, but someone must be printing and distributing it. And every now and then, one of our air force officers takes a plane and defects to the mainland.

The Communists are clever. They work on people who long to return to their original homes. Recently, I read in the papers that an old Mainlander taxidriver was arrested for spreading Communist propaganda. Sometimes the police report finding caches of guns and knives. Are they for gangsters, for Communists, or for some Taiwanese secret opposition? Things are very, very complicated when you look beneath the surface. Generally, it is best not to discuss such matters.

I was very sick three years ago with a kidney ailment. They operated on me for more than eight hours, removing my kidney. I didn't come to for three days after that, but then it wasn't too bad. However they fed me intravenously for nearly a month afterward. My health has returned now, and I am still strong. Because I'm a veteran, my stay at the veteran's hospital was free. If I had family members here, they would pay half-rates at that hospital. If I weren't a veteran, I could have labor insurance at this job, which would pay some of the expense. As far as health goes, I'm taken care of.

However, when I get too old to work things will be difficult. The pension

3. A group of supporters of a recently banned Taiwanese magazine rallied in Gaoxiong City on December 10, 1979, to demand freedom of the press and human rights. Riot police surrounded them, a struggle ensued, and the protesters were jailed. The imprisonment of the most famous participant, Shi Mingde, is viewed by Amnesty International as a purely political act (Formosan Association for Human Rights 1985:39).

I'll get from the library—NT$1,800 (U.S.$45) a month—will be enough for food but for nothing else. I guess I may have to go to a veterans' old folks' home. I'd rather not live there—it might be possible to live nearby and go there for meals. Anyway, I'm only sixty-one years old, so I have a few more years of good health.

Life really is easier for me here in Taiwan now than my whole life before. This island is very prosperous; so many advances have been made in providing good food and a good life for people. Take apples—we used to have to import them, and they were expensive! Now we can buy a whole pile of local ones for the price of a meal. They haven't managed nearly as well on the mainland. I see the newspaper accounts, and you can tell that there are a lot of shortcomings. I will say this, though—the present bunch they've got running the mainland[4] is a great improvement over the way they were before, under Mao Zedong. They're talking about having a proper legal system and doing business in the regular way—naturally that's an improvement. They just did whatever they wanted to in the past—not at all scientific.

Ong Siukim: A Mother after All

Ong Siukim is Taiwanese, in her mid-thirties, and remarkable. She is married but keeps her maiden name for old friends, as the more educated Chinese women often do, and she still astonishes me with her Chinese version of true grit. With a minimum of external help and some very well-timed luck she has overcome family insanity, dire poverty, and paraplegia to become a self-supporting craftswoman, a wife, and a mother, her life a Buddhist fable of undeserved punishments and unexpected rewards. Her style of speaking, and even more of writing, contributes to this religious image, for she has been deeply influenced by inspirational literature, from Buddhist sutras[5] to Dale Carnegie.

There is nothing visibly "spiritual" about her, however. A solid-looking woman with a square, thickening face and home-cut hair, she beetles her brows to see clearly through eye-exaggerating and ill-fitting glasses. Having seen little of the world, and having had few choices because of real poverty, she dresses in oddly assorted bright colors, looking gay in her dark rooms. With her serene, meaty baby on her lap, she is a sturdy, pyramidal madonna, a tough plant surviving in a crack in the concrete.

4. Led by Deng Xiaoping.
5. Religious writings.

[164]

The apartment she came to in married life is one of hundreds in her industrial suburb, all five stories tall and crammed into every available space around a huge American-owned electronics factory. These sleazily constructed complexes house thousands of persons per acre in small dark rooms with heavily barred windows. Ground-floor apartments are colonized by tiny industries and shops; the hum of machinery and the convenience of local marketing and haircuts are built into the neighborhood. On days when the air pollution is low enough, the graves of the dead can be seen packed as densely on the brushy hills above this little valley as the living are below.

The apartment, newly furnished in inexpensive modern furniture—a plastic-upholstered sofa and chairs, a coffee table, Western beds in the bedrooms, a refrigerator—is far grander than Miss Ong's natal home, with its homemade benches, bedrooms floored in tattered tatami matting, and smoke-stained rafters. The new rooms were wallpapered by the builder in a large, olive-drab pattern, but the paper is peeling from the top, and for some weeks it hung in great festoons from the ten-foot ceiling. Zhang Wenlong, her husband, finally ripped most of it off above eye level. The kitchen—a sink with a cold tap, two gas rings on a low concrete platform, a few shelves—is a tiny alcove opposite the Western-style bathroom. Both are thoroughly grubby, a consequence of Miss Ong's busyness and physical limitations, of the unwillingness of her husband and sister to tend to such matters, and of the toleration for dirt and disorder the poor are forced to develop in their crowded and inadequately plumbed dwellings. As in any large city where housing density makes extermination impossible, vermin flourish, with roaches and rats the most conspicuous among them. The family washes its clothes in the bathtub, where a small gas-heated contraption supplies water for bathing, and hangs them on bamboo poles in the dank air-shaft courtyard.

Miss Ong's art is displayed casually in the living room, pictures lined up along the walls, as yet unhung. The bedroom she, her husband, and the baby share is bright with the colorful bedding Chinese brides require (to keep their spirits up, one suspects) and with photographs and small, treasured souvenirs of her wedding trip. Her sister's room, like any teenager's, is plastered with magazine pictures of the pale, infantile, and pampered cuties marketed as movie stars and pop singers in Taiwan. As in most cheap housing, there are no closets, so the meagerness of her possessions is apparent, though young Taiwanese women are mad for clothes, especially shoes.

All this is Miss Ong's domain, and she knows it. Her husband, well on his way to gangsterhood, has done nothing yet to match the contribution to the

[165]

household made by his wife's dowry and income. She is boss, although she tries, before company, to defer to his presumed masculine authority. The birth of her son insures her against his opportunism, for he loves both the child and the idea of his own fatherhood, though his affection for his wife is waning. Against all odds, Miss Ong has won.

Because she is confined to her home by her handicap and is younger than the other subjects, she knows less than they about Taiwan's recent social history. Until she married, she had hardly ever been out of the house in which she was born. But her experiences reveal something of the lives of people who do not even have the advantage of a fully functioning body in a society where the poor must usually labor for a living. Miss Ong's unusual marriage and motherhood underline the importance people attach to founding one's own family; her conversion to an underground religion shows the desire to explore philosophical questions which is characteristic of many Chinese with the leisure to read and think. Recent events in her family expose the workings of inheritance patterns, and her husband's activities give us a glimpse of Taiwan's underworld. Although her economic future is uncertain, her self-reliance and family ties continue to sustain her.

In my life, I have always tried to learn from good and famous people. Hellen Keller especially has been a model for me. Think what she was able to accomplish, with all her handicaps! So I have always striven to overcome my crippled condition and to achieve something in life. Reading books about great lives has been my help and inspiration.

I want to do everything for myself that I can, so that I will burden no one. Self-reliance is very important to me; I do not want to be pitied. Life offers great challenges to everyone, and great difficulties. It is by conquering these that we perfect ourselves and become strong characters.

Our family lived for many generations in Prosperity Settlement,[6] where we had a two-story brick house. My father was a carpenter. He could build houses and carve wood beautifully, so he earned good wages. Although his only education was a few years' study in an old-fashioned Chinese school, he admired beauty. He gave us girls refined names: mine is Elegant Lute.

He and my mother had nine children, of which the first three were boys. My eldest brother began to help Father at an early age, so both were often living away from home for weeks on distant construction sites. When Mother had her last child, she became paralyzed from the waist down, slowly became insane, and died after a few years. Because of this, my second brother had to assume daily responsibility for the household when

---

6. A few doors from Mrs. Lim (Chapter 8).

he was about fourteen. He tried to care for our mother and the younger children, to keep going to school, which he really loved, and also to work and earn money for us all. After a few years he also became insane. In a period of deep depression when he threatened suicide and began to run wildly about with knives, it became necessary to lock him up. In time we sent him to a mental institution—that was about the time our mother died.

He frequently ran away, so the institution required us to send a family member to live with him and care for him. We sent my fourth brother, the one just younger than I. This bad environment affected him so strongly that he too began to act strangely and had to be institutionalized. Now they are both there, but I know nothing about them anymore.

Mother died when I was about seven years old. Shortly after that, I contracted polio, which resulted in my legs becoming paralyzed. They stayed small as I grew, so I had to pull myself around with my arms, crawling on the floor. I lived upstairs and hardly ever came down for several years. I remember it was usually dark and somewhat frightening up there. My older sister sometimes brought me her schoolbooks, which is how I began to learn to read. That was a dark time for me.

My happiest moments were at our neighborhood's celebrations of the gods' birthdays, which people sometimes call *toa paipai* (T). You have seen these. To my eyes as a little girl, they were really wonderful, although at that time, they were probably less colorful and lively than they became when people got richer. We celebrated the birthday of the Earth God and his wife who lived in our little temple in Prosperity Settlement, and sometimes other gods' birthdays, too. The gods were carried out of their temple in small sedan chairs by local young men, who had to be very clean and pure for the occasion—carried right around the whole neighborhood to inspect it. I never followed the procession but some children did—for the fun of hearing all the firecrackers people set off when the gods passed their houses.

Afterward, the gods were placed in a beautifully decorated temporary shed out-of-doors so they could attend the celebration. Other gods' images were brought by our villagers from their family altars or from nearby temples to be guests of our god. All of them, displayed in their bright colors, with flowers, candles, and the scent of incense, made a splendid sight. Or that's how I felt then.

The neighborhood leaders collected money—just a few New Taiwan dollars from each family, so that every household could afford to be represented—to hire a Taiwanese opera to entertain both the gods and their guests and the people and their guests. It played several hours each afternoon and evening for two or three days. The costumes, the singing, and the music of the horns and gongs were a treat I really looked forward to. I learned a lot of the old stories, in which the evil were punished and the just rewarded, and laughed at the jokes the actors inserted into plays that seemed too serious.

The big event of a *toa paipai* was the feast each family gave its friends and relatives from other parts of the city. We couldn't afford it, after Mother got sick, but some families invited five or six tables of guests, with ten or twelve people eating at each table with its bright red cloth. It cost a lot, but it was almost the only time that ordinary people had really good things to eat, except for the New Year. I used to hear the guests arriving, their hosts greeting them, then toasting while everyone ate and drank. Soon a lot of the men were a little drunk, playing noisy word games and singing loudly. Then I'd hear the firecrackers and music for the opera start up, and all the guests would go to watch. Sometimes my brother carried me out on his back to watch, too. *Toa paipai* are superstitious, but I didn't know it then. I thought they were wonderful.

About 1960, when I was twelve, things became a little better for our family. There was more construction work near our home, so Father and First Older Brother were home more often and earned more money.

Then, some really good fortune came to me from a Mainlander lady who moved into the new houses that were being built in the fields around Prosperity Settlement. She learned about my condition, came to see me, and paid for me to go to a drawing school to learn to make portraits from photographs. My elder brother carried me piggyback every day to school, and afterward he brought me home. I will always be grateful to that lady, because she made me able to contribute to our family's needs. She has moved to Hong Kong, but I still hear from her sometimes. After I learned how to do portraits, Father rebuilt the front of our house so I could have a workshop where people could easily come and buy. My bedroom, which I shared with my sisters, was right behind it, so I could easily go out to work or in to rest, without having to ask to be carried. It was much nicer for me then, as I could see the passers-by and talk to our neighbors. I began to read more to improve myself, and I began to understand the spiritual side of life.

The reason for copying photographs is that people like to have a large portrait of a relative who has died to use in the funeral ceremonies or to hang on the wall, but they may have only a small snapshot of the person. I learned to copy these on a bigger scale, by making many little dots of ink on the paper. It is a fairly good business—I used to charge two or three hundred New Taiwan dollars each (U.S.\$5 to \$7.50), and now it's up to NT\$1,800 (U.S.\$45). I can do one in two or three days.

I did my very best at this work and got quite a few customers. A few years ago, out of gratitude that I had the opportunity to work and not just be worthless, I did a portrait of our old president, Jiang Jieshi. When I put it in the front of the shop to attract customers, a newspaper reporter saw it and did a story on me in the *United Daily News*. There was a photograph, too, of me and the president's portrait. I still have it with my other valuable possessions. When I was not busy, I did other portraits, especially of movie stars and famous personages. I've made some attempts at more artistic pictures too, which I make by copying from magazines. I like beautiful scenes of the ocean, of gardens, and of mountains.

Someone put us in contact with a charitable organization in 1974, and I was able to obtain a wheelchair. That was about the time the American television program "Ironside," about a policeman in a wheelchair, was very popular. "Ironside" showed that people like me can accomplish great things in spite of our handicaps. It was not easy for me to use the wheelchair, because there are so many steps and uneven places on the streets, but on a few occasions, a relative or friend took me out for a ride. I remember how happy I was when you took me to the University grounds to see the azaleas in blossom!

As I became known and began to earn more, my family could depend on the income I earned. My eldest brother stopped working with Father and began to drive a taxi. When he married, he and his wife moved into a rented apartment next door, and Sister-in-Law set up a barbershop there. We "divided the stove,"[7] with them becoming financially separate from our household, setting up an independent household registration with the police, and keeping more to themselves.

Over the years, Father had become very silent. When Mother died, he took all of the gods on our family altar, some of which he had carved himself, and burned them. He never carved things after that, though he was a fine craftsman, but just got quieter and quieter.

Our two eldest brothers and fourth brother were gone from our house. The third, after his military service, tried to start an electric-fan repair shop on one side of my workshop, but he never made much money. He did get married, though, so I had a sister-in-law at home and, after a while, two little nephews. We were able to marry my elder sister out in a quiet way, and one of my younger sisters drifted away to live somewhere else. She had a baby about ten years ago who has no father. That left seven of us still living together when our father died in 1979.

That was the year the Taibei City government started to widen Roosevelt

7. That is, legally divided the brother's household from the father's.

Road again. The change required that we lose half of our property and tear down our house. Everything was very confused about our land, which was not a neat rectangle in shape but rather an irregular chunk. There is no way to build a new, modern building following those crooked lot lines. Besides, even with the compensation, we didn't have the money to rebuild. So we sold the whole property, took the compensation, and divided the money.

First Older Brother received one-third, because even though he had separated from our household, he had helped us sometimes and he is still the eldest, with sons of his own.[8] My third brother got one-third, which he used to buy a new apartment for his family and his wife's mother. And I received one-third, because I had helped the family financially for many years.

My share was NT$100,000 (U.S.$2,500). I borrowed another NT$30,000 (U.S.$750) from my eldest brother's family and bought this apartment downstairs from Third Brother's. I have to continue to pay NT$1,800 (U.S.$45) a month until I make up the remaining NT$300,000 (U.S.$7,500) that is owing. My youngest sister lives with us to help me with shopping. Her job is very low-paying, so I don't take her money. She often eats outside.

Before Father died, another piece of good fortune occurred for me when I met my husband. Because he lived nearby and often walked past my shop, we began to have conversations. He has many dreams for his future, which he told me. I felt I could tell him my ideas, what I had learned from books. We became friends, but I never thought of marriage, because in our Chinese society, crippled people, whose children might also be imperfect, almost never marry.

My husband was born a Taiwanese but was adopted at an early age by a Mainland soldier who had no family in Taiwan. He grew up speaking the national language and had to learn Taiwanese from me. At twenty-five, he is six years younger than I am. My husband has very big ideas, but he did not like to study books. Although his adoptive father wanted him to attend university, he could not pass the entrance examinations. After completing his military service, he again tried to pass and failed three years in a row. It was during those years of rootless study that we met and began to feel love for each other.

Our wedding was a very quiet one, because I did not want to be too conspicuous, and because his family thought our marriage unsuitable. But

8. First Older Brother had not received the usual first son's share of the family property when the two households "divided the stove," because they owned nothing of value but the house itself at that time.

Wenlong and I did have a honeymoon, like other couples. What an experience! We did more traveling than I have ever done before, with me on the back of his motorcycle. He took me to see all the famous sights of Taibei City and even to the Mountain People's village at Wulai. We could not, of course, go to climb Mount A Li or visit the southern cities, but we had a wonderful time seeing the sights and eating at restaurants.

Our marriage was made possible when my family sold our property. There were advantages for both of us in marrying. My husband is very interested in our country's youth and thinks that he should help them prepare for the future by studying martial arts and making strong ties and connections among them. Sometimes he works at petty trading, and he was a night watchman for a while, but mostly he spends time with his friends. It is hard to get a good job that suits his ideas about himself.

There are many young men out of work in this neighborhood who do not have very much to do. Some of them find a woman who has a job in a factory, or some unpleasant kind of job,[9] and live on the money their girlfriends provide. The women are being used, really, but they are afraid their boyfriends will leave them, especially if they have children. In time, perhaps, these wild youths will settle down to take care of their families.

So I think this neighborhood is less desirable than my old home, Prosperity Settlement. There, there was community spirit, people held the local temple festivals, and very little crime occurred. Here, I hear of knife fights, even at the high school behind our apartment. My husband came home cut up from a bottle fight last week, and he is always going off to stick-and-chain fight competitions with his gang of friends.

Sometimes I really miss Prosperity Settlement, because it was more neighborly and I could see some things of the world passing by on the main road. Here in this enclosed back street, I rarely see visitors. Roosevelt Road was better for business, too, but of course that is why the property was so valuable there. There is no easy way for new customers to find me here. I need at least five or six portraits a month to support us.

But all in all, I am really fortunate to have my own home, something I never dreamed of when I was younger. This apartment has a bedroom for my sister and one for us, with a large living room all wallpapered, and a modern kitchen and bathroom. Because we are inside an air shaft, it is quite clean and quiet compared to Roosevelt Road, even though there is a large factory in the next street. The neighbor's children come by sometimes, so I can always send one of them for my relatives upstairs, who even have a telephone now.

9. That is, prostitution.

[171]

The other good fortune I have had, of course, is this baby of ours. When I married, I didn't know if I would have a baby or not, or if I had one, if it would be crippled like me. I didn't know anything about birth prevention, but what could I do about it anyway? I left everything to my husband, and he left everything to fate! After a few months, I began to think I might be pregnant, because my periods stopped. I began to be very afraid, so afraid that I couldn't sleep or think, too afraid to tell anyone. What would happen to me, to my body, if everything wasn't normal? And what about the baby? Would it be healthy?

When I was in my seventh month, my husband took me on the motorcycle to see a doctor. He examined me, tested my blood and urine, and told me the baby seemed normal. I would have to have an operation to birth the child, however. So I was more afraid than ever! It was then that I really started to chant sutras regularly, to protect myself and the baby, and to give me peace of mind.

When I began labor, my husband and sister took me to the doctor's little obstetrical hospital with room for three or four women to give birth. It's very common even for normal births to be in the hospital in Taiwan, because giving birth is a very dirty business, and no one wants that in the house if they can afford a hospital. In my case, of course, I had to go because of my need for the Caesarean section. I don't remember much about any of it; I was just too frightened, but I remember when they told me my son was healthy.

I came home from the hospital after a week. Here I was, with a baby, and too sore to move. My sister-in-law from upstairs came and helped, and of course, so did my sister and husband. My husband was really happy to have a child of his own. He is a very good father.

His family, who had opposed our marriage at first, changed their feelings toward us when they saw I had a healthy baby. My father-in-law had recently married, and my mother-in-law also came and helped me with the baby while I recovered. They have now adopted a Vietnamese orphan boy—basically very kindhearted people.

When you have a baby, you are supposed to follow a lot of rules in the first month for the health of the mother and baby. For example, you shouldn't wash much, and only in very hot water. After I had my baby, I often felt dirty and wanted to wash. Besides, it was midsummer and *very* hot. When I tried to follow the rules, I found that different people told me different things—Mother-in-law's and Sister-in-law's ideas were not at all the same. I suppose that what we did was all right, though, because the baby is fat and lively.

Now I have begun to wonder what I should do about birth prevention. I don't want to have another baby right away, not until my husband gets a job at least. What I've been doing is pretending that I'm asleep when he comes to bed. He seems to be staying out late at nights more now. There are many women who don't care what they do. I've heard that birth-prevention pills can prevent women from ever getting pregnant again, so I don't want that. I would like to have one more child, but not just now. I'm really not sure what to do about this problem.

One thing that has helped me keep a more peaceful heart through these difficulties has been my conversion to a new faith. Our family ceased to worship the gods after mother died, nor did we make much effort to remember our ancestors, with no adult woman in the house to prepare the offerings. We were too poor and disorganized. When things were very bad for our family, though, Mr. Kho[10] came to teach us about a new way of worshiping the Buddha. This religion has no offerings or superstitious beliefs or big festivals. In fact, it is only a private religion, performed in the home, not in temples. It began in Japan, so our government does not permit it to be a public religion, but it is only for good. It helps people to think pure, good thoughts, have peaceful hearts, and be kind to others.

The worship is simple. Mr. Kho used to come to our house in Prosperity Settlement and talk to us about forgetting the sad and difficult parts of our lives, focusing only on good and on the Buddha. He taught us to chant a sutra that calms the heart and brings us closer to God. I used to chant the sutra often, and it always helped. When I was pregnant, I chanted it hundreds of times a day! When we chant, we place our hands in a special position, wrap the rosary beads around them, and chant a sutra for each bead.

At the old house, I just chanted anywhere. When I got this house and new furniture, I bought a shrine with the names of Buddha written on a paper inside. Over it, I've hung a picture of the religion's main temple in Japan, on Mount Fuji. We put white candles up. I have a book with many different sutras in it, and I try to read them all over at least once a day, though I've done it less often since the baby became so active.

It was Mr. Kho who suggested that my family move here and buy apartments in his building. I like living near him. He often drops over to see me, to teach me. He is a saintly man who has helped many unfortunate people by introducing them to this religion. I think it is because I slowly came to this religion that I was able to marry, buy my own house, and have

10. Mr. Kho's life is related in the next chapter.

my baby. Even a person with nothing, with handicaps, can have a good life if she works to be a good person and has faith. I have troubles, but I am also blessed.

Postscript, 1985

Miss Ong's picture business did so badly in the new apartment that she began to think there was something seriously wrong with her fate; she decided to take both mystical and practical action to change it. After studying books about the effects on one's fortune of one's name, she found a more auspicious one for herself, and adopted it. Then, her husband sought out a safe and relatively weatherproof location where many prospective customers could see her wares. He found the perfect spot in the lighted, tiled pedestrian underpass leading across a main road to a large, flourishing temple. His connections secured her a place to spread a mat and sign among the sellers of fruit, flowers, incense and spirit money, lottery ticket vendors and other fortune-tellers that crowd this profitable venue. She and her lively little boy set out every day behind Wenlong on the motorcycle to take picture orders and tell fortunes on the basis of the Chinese characters of the customers' names. Now her skillful hands and flowery language earn them a decent living from pious passers-by.

[8]

Folk Religions, Old and New

The folk religion practiced by Taiwanese people is a local variant of the many that historically emerged all over China. Although the imperial state imposed some controls on religious customs that challenged authority by growing too unorthodox, Chinese working people have experimented freely with their traditions, adding or dropping elements, reformulating ideas about supernatural beings and their relations with human beings, or inventing and elaborating rituals that express local concerns. In Taiwan, Buddhist and Daoist temples, monasteries, convents, and private religious specialists are locally influential, but there are no strong religious organizations that can unify ritual practice or set dogma. Some Buddhist associations that are dominated by Mainlander clergy, however, make attempts to "purify" local folk ritual to conform to government policy and the customs of their mainland religious training. At times, Japanese and Nationalist officials have tried directly to limit or eliminate certain folk religious customs (see Weller 1985, 1987). By and large, however, folk religion has flourished freely and illuminates exceptionally well the ways Taiwanese people organize themselves and view their world when they are allowed to shape their own institutions.

The little communities in which working-class families prefer to live generally symbolize their unity through worship of a supernatural patron believed to have a special attachment to the area and a concern for its people. Even in Taibei, the largest and most rapidlly growing of Taiwan's cities, urban neighborhoods that have engulfed older town or village nuclei often contain old shrines or temples around which religious activities cluster.

These temples are of varied origins. In the most common, the Earth God (and Madam Earth God, in some cases) is worshiped. These represent, people say, the lowest level of a heavenly bureaucracy that parallels Taiwan's government. At the top of the government, President Jiang; at the top of Heaven, the Jade Emperor; at the bottom of the government, the neighborhood police station; at the bottom of the hierarchy of gods, the Earth God, responsible for the neighborhood people over which he has been given authority. Between these levels are many earthly and heavenly bureaucrats and ministers, each supernatural with a retinue of spirit generals and soldiers who enforce his will. (Beneath the earth lies another supernatural realm that is "just like Taiwan" except that it is populated by the spirits of the dead and ruled by monstrous spirits who punish their sins.) As the country is divided into administrative units governed by officials, so every neighborhood ought to have its Earth God to report back to his superiors on people's behavior. The various Earth Gods were once human beings of superior virtue. If they conduct themselves well in their posts as Earth Gods, they will be promoted to a higher rank in Heaven. These gods, who are represented by small, brightly painted wooden images of a seated old gentleman in imperial court costume, are housed in small temples that serve as the focus for much community worship.

Some neighborhoods worship other supernatural beings, in addition to or instead of an Earth God, such as higher-ranking gods with larger temples. Communities sometimes also worship dangerous, low-ranking spirits. Little shrines for those who died in battle—against the Aborigines or in the clan wars—are often built over historical mass graves. At a site where someone died violently and unhappily, the ghost may linger in a bad temper, causing harm and illness until it is given a tablet, shelter, and offerings (Harrell 1974). One such shrine, built in the form of a colorful little pagoda, stands not far from Prosperity Settlement, a physical home for the spirit of a slave girl who was beaten to death on the spot by her master nearly a hundred years ago. In the decades since neighborhood people began to pay her spirit respectful attentions, she has become well disposed and protective; they now describe her not as a *gui*, or ghost, a term with unpleasant connotations, but instead as a *shen*, a god (see Jordan 1972; A. Wolf 1974).

By conceiving of the "other," supernatural world as organized into a single hierarchy of power and authority, the Taiwanese express their understanding that society itself is structured hierarchically. Inequalities are part of the nature of the cosmos. Everything on earth, in heaven, and in the underworld is included in this schema: no evasion of its principles is possible. Humans must obey their superiors and do their duty by those dependent on them.

In Taiwan, where human beings may become gods after death and where any individual or community may decide to worship such a spirit, there are many ways in which a small shrine may grow up. Even a newly developed working-class urban area is likely to be close to an older religious center, or it may establish a new one of its own. Typically, at least once a year the people of the neighborhood celebrate the "birthday" of the patron god or goddess in a festival that strengthens and expands their social ties, "putting the neighborhood on the map" for the rest of society.

Prosperity Settlement, home of about two thousand people, including Mrs. Lim (Chapter 9) and formerly Miss Ong, holds two such festivals each year. Another festival, managed privately for many years by a resident household, also drew heavily on neighborhood support for its success until the manager moved away in the mid-1970s.

On the fifteenth day of the first lunar month of 1972, Prosperity Settlement families celebrated the birthdays of their Earth God and Madam Earth God with the longest and most expensive festival they had ever sponsored, in honor of the new temple they had just built. In preparation for this event an "incense pot master" and four assistants had been chosen the previous year from among the female and male household heads of the community. The god himself selected them, indicating his intentions by the positions of two red wooden blocks thrown repeatedly by the candidates: the person receiving the most "votes" from the god became incense pot master, and those ranking next, his assistants. Families that were impure through death, or women through childbirth, were not eligible to participate.

This group of solid citizens was responsible for planning and supervising the festival, including hiring the Daoist who would perform a necessary ritual. They requested permission from the local police station to hold the event, as no unregistered public gathering was permitted under Taiwan's martial law. Mr. Dan, the incense pot master, filled out the necessary forms and paid the police the necessary bribe. After careful consultation with the others, one of the assistants was deputed to hire three different opera companies for the anticipated fifteen days and nights of performances. These companies were chosen on the basis of reputation and familiarity from one of the many small opera troupes whose members fill in between engagements with other forms of day labor, including funeral miming.

Ten days before the festival date, the leaders visited every Taiwanese household in Prosperity Settlement except for a few extremely im-

[177]

poverished ones, approaching even a few sympathetic Mainlander households. From each family they requested a token donation of NT$4
(U.S.$0.10) for each man, woman, and child, listing the family by number
of males and number of females under the full name of the household head.
Because this sum fell short of the expected costs, the leaders made a second
circuit, this time tapping all the owners of the nearby small factories. One,
whose paint factory always dumped the last of its current batch of coloring
into Prosperity's stream, causing it to flow green, purple, or pink by turns,
gave the NT$3,000 (U.S.$75) necessary for a whole evening in gratitude for
the past year's good business. By concentrating their efforts among the
better-off, the leaders were able to reduce their deficit to only a few
hundred New Taiwan dollars.

Though a few Mainlanders join the ritual community by making contributions, these celebrations flourish mostly among working-class Taiwanese;
many Mainlanders disdain Taiwanese festivals as supersititious and old-
fashioned, and either ignore or criticize them as wasteful, as do more
educated Taiwanese like Mrs. Lim (Chapter 9) and Mr. Kho (this chapter).

Two days before the festival, a hired crew erected a bamboo and canvas
opera stage facing the brilliantly tiled new temple. The neighborhood
children immediately took possession, swarming over, swinging from, and
jumping off it with great glee.

The morning of the fifteenth, the weather showed a welcome break in the
midwinter rains. Very early, the leaders, free from any sexual taint and
dressed in freshly washed clothes, walked to a lovely old Goddess of Mercy
temple nearby to invite one of her many images to attend the celebration as
the community's and the Earth God's guest. After burning incense, the
incense pot master invited the goddess to accompany them to Prosperity
Settlement, obtaining her assent by throwing the wooden blocks and
observing their positions. (Should the answer have been "No," I was told,
they would renew their request, ever more respectfully, until a positive
answer turned up.) Placing the small wooden image on a stack of spirit
money to maintain its purity, the incense pot master carried her out of the
temple and back to Prosperity. Here, welcomed with firecrackers, she was
installed in the position of an honored guest on the Earth God's altar.

On this important occasion, the altar was particularly beautiful, decorated with symmetrical vases of bright gladiolus and fragrant ginger
flowers, fresh candles, and large platters of beautifully colored fruit. On one
wall glowed a cheerful neon sign of a peach and the character for "long life"
which a local businessman always lends. Over the door hung a red "Eight
Immortals" banner, embroidered with legendary Daoist figures. The older
women and men of the neighborhood bustled in and out, offering un-

solicited advice and unstinted criticism, carefully depositing their own god images, hanging up a great incense coil as a family offering to the assembled supernaturals, and generally having their say. There are rules for rituals, but as few people completely agree on what they are, there was plenty of room for rearrangement, additions, and the airing of opinions. Many settled in for a few minutes to sit on a bench or stool by the door and enjoy the "hot noise" of a lively, happy crowd.

Meanwhile, outside the temple, a muscle-bound butcher prepared two large pigs as offerings. While in the old days, Prosperity people raised their own pig sacrifices, it was now illegal to keep livestock in the city limits, so the pigs arrived with the hired butcher as gutted carcasses paid for by two competitive groups of neighbors. In front of the temple, the butcher maneuvered them over the temple's stretching racks, making them appear twice as fat as they were, and began to decorate them. Already covered from snout to hams with red slaughter-tax seals, they were adorned with small pineapples in their mouths, live, flapping fish suspended from their jaws, necklaces of old coins and new money, and a prickly scatter of national flags stuck into their shoulders. Through the morning, they stood as symbols of spiritual salvation—even a lowly pig can become a worthy offering to the gods—the grandest sacrifice a god can receive (Ahern 1981a). By the afternoon, the butcher was rapidly disassembling these handsome beasts into neat, numbered, and precisely equal piles. As dusk fell, they were distributed by lottery and soon converted into dinner.

Meanwhile, during the afternoon, the opera began. The loud music and firecrackers that announced it drew people from their houses, the older ones carrying chairs or stools for comfort. During the day, old people and preschool children formed an appreciative audience for historical moralistic tales, while the younger evening crowd preferred romantic operas laced with satire and wit.

Toward evening, as the opera tootled and gonged its way through a Confucian plot, mothers-in-law and wives began to appear to set their family's special festival dinner down before the gods as an offering. A whole cooked chicken, a duck, and a big chunk of pork was the usual offering, symbolizing, by the largeness and wholeness of the animals, a hope for abundance and family unity in the year ahead. Most women offered small cups of wine as well, drawing the gods' attention to the food and liquor with prayers and incense. When an incense stick had burned down, the donor assumed that the gods had had time to consume the essence of the food. She then repacked the remaining part into a carrying basket, poured the wine back into the bottle, and took the whole kit home for dinner.

People in Prosperity made other offerings, too. Red cakes two feet long in the shape of turtles were offered, but these were left on the altar and not taken home. A person seeking to improve her family's wealth, health, or fertility could take a turtle home to share with her family, promising the god that if he helped them, they would return two turtles the next year. Typically, in reality, people returned one and contributed an equivalent in money to the incense master's fund. The temple's records for these transactions in Prosperity go back to 1952, showing increasing expenditure on turtles through the years (Rohsenow 1973:125–26).

The second and succeeding days of the celebration were less lively, for the special offerings were completed. The operas continued, however, providing an opportunity for local people, guests, and gods to savor this traditional and well-loved entertainment.

Toward the end of the festivities, a Daoist arrived to address the god formally in archaic spoken Taiwanese, calling his attention to the contributions people had made. He read off the entire list of household heads, along with the number of males and females in each household and the amount of money they had given, so the Earth God would know the people who were included in his jurisdiction for the next year and would take proper care of them. The list, on red paper, was burned, thereby sending it to Heaven, where the households received proper credit for their individual sums. A second copy was posted on the temple wall for all to see, so there could be no accusations of embezzlement. Settlement people celebrate in this fashion every year at this time, albeit on a smaller scale, as do many neighborhoods throughout the island, each in its own fashion.

Prosperity Settlement's second yearly festival, held on the fifteenth day of the tenth lunar month, celebrates the birthday of a tripartite god, or group of three brother gods, named Sam Gai Gong. Sam Gai Gong has no temple and no image but is represented by an incense pot that "lives" in the house of the current incense pot master. The celebration is similar in most respects to that for the Earth God, except that pigs and turtles are not offered and that on this date Prosperity families invite human guests to feast and watch their opera.

Ordinary households invite two or three tables of guests—two or three dozen people—while the well-to-do in the neighborhood may invite five tables—sixty or more guests. Married-out daughters or sons who live separately, senior collateral relatives, and good friends are invited along with those with whom the family wishes to form a closer relationship: a child's teacher, the business's wholesaler, a handy contact in a government bureau, someone who is owed a favor, someone the family wishes to ask for a favor in the future. These feasts are very important to the family's social and business network, and the household spares no expense to provide lavish food, liquor, and cigarettes. The stiffness Chinese often show when strangers gather is greatly loosened by drink, giving the guests opportunities to make new and useful friends. When people speak of festivals, what is central is the food and the sociability of eating together in the honorable relationship of host and guest. As a respected Prosperity family head once said, "Some people really aren't very great believers in the gods. But when a community celebrates this way, it makes us all better neighbors."

Offerings of food and entertainment made to gods convey information about the real world, too. If society is a hierarchy of power, ordinary folk may need the support and protection of important people who can be brought to benevolence by offering them gifts and deference. As Emily Martin [Ahern] has pointed out, the etiquette of dealing with human superiors is codified and taught even to working people through the formal rituals appropriate for petitioning gods (Ahern 1981b).

Large temples, of which there are dozens in Taibei and hundreds on the whole island, hold similar "birthday" celebrations on a grander scale and sponsor other rituals as well. Just as leaders from small neighborhood temples borrow images from larger ones, so do the leaders of medium-ranked temples borrow from the oldest and most famous. Hundreds of gods "go visiting" every year from a few temples thought to be especially spiritually powerful, and the leaders who escort them develop relationships that reach throughout the island. At the most famous of these, the Beigang temple to Mazu, a goddess often associated with the sea, the celebrations draw visitors from as far away as the emigrant Taiwanese community in Japan. When thousands of eager pilgrims converge on the dusty little town to watch its dramatic religious processions and to worship in Mazu's riotously ornate main temple, it becomes clear that this totally decentralized folk religion in fact links Taiwanese people into a huge, loose, but very significant organization. Much of the continuing sense of Taiwanese ethnic identity is formed in the ritually defined temple communities with their colorful celebrations stressing locality and sociability.

Working-class Taiwanese often approach their gods to pray for assistance in family matters, getting a job, or bearing a child. Some, however, find the temple setting too impersonal or fear that the gods in them will be too busy to attend to their problems. Or, they may have prayed earnestly to several gods and received no help. Such people often turn to spirit mediums like Mr. Go (this chapter), women and men who, in a trance state, are believed to be possessed by a god who either speaks, writes, or in some other way conveys the god's answers to those who ask him questions.

Mediums are extremely common in Taiwan: there are three or four within a few minutes' walk of Prosperity Settlement, which is not exceptional. Many set up as small businesses, charging a fee for consultations. Some seem fraudulent, but many give helpful, sensible advice and reassurance and are apparently sincere. One medium whose advice I came to respect warned a client who wanted a charm to protect her toddler from fire that a charm would not help the child. She, the mother, must be vigilant in keeping her away from the low gas rings and charcoal stoves on which Taiwanese women cook. He would, however, give the *mother* a charm to help her be alert to danger. While some people believe very strongly in certain mediums' abilities to transmit supernatural messages, many are skeptical, assuming that most of these practitioners are merely "doing business."

A clever and effective medium can do a great deal toward raising the prestige of a local god or temple, as Mr. Go did in his neighborhood's Earth God temple. Prosperity Settlement's privately managed festival attracted visitors from distant parts of the city because of its association with a medium who was believed to transmit the patron god's healing powers to worshippers.

Although most variants of folk religion, like those of Beigang and Prosperity Settlement, fit into patterns acceptable to the government, others take on unorthodox or even subversive elements and are banned. Some of these, such as an underground cult called the Duck Egg Religion, invert traditional folk symbolism—using white candles instead of the customary red and allegedly requiring nudity instead of the sexual propriety of orthodox religion—and are officially believed to be corrupting to good social morality. Others, like the Soka Gakkai to which Miss Ong and Mr. Kho (this chapter) are converts, are banned because they might, as in Japan, organize a political party that would successfully compete with the Nationalists.

Christians, who make up about 5 percent of Taiwan's population, are divided among Catholics—mostly Mainlander, conservative, and very acceptable to the government; Presbyterians, mostly elite Taiwanese, sensitive to political repression and objects of suspicion to the government; and a fantastic assortment of other minor sects.[1] While working-class Mainlanders are often Catholic or atheist, most permanently settled working-class Taiwanese follow community temple ritual. That transients and squatters

---

1. Since the early 1950s, Taiwan has had a great superfluity of missionaries who were formerly posted to the mainland. Although they are not successful in making converts, many American churches keep them on in Taiwan in hopes of gaining a share in anticipated future repayments for mainland church properties seized in the 1949 revolution.

like Mrs. Lo and Miss Guo do not participate in such activities indicates how much the gods stand as symbols for orderly, settled communities.

Community folk ceremony remains a powerful force in Taiwanese society despite the relative shallowness or even absence of religious belief among its adherents, if only because of its numerous and obvious social functions. Temples define the neighborhoods into which mobile urban people move, and offer them and older residents the opportunity to participate in a virtuous collective endeavor. The genuinely poor can participate in token ways that preserve their dignity and community membership, or they may forgo involvement altogether without being criticized. Suspicious strangers are transformed into known, potentially friendly neighbors, contacts are made with guests from other areas, and the neighborhood's existence, prosperity, and upright morals are advertised. The widely shared foundations of belief are easily restructured or created anew to meet local and individual needs, so even newly built residential areas may choose to become ritual communities. Because many families earn their livelihood as religious specialists, as manufacturers of ritual equipment, and, in pilgrimage centers, from the tourist trade, folk religion is an asset to the working-class economy by redistributing some of the better-off families' wealth to others in the form of food, entertainment, and contacts. From the symbolism and rituals of folk religion, too, people read certain tried-and-true conclusions about the world: that women and men are deeply different; that hierarchies of power are inevitable and sanctioned by the gods themselves; that by careful etiquette, gift giving, and sharing of food the ordinary people can extend their social networks to enlist the aid of the mighty.

Mr. Go and Mr. Kho, whose life histories follow, are unusually involved in religion: most Taiwanese do not become spirit mediums, nor do they worship in underground sects. But they also illustrate very characteristic patterns of belief among Chinese men. Mr. Go, through organizing and participating in ritual, has made something of a late-life career of folk religion. All the temples and cults of Taiwan are kept alive by the partially self-serving actions of such men, and of rather fewer women. Mr. Kho, like many better-educated Chinese, sees folk religion as childish superstition and has sought a more spiritualized faith. True in spirit, if not in detail, to the Confucian tradition of self-cultivation through reading, philosophizing, and upright personal conduct, Mr. Kho's "foreign" religion in fact permits him to follow the traditional path of the Chinese gentleman.

Miss Ong's religious impulses are also revealing. Like many Chinese working-class women, Miss Ong searches among the religious options open to her for help in bearing an often difficult life. From an enthusiast of

[183]

community festivals, she became a high-minded convert to Mr. Kho's sect and is now a fortune-teller. Taiwan's temples see millions of such women and men, sometimes searching for the meaning of life, sometimes desperate for assistance for the present moment.

Go Cala: Temple Master

"Did you come to worship the goddess? Today is Mazu's birthday, a great celebration. If you pray to her, she will give you what you ask," said Mr. Go, eager to welcome an unusual American visitor to his small temple's most important event of 1970.

Above the murmuring of neighborhood worshipers, the joyful noise of the opera performing a few yards away, and the racket of nearby traffic, Mr. Go told me a bit about the three-hundred-year-old Earth God temple that he was planning to expand into a center of worship of Taiwan's favorite goddess, Mazu. For the next ten years, as a retired patriarch in his sixties, Mr. Go planned, raised money, organized work groups, leaned a little on local politicians for donations, rebuilt the temple, and expanded it to include a sort of chapel for Mazu; that accomplished, he led pilgrimages to greater Mazu temples throughout the island to give greater sanctity to her images housed in his temple, trained a group of young men in ritual drum and gong music to play in processions and festivals, and built up a small but flourishing center of Mazu worship over which he presided with expansive geniality.

A short, slight man with small features and hair dyed jet-black, Mr. Go always wears a business suit when he leaves home, careful of the impression he makes on the world. As I visited him over the years to follow the development of the temple and the changes in its neighborhood, we always met rather formally at his little office in the temple. This was his place of business, and he had its dignity as well as his own to consider.

Taiwan's temples are pleasant, shady places to sit and talk on nonfestival days. They smell of incense and, like this one, often have space for a tiny garden, bright amid the bricks and concrete of its old-fashioned working-class surroundings. The Earth God's temple itself is too small to sit in comfortably, for the altar tables take up most of its 12-foot depth. To me, the white-tilted interior looks a bit like a bathroom, but local people admire it as bright, easy to clean, and pleasingly modern. I preferred to sit outside, in a space that Mr. Go's efforts have provided with a decorated roof upheld by pillars. This shelter, larger than the temple itself, protects its doorway and makes a breezy but rain-free spot for conversation or for displaying festival offerings. On the left side, in a glass-fronted shallow room, stand about twenty images of Mazu, plumply benevolent behind fierce spirit generals. Mr. Go's office is squeezed beside them, just leaving space for the narrow alley that leads past several front doors to the street.

When I visited, several other people often sat down to enjoy the relative quiet: an old caretaker, who lived nearby and kept an eye on things when Mr. Go was elsewhere; a few young men, between jobs or looking for a favor from the temple master; a couple of older women escaping the heat of their daughters-in-law's kitchens. It seemed natural to meet there, at Mr. Go's principal place of business. But, despite our many chats, I realized when I decided to include him in this study that I knew little of Mr. Go's personal life outside the temple.

When in 1980 I asked to record his life history, Mr. Go was amused but willing to tell me something of his past. But luck was not with us. One day I missed him, on another my assistant was ill, on a third occasion he was unexpectedly busy. Suspecting that, after all, my request had been politely rejected, I dropped the project. When I returned to say good-bye before returning to the United States, I found him offended that I had not persisted and actually recorded his life. Finally, early in 1985, I was able to complete the task through the kind assistance of Ms. Wang Chunhua, whom he knew as my friend from many earlier visits. She guided the interview with a list of my written questions.

Many men like Mr. Go, after an early life of hard work and raising sons to care for them, retire to a more leisurely career managing and manipulating people. Mr. Go was reserved about his network of patrons and followers, but his account of his life reveals a little about the social groups that gave him a local power base. First, and most obviously, his religious connections were numerous. Virtually anyone, old or young, female or male, can use one of Taiwan's many temples as an arena to attain a degree of local fame (or notoriety). Many young men, and, more rarely, women, become spirit mediums through whom gods speak, offering these services either freely or for pay to the public as Mr. Go did for a time. Older men (and, occasionally, women) are more likely to do as Mr. Go did when he felt that his physical strength was waning and his local power base was broad enough: they build up some local temple by expanding and decorating its buildings, organize bigger and more spectacular festivals, persuade popular spirit mediums to attend them, and arrange for pilgrimages. These activities bring them into contact with many people, including similar men and women in other neighborhoods and communities. Such religious leaders depend on a network of useful social ties, while fund-raising and the giving and receiving of favors extend those ties. As a long-time resident of a neighborhood with an established temple, Mr. Go had a natural base. By shifting the focus of local worship to the popular goddess Mazu, he was able to take advantage of the enthusiasm of older women for religiously sanctioned travel and turn a static local Earth God temple into the center of expanding social significance.

His colleagues in the building trades were the second group on which he drew for support. Urbanization in Taiwan since the fifties meant prosperity for builders and importance for the older men among them who knew where the jobs were, who could organize work gangs, and who could pass on skills and knowledge to younger men. Mr. Go, as a minor contractor for carpentering jobs, was such a man: he also knew how to pay off the police, building inspectors, and officials who grant building permits in a system where such knowledge is an essential business skill.

These contacts brought him into a political network: the police and other low-level Nationalist officials of Taiwan's large government/party leadership. Men like Mr. Go are essential to Nationalist electoral success in Taiwan, for it is they who deliver the votes of the working-class population. In the 1980 elections the going price of a vote was $NT200 (U.S.$5), paid out through established, reliable community leaders who have clout with their neighbors, who can judge dependably which of them will vote as they have been paid to do, and who have too much to lose to attempt to deceive the party men who supply the funds. Those who can dispense this patronage naturally increase their ability to attract donations for temples and find it easier to clear away red tape in the construction business. Mr. Go appears to have benefited from such linkages in his rise as temple master.

I was born in Great Prosperity, on Eternal Spring Street. My family has lived here since they came to Taiwan about one hundred years previously. There have been houses and businesses in Prosperity Settlement and Great Prosperity for many years—since before the Japanese came. We were not farmers here, but workers like carpenters and miners or shopkeepers. My grandfather was a carpenter who made wardrobes and closets, my father followed his trade, and so did my elder brother and I. For three generations in our family we have done the same thing. Grandfather and Father ran their own businesses, as did I before I retired. But while Grandfather got rich, Father became poor. He just got by, from day to day, and couldn't hope to have savings.

We were three brothers—one older than I and one younger. Though I used to have relatives living around here, now everyone has bought his own house and moved away. My mother didn't work outside the home; in the past, women stayed home taking care of the children, and didn't work at all.

I didn't go to school, but got into business peddling very young. I sold cakes and small things on the street. It was like today's street peddlers—I had to keep moving to make sales, and when the police came, I ran away. I tried a lot of different things—everything I could think of. My older brother was building houses, so I learned to do that. We built Japanese-style houses, all one floor.

But for a while, when I was about twenty, I belonged to a *zhentou*—an old-fashioned Taiwanese band that played opera at festivals. When people hired us, I played. It was irregular work. I also acted in operas, learning one role at a time, altogether learning only two or three operas. I played women's parts, because at that time, there were no women actors. Younger men played women's roles. It was fun, for a while, for me and for the villagers we played for. I didn't have any pictures taken of me acting at that time; it would have been more than forty years ago.

That was during the Japanese time. I knew some Japanese people and generally admired them. They were straightforward, and when something needed doing, they went ahead and did it. Life was not so easy for me then, though, especially during the war.

In the years before the war, I worked again building Japanese houses. After Retrocession I built both Japanese and Chinese styles. When we built, a head craftsman told us what to do. I sometimes think that he didn't need to have a specific skill—he just did the design. Before the war, there was a lot of house-building, so we had a lot of business. During the war, there wasn't any building, so I went back to work as a miner. I didn't go back to building until the economy got better in the fifties.

I worked as a coal miner in Shiwufen, in Taibei County. It was an hour's walk from our house; there were no cars then, so I walked to work. I did that for seven years. As a coal miner, I earned between sixty and seventy yen a month, two or three yen a day. That was a good job, better than being a house-construction worker where I earned only a little more than thirty yen a month—1.1 yen a day. Unskilled workers got 0.48 yen a day, but most people were skilled and earned 1.1.

Late in the war, I went into the Japanese Navy, serving for six months. I was the only man in my family to be in the service, and one of only eighty-seven men in the whole city of Taibei who were in the navy. It was pretty good. It paid 5.50 yen a day. I made airplanes in the south of Taiwan and was stationed in Yilan for a couple of weeks.

During the war the government allocated food to people, including the Japanese—pork and other kinds of food. They gave enough for about twenty days out of the month—the other ten days' food people had to get what they could for themselves. My family would buy sweet potatoes from the south in the Wanhua district of Taibei. During the war there was never enough food. The Japanese were just the same to us in the war as they always had been.

After the war was over, seventy bandit soldiers came to our neighborhood, sent by Chen Yi.[2] Many people were killed when the soldiers stole the people's food. My family didn't get hurt, because I made friends with the bandit soldiers by fixing up a building for them to use when they needed a carpenter. So we became good friends, and they were afraid to hurt my family. Later, the "2:28 incident" happened. An old woman was selling cigarettes illegally in downtown Taibei. There was a fight. Many people died. After the 2:28 incident, things got better. The Japanese and the Nationalist Chinese were about the same, really.

Before the war, I married my wife, A Kim. She had nine children—four girls and five boys. Our first son lives nearby and runs a small dog-meat shop. The second, who is divorced, works in a restaurant. He and his two children live at our house. The third son has a small company, the fourth owns an ironworking business, and the fifth is in the navy. Our four daughters are all married. We married the second to a much older Mainlander because it was necessary to help the family at that time. The Mainlander gave us some money for her; my wife managed the whole thing. The youngest daughter is getting divorced because her husband has a girlfriend.

I got seriously interested in religion only after the Nationalists came. In the war, the gods really showed their power, protecting us from bombs, so I started to believe in them. I didn't really believe when I was young, but I believe more and more as I get older.

About twenty years ago, I began to have spiritual powers: I became a *tang ki* (T).[3] I knew many men who became *tang ki*. Different gods would possess them so they could walk through fire or beat their backs with spiked balls, but not be hurt. I could do those things—I still have the sword I used to use leading the firewalks—but my greatest power was different, and very unusual.

With the help of the gods, my spirit could travel to the underworld to help people solve their problems. I could only ask help there from the ghosts of people whom I had known while they were alive. Ghosts who had been strangers to me in life wouldn't recognize me, and so wouldn't answer questions. A family might be having a lot of sickness or losing money, and

2. Chen Yi was the first Guomindang commander in Taiwan after Retrocession, and later Jiang's scapegoat for 2:28.
3. A spirit medium.

they'd ask me to go and ask their grandfather why they were so unlucky. Maybe they had been neglecting his spirit, so he was holding back their fortune. I'd ask, and tell them, and they'd make offerings to the unhappy spirit. Then their luck would change. Or a woman would want to know if she would have sons. Down below, each living woman has a flowering tree. Each flower is a child. I couldn't change the number or sex of her children; that is each woman's fate. But I could prop up or replant the tree to make it healthier, foretell the sex of her children from the color of the flowers, and keep weak flowers and branches from falling off.

The world of the spirits is just like here in Taiwan: there are cars, streets, everything just like here. There are even temples. But there are more old-style houses than we have now. And the rivers are full of drowned corpses of people who have not been properly buried on earth. People whose zodiac animals are grass eaters, like the ox, can manage there more conveniently than others, as grass grows everywhere, even there, for them to eat. But human food is provided only by the offerings from the living.

While a *tang ki's* spirit is in the underworld, his body on earth acts out the things he does and sees below—like games or operas. He must be careful not to be enticed by women, though. He could lose his power and not be able to get back. When he comes up, he is exhausted. Helpers who interpret for the *tang ki* should be "strong-fated" and lucky so they can fend off ghosts. If the helper is not like that, the *tang ki* may not be able to get back to this world. I knew a man who lost his soul that way and died in trance. The helpers have to have special training. I stopped trancing about ten years ago. I am past sixty and no longer have the strength. It's too dangerous.

The images of the gods that helped me do these things are still in my house—I used that as my office then. After I stopped trancing, I still wanted to promote belief in gods, so I began to build up this Earth God temple.

Our little Earth God temple is over three hundred years old. It was there in the time of my eighty-year-old neighbor's grandmother's childhood. When people first settled around here, most of them were farmers. Once, when harvests were bad, they were advised to build a temple for his worship. They had an image made, brought it to a pure and auspicious location, opened the god's eyes, and brought him back to the temple. There's a Madam Earth God, too, of course—you can't have the Earth God without his wife.

Later, they added other gods. After the war, Great Prosperity invited an image of Mazu from Beigang to be a guest at their festival. We borrowed her for a while. The next year, they didn't invite her, so we invited her

[189]

ourselves. We did that for some years, then finally had an image of her made and had her eyes opened. She stays here, but she's like a married woman: each year at lunar New Year, she returns to her "mother's home" in Beigang. We've also had images made of Mazu from Lugang and other famous places, and of a Goddess of Mercy from the very old temple at Great Prosperity, which is one of the oldest temples in the island. When we had her eyes opened, the Daoist didn't use blood, because she is a vegetarian.

When a god's eyes are opened with blood—from a white rooster's comb, or sometimes from a duck—the animal is still alive while the blood is drawn. Devotees don't eat the meat of these fowl, but give them to the helpers who open the eyes. Women may not be present at eye openings.

The temple the old people built was very small. In the year of the restoration of Chinese rule, I started to take responsibility for caring for it. I had just moved my family from Great Prosperity over here to this street and noticed the activity at the temple for the Earth God's birthday, which we celebrate in the first lunar month. Some pious person had left oranges and turtle cakes for others to take home to bring their families a peaceful year. Those who took them asked the god for a favor. The next year, those who had taken them returned a gift of food or money to the temple, especially if the god had helped them. It seemed like a good temple, with sincere worshipers. They needed someone to act as head of the temple, so I took on the responsibility. The man who had been in charge before had been the *bao zhang* for the Japanese, but he didn't do much anymore. So the local people asked me to take over.

About ten years ago, the old roof was so full of termites and the building was so small—only 8 or 9 feet square—that I hired a knowledgeable temple builder to reconstruct and expand it. When I started to take the small temple down, local believers volunteered money to help build it. I didn't go around asking people for money. The people of eight neighborhoods all joined in. I gave a lot myself, and a policeman friend of mine, a rich man, gave NT$40,000 (U.S.$1,000).

After the temple was nicely fixed up, in 1975, we formed a committee to register it with the Ministry of the Interior to change it from private to public property. Then we would not have to pay taxes on the temple's land. We had a big meeting with twelve tables of local household heads who came to choose the committee. Each person contributed NT$200 (U.S.$5) to pay for the feast—we didn't eat from the temple's money! It was very democratic, with speeches and voting. My friend the policeman and I were chosen to head the committee, along with twelve committee members and two accountants—one for expenses, the other for income. We filed our application with the police, who sent it up to the City Government, who sent it up to the Ministry. After a few months, the Ministry sent an investigator to see if the leadership was respectable, honest, and owned some property. He assessed the temple's value and registered it for us. Now we are an official temple.

I stopped working after I became temple master; I haven't worked as a carpenter now for more than thirty years, though I do a little contracting. My family expenses came from buying and selling houses. I spent most of my time in the temple. People often came to drink "old people's tea."[4] The police would come around and we'd drink tea and I'd get to know them. People were always dropping by—they knew I had an office there.

Every few years, I'd add something new to the temple and the believers always helped with money. I built the roof out in front of the temple so people can leave their offerings on big festival days without fear of rain. I built the altar room on the side to house our many images of Mazu and the "generals" who were forced out of the Xian Gong temple up the road.[5] When these things were built, I arranged for Daoists to come and consecrate them. When men began to make more money, their wives wanted to go on pilgrimages to visit Mazu's temples in Beigang, Lugang, and other famous places. So I organized those, which brought many believers to a more sincere worship of the goddess. When young men in our neighborhood asked me how they could organize to serve society, I helped them form a musical group. They played for our festivals and were invited to play for festivals in other neighborhoods. Professor Gates came to some of them and took a lot of pictures of our group. Membership is good for young men. It encourages virtuous behavior and helps them earn a little extra money. The temple has become larger and more beautiful, and has been well supported by local believers, all because they have faith in Mazu and the gods.

Our Taiwanese religion is good for people. The gods teach us to do good, to be honest, to fulfill our responsibilities. They can cure sickness and mental illness, and they help us to prosper. We must show our gratitude by worshiping them. Where people worship the gods, there is less social trouble like robbery and killing. People who criticize religion should think about this.

---

4. Tea drunk in temples, for recreation.

5. This medium-sized old temple, built on land claimed by the government, was subjected to considerable pressure to close during the early sixties. Though local resistance has kept it open, a government-controlled Buddhist association installed a non-Taiwanese Buddhist priest as temple head. He has attempted to encourage a more patriotic tone in festivals, and has purged the temple of folk images and practices he considers unorthodox. Mr. Go's temple houses these orphan images.

Our neighborhood has an unusual reputation. Many Taiwanese girls have married Mainlander men from a nearby army base, but they have Taiwanese lovers and all three live together. Some of the young men are good fighters and can do what they like. A young relative of mine lives in a household like that, and one of the young men in the musical group was just thrown out by his girlfriend's husband. There are others, too—this place is famous for it. There is some theft here, too. My friend the policeman gave two gold votive offerings to the Earth God, and they have already been stolen by a cat burglar who must have crept in through the window at night. So you see, people need to have the gods to control them.

I am nearly seventy, and Taiwan has changed a lot since I was a child. There are more houses, wider roads, lots more industry. People have washing machines, television, refrigerators. We can keep food for days now. Life is more comfortable. Life is freer, too, because if you have money, you can buy whatever you want. During the war, even if you had money, you couldn't buy things.

It was easier to do street peddling in the Japanese period. The government made it clear where and when you could sell things. Now, there is no set place. If the police want to take your things, they do, and then you have to go to the police station to pay to get them back. There was some crime in the Japanese period, but it was different from today. Today, the government arrests a lot of people, but some just pay them off and go on doing whatever they want. Japanese society was much better, more stable. Under the Japanese, when people did bad things, they went into hiding. Now people who have committed crimes just walk around on the streets, good friends with the police. If you are poor, people laugh at you. If you are rich, no one cares how you got your money.

If a young person asked me how to lead a good life, I would tell him to get a job and work, and don't go into gang life. Try to have a house, get married, and have food to eat: that's enough. When I was young, I wanted to have a house and see my children grow up. My wishes have been achieved. My sons have their own houses, except for the youngest, who is still unmarried. My daughters are married. I live on my savings, and my sons give me money sometimes. I grow a few vegetables in front of my house and help take care of my grandchildren. Live a stable life, month by month—that's the best.

I don't go to our temple much any more. Too many people wanted to be temple master, and things began to change. Now they don't have Taiwanese opera there anymore at festivals, just puppet shows in the afternoon and movies in the evening. The times have changed.

When I was a younger man, I didn't get along well with my wife—I'd go to Beitou and bring opera girls back to the house, and she'd get mad. But we're old now. When I go to Wanhua to drink tea, I sometimes take her along. There are some nice tearooms there.

Kho Teklun: Saved by the Buddha

Mr. Kho, at seventy, is a vigorous and successful old gentleman. Born in Taiwan, he spent his youth competing in the Japanese-run educational system, winning the kind of well-paid and well-respected lower-level government job that was becoming more and more available to Taiwanese in the thirties. When the arrival of the Nationalists erased the value of his Japanese-language education, he turned to small business as a way of earning a living. A capable man, he did well at that, too, for he chose construction—one of the few reliably expanding businesses of the fifties. With a much-loved wife, whose death is still too painful for him to discuss, he raised two prosperous sons and married off three well-educated daughters. Perhaps because of the breadth of his early education, these traditional fulfillments were not enough. In his forties, he turned his mind to religion.

Before I was able to meet Kho Teklun, I had heard of him for years through my old friend Ong Siukim as a kind of guardian angel to her unhappy family. Motivated by religious belief resulting from his conversion to a Japanese form of Buddhism, Mr. Kho quietly seeks out and helps those in trouble, persuading them, when he can, to embrace his religion. Because he sounded like an interesting and knowledgeable man, I hoped to meet him, trying several times on my first field trip to have Miss Ong arrange this. When I was unsuccessful, I concluded—rightly—that he was unwilling to know me. Before long, I discovered why.

The Buddhist sect that Mr. Kho had joined and was quietly propagating is illegal in Taiwan, banned by the government. It is Soka Gakkai, a religion that became tremendously popular in Japan after World War II among working-class people and new migrants to the cities. More than a religion, Soka Gakkai has amassed considerable property, and successfully backs the populist Clean Government party in Japan's national politics (White 1970). The Nationalist government in Taiwan refuses to permit the emergence of a religion with such potential for social and political power; in consequence, the sect and its members remain secretive about their organization and cautious about connections with strangers. My eventual success in gaining hs confidence was due to Miss Ong vouching for me as, by now, an old friend.

[193]

Mr. Kho receives his many visitors in a cluttered living room above the small first-floor grocery his family runs. The clutter is fascinating evidence of a well-rewarded life: framed Japanese-language school certificates, official awards, gracefully phrased calligraphic couplets celebrating family and business events, and souvenirs of travel and meetings with important people. Among the treasures are family heirlooms, such as his grandmother's three-inch-long slipper for a foot bound in infancy, a lovely teapot from an ancestress' dowry, a porcelain wine bottle from a special feast.

Fine-featured and iron-gray, Mr. Kho looks years younger than his age. His energy carries him on long walks nearly every day on business or charitable errands, but he is at home most afternoons after the midday nap, which all in Taiwan try to squeeze into their routines. Visitors, mostly younger men seeking favors or fellow members of Soka Gakkai, frequently interrupted or terminated our interviews.

Skill at managing a thick skein of human relationships is the most prized talent in Chinese society. It allows its possessor to create a sufficiently wide network of well-placed people to achieve his ends—any ends—gracefully, efficiently, and without excessive expense. Do you need a team of reinforced-concrete workers to put up a building? A man is found who is sufficiently obligated that he will reliably supply them, at a reasonable price. Are you in difficulties with the police? Someone's uncle is related to the police chief, and will speak to him. Do you want to buy a refrigerator? An old schoolmate's son will sell you one wholesale. Would you like your less-than-brilliant son to enter a respectable college? The right combination of cash and acquaintanceship can, perhaps, achieve this end. Is becoming a U.S. citizen your goal? An old friend's elder brother now with the diplomatic mission in the States can get you on a list for a green card. A person's power is based on his ability to deliver a well-disposed contact to someone with a request—who, in turn, becomes an indebted source of future favors for other supplicants. The man in the middle, "the person who has a way," gains with each transaction, and spreads his network ever farther.

This is a demanding life. Men who use these networks to become elected politicians are expected by their constituents to be on twenty-four-hour call to solve their problems; a popular mayor boasts that he sleeps in his office, supremely available. Mr. Kho is only an amateur, not very wealthy, and holder of no high office. He could not (I believe) help anyone emigrate to the United States, or bribe a friend's son into a university. But to anyone who can presume on his acquaintance, he is a valuable source of connections and information about who is who, and who can do what, in local government and civil service, in the construction trades in south Taibei, and in a number of other useful areas of expertise.

Unlike many men of his age and in his line of work, Mr. Kho has kept clear of the underworld of gangsterism, mainly for religious reasons. This may be why the political career of this wise and influential man has been limited to election to a minor neighborhood post. Spreading the blessings of his religious belief to others also absorbs much of the time a political career would have required him to spend mingling with the marginal characters whose vote-buying activities are essential to the Nationalists' continued success. While Mr. Kho clearly regrets his exclusion from public power, he sees mostly venality in those who do hold it. By choosing to dedicate his time to the practice and propagation of an illegal Japanese sect known for its political and social activism, Mr. Kho rebels, a little, against the political system that so changed his life.

My ancestors came from An Qi county of Fujian province. They were surnamed Kho. About one hundred years ago, my great-grandfather came to north Taiwan with his wife to cultivate sweet potatoes and tea on uninhabited land. They planted sweet potatoes first, to have something to eat, and slowly began to raise tea, pigs, chickens, and ducks. They worked very hard.

The Mountain People used to kill us plains people to offer our heads as sacrifices. Therefore, every day before leaving the house, our ancestors asked the god's guidance. If they didn't get a positive answer from thrown divining blocks they stayed in that day! If the Mountain People saw you, they'd kill you. We had no guns or knives, but outsmarted them by running away. There were tigers, bears, and bandits then, too; those were harsh times. Our people ate mountain products, and there were no good things to eat.

Then, in the time of my grandfather, Kho Toakim, the Japanese came to Taiwan and took control. The Japanese fought the Aborigines back into the mountains, to Mount A Li, to Wulai, places like that. From this began a time of peace.

Grandfather grew tea, which is very hard work. He slept only four hours a night so he could work to earn money to buy his land, as people were not allowed simply to occupy the uninhabited areas without paying for them. He grew rice and tea, and built a house of straw and clay. Snakes used to come into the house sometimes.

In Grandfather's time there was peace, but the Japanese made living harder for us in some ways. They taxed at a high rate and discriminated against us Chinese people. They made Taiwanese build the public buildings, roads, and bridges made out of layers of soil, then wood, then clay. There were land taxes and household taxes, though the taxes were not as heavy as they are now. Mostly the Japanese made use of our labor by requiring people to work without pay. The land tax on cultivated and uncultivated land and houses for our family came twice a year—ten yen each time.

At that time, women bound their feet—the smaller their feet became, the more admirable they were thought to be. I still have my mother's shoes, which are only three inches long. Even in the countryside, women did this. Their work was cooking, caring for children, in the house because most women didn't go into the fields. Only servant women didn't bind their feet. The Japanese forbade this custom, however, which they said was unhealthy. Taiwanese people couldn't oppose the prohibition against foot binding, although they were angry about it, because the Japanese had a good system of household registration, and they inspected every house for illegal foot binding, for vaccination, and even for cleanliness.

In school, you were equal with the Japanese if you were clever and got high grades. If you graduated with good grades, you could get high official positions—in the police, as mayor, as head of a school. They didn't discriminate in this, because they were afraid we would rebel.

My grandfather started to buy fields around here in Xindian, as he was making a good living. At that time, agriculture was all done with human labor. Men cultivated fields and built irrigation works by themselves, until the time of my father. Then the Japanese built irrigation works, charging fees twice a year for the use of the water.

When he was young, my father was a guard protecting a Japanese area against Aborigine attacks. He got a gun, a uniform, and a salary and was nearly killed by one of the Mountain People when he was thirty-seven. After he married at thirty eight, he stopped being a guard to grow tea and rice. When we were seven or eight years old my two brothers and I began to help in the fields and to watch the water buffalo. We didn't have shoes, so our feet nearly froze in winter. Father bought an old straw and mud house, and later he rebuilt it of bricks.

The Japanese interviewed my father in an official search for model farmers, and rewarded him for his hard work. We were prosperous when others were poor because we worked ourselves so hard, didn't hire labor, and saved money. So father was appointed *baozhang*. We then had between three and four *jia*[6] of land in this area.

About then, my eldest brother was also successfully growing tea, but he drank some ditch water, which gave him tuberculosis. He died at fifty-eight, with five children—there was no cure for his illness during the

6. One *jia* equals approximately two and one-half acres.

Japanese period. My younger sister also died, of throat cancer. I had malaria at the age of twenty-six, and it almost killed me. Later the Japanese eliminated malaria, but in the early years of my life, many illnesses were fatal.

When I was young, there were no nearby hospitals and no public health stations such as we have now; if you were really sick, there was Taiwan University Hospital in town. Both Western-style and Chinese pharmacies dispensed medicines according to the diagnosis of the pharmacist. Most were traditional Chinese pharmacies. The Western ones were brought by the Japanese. The Japanese stationed public doctors, who worked out of offices in their houses, at Xindian and at many other small towns. Some of these doctors were Japanese, some Taiwanese. Their medicines were cheaper than those in the pharmacies. People doctored themselves with herbs unless they were very ill and rarely went to doctors.

My father sent us three brothers to school, but our two sisters didn't have the opportunity to study. I remember being very afraid on my first day at school. I wanted to get out of there and follow my mother home! If there hadn't been so many others there, I would have cried. Until I was in the fifth or sixth grade, I was always in fights.

In the first grade, we were allowed to speak Taiwanese, but by the end of the fourth grade, everything was in Japanese. If we spoke any Taiwanese at school after that, we were beaten with a wooden paddle. From there, I took the entrance examinations, passed, and went on to three years of middle school, where four of my teachers were Taiwanese, and two Japanese, four male, and two female. We wore uniforms and shoes and paid a school tuition fee. If a person could pass the entrance exam but was too poor to pay the tuition, he (or she) could apply to the education office and have the fee waived. This money came from our taxes. Tuition was fairly cheap—2.6 yen a semester, when pork cost less than 20 sen a pound. Students had to supply their own books. The middle school had a small health station, too.

After graduating from middle school, I passed an exam to enter a three-year government-run tea agronomy institute. There were two to three hundred students, half Taiwanese and half Japanese. The Japanese were trying to improve the quality and quantity of Taiwanese teas, which were already very famous. I thought this would be interesting and wanted to study there, even though there was no guarantee of a job afterward. Before graduation we had to undergo three months of hard practical training, going out to the countryside to instruct farmers in tea growing. Those who passed with high scores and good recommendations were sent by the principal to jobs in the tea sections of various administrative offices in north Taiwan. My grades were high, and I got good recommendations from a

Japanese friend, from a teacher, and from a rich man in our village, so I was given a job in a high-level office here in Xindian. I eventually became chief of the agricultural section.

The government sent me to Hainan Island for a while when I was twenty-seven, to supervise the agricultural practices of the many Taiwanese who were growing rice there. My back gave me such trouble, though, that they had to send me home. At thirty, I married my wife, whom I had met as a tea-picking maiden in Xindian. Tenants farmed my fields, and I continued my work in tea agronomy until after World War II, when the present Chinese government arrived.

As World War II became worse, Taiwanese people were ordered to serve in the military in the South Pacific where a lot of them died of malaria. My second elder brother was sent abroad and suffered great hardships.

It was hard to survive during those years. As soon as your harvest was dried, you handed it over to the government, and they gave back a daily ration of six ounces of rice for each person in your household. You would be shot if you kept rice at home secretly. There was not enough rice to eat, so we grew sweet potatoes to feed ourselves—we were allowed to keep those. The Japanese shot a few people as an example, so people dared not keep the rice. The authorities knew how much rice could be harvested from one *jia* of land, so there was no deception.

War is a great misfortune for people. When people are satisfied with what they have, there will be no more war. I don't blame the Japanese for the war, though, and I'm not angry with them, even though they killed Taiwanese, because they were trying to make the Japanese empire great.

The relationship between Taiwanese and Japanese people was not a simple one. The Japanese are a very civilized people and did many things to build up Taiwan, improving life here very much. At the same time, we were not treated as equals. We were an occupied country, more like their adopted sons than their own sons. Even though I studied Japanese, I was always made to feel different. Our surnames were different from theirs, and this marked us as Taiwanese, no matter what we did to learn Japanese ways. During World War II, Taiwanese were told to change their surnames to Japanese ones, but by then, I didn't want to. Especially during the war, we became conscious of our Chinese origins as we heard of the fighting between Chinese and Japanese on the mainland. After all, each generation is taught where their ancestors came from in China, so I grew up with knowledge of my Chinese origins, even while my life was somewhat Japanese.

In 1945 Japan surrendered. I couldn't write Chinese, so I had to quit my job. I had no capital, but we fixed up a house that had been bombed to live in with our two children. Though my land was tenanted, I couldn't get any money from it—the tenants were too poor. So I started a construction business, and sometimes the gold just rolled in because so much rebuilding was necessary after the war. After a year in the construction business, I started a grocery store at South Gate in Taibei and ran that till I was forty-nine.

Then I got sick. My face and body turned yellow, and I nearly died. So I came back to my wife's family to rest up, because the doctor said nothing could be done to cure me. The necessary medicines were simply not available in Taiwan then.

Just then, I read in a newspaper about a sutra in Japan which could save people if they repeated it. I learned the sutra from the Japanese news-papers that we could still get then, and repeated it three or four times every day. When I returned to my doctor, he couldn't believe I was still alive. The meaning of the sutra is that you can become harmonious with the great universe. Reciting the sutra improves our characters, making up for our personal shortcomings. I've prayed using this sutra from when I was forty-nine until now, in my seventieth year. No one taught me, but I often buy books to study more deeply in religious matters. Now I am healthy enough to carry a fifty-kilo bag of rice to the second floor.

I extend my life by praying "*o mi to fo*," by reciting the special sutra of our faith. There's no organization for this religion in Taiwan, but there's a school of it in Japan. It is proscribed in Taiwan because it is Japanese. I have taught a little of it to a few people, not asking for donations, and some of us help poor people. Otherwise, who would save the disabled, like our crippled friend Miss Ong? After she began to recite this sutra, she had the chance to marry, and now she has a son.

There is freedom of religion here in Taiwan. What this means is that the government forbids evil religions, and we are not allowed to organize people who pray using this sutra—it is against the law. We preach our belief by personal contact, and by helping people. We don't need to organize or evangelize. I don't know how many believers there are around here; perhaps not many, but it is hard to know.

Folk religion is naive by comparison, using pictures and statues as objects of worship. Buddha said people could do this for a thousand years, after which there would be a new way, taught by a new sutra. The religion I follow, and the God, are the same as this older form of Buddhism, only clearer, just as the sutra is the same, though it was once Sanskrit and has been translated into Chinese. We followers of Soka Gakkai worship a different state of the Buddha with a different sutra.

This faith is a great improvement over traditional folk religion because it has a systematic explanation of things. Our Fahua Sutra divides humans into ten categories. We have a choice which category to belong to—you can be good, do right, if you choose. This religion, originally Indian, spread to Japan and is now spreading even in the United States. There is a new Buddha for each thousand years. The next new state of the Buddha will be in Japan, because Japan is in the center of the solar system, and because it is a nation without knowledge of the true way of religion and therefore needs a new path to follow. So a Buddha will be born there as a fisherman, among the common people, after which Soka Gakkai will become the main religion of Japan and the world.

From the Fahua Sutra, you can learn to be a virtuous person. You simply recite the sutra as many times as you need to. It's necessary to be educated, so as to be able to read the sutra, of course. As you worship, you train yourself, asking yourself whether you are filial and honest, and if you are behaving legally and helping to preach our discipline.

If anyone asks me why I am so healthy and long-lived, I tell him it is because I recite our sutra, and I urge him to do so, too. Through personal contact and example, we can help others to have a better chance in life by behaving well. If all humans did this, believing in Buddha, there would be peace instead of war. War is a terrible thing.

Traditional religion is not actually bad—I was always in the parades for the gods at the main Xindian temple when I was young, and I enjoyed the feasting and opera—but its goals are simple. People enjoyed the entertainment, but now there are many forms of recreation, like hiking and exercise, which are better for you. Worshiping in order to hold big feasts makes no sense now that people eat well every day. This old form of religion is regressive superstition. It is foolish to mix up the worship of Buddha with that of the old gods. That's naive.

After World War II, for a time people became very evil, robbing, killing, and insulting women. This was the result of the population increase as people fled from the mainland. Many were ambitious, greedy, and wanted to have a good life without working hard. In education, a prince was the same as a common person under the Japanese; under the Chinese, this was not so. The Japanese law was compulsory, binding on everyone. The way Chinese law is applied depends more on who you are.

Right after the surrender, on October 25, 1945, when the Chinese government had not yet reached Taiwan, we educated Taiwanese took over all official business as the Japanese gradually returned home. We ran the provincial, county, and local levels of government for about a month until General Chen Yi arrived with his soldiers.

Those troops behaved abominably. Everything bad you can think of, they did. Before all the Japanese left, they opened their storehouses of several years of food and supplies to give to the people, as there would be no more imports. A lot of that was looted by the Mainland troops.

By 1947 the behavior of the Mainland people was so bad that the February twenty-eighth uprising—2:28—occurred as Taiwanese resisted the corruption and oppression of the Mainlanders. I was an elected Neighborhood Head in South Gate at the time, a part of Taibei that saw much fighting, as Mainlander soldiers shot civilians and Taiwanese attacked Mainlanders with swords. I used my position to keep people in our neighborhood from killing Mainlanders; no good could come of it. People were being shot indiscriminately in the street by troops as the days went on. It was months before all the resisters were killed or imprisoned.

General Chen Yi lied about these events, saying that the Taiwanese had revolted, but we were only defending ourselves against his troops. General Bai Chongxi[7], chief of the Defense Department, went out and moved among the people, standing in a bus line in Jilong, and watching people work as usual. So *he* knew that General Chen had lied. Later, General Bai distributed awards to people like myself who did not fight against the Mainlanders.

After Mr. Chen Cheng[8] became governor in 1949, life improved. He was a responsible official, who went into the streets and markets and temples to see the quality of people's lives, to make reforms and improvements. Even the poor had rice again. When he died, he was greatly mourned. People walked five days and nights from southern Taiwan to come to his funeral. That is the right kind of official; these time-servers who wait around in offices to collect their salaries are bad officials who harm the people.

Another very serious problem after the Chinese took over was inflation. Because they wanted Taiwan's wealth, the Japanese had changed our original money system based on gold and silver, giving us paper money in its place. There were various denominations, and people saved the paper money in banks and postal savings accounts when they could afford to.

After Japan lost its battle, for a while we used Japanese money, but it was said it would soon be declared valueless. The Chinese government set a period of a month or two during which people could exchange their Japanese cash for Chinese notes, but it wasn't possible to draw savings out and exchange that. Some people read the announcement; some didn't.

---

7. An official of known integrity, General Bai Zhongxi is remembered as an opponent within the Mainlander group of the dominant Jiang family.

8. An unusually respected Nationalist official, Chen Cheng served as governor and in other high Taiwan offices from 1949 to 1963.

Some people, peasants mostly, heard that *all* the Japanese money was valueless after surrender, and burnt even their cash, losing everything. All insurance savings were also lost. Some of our officials suggested that Japan ought to return the money people lost in banks, postal savings, and insurance, but nothing was done. Japan lost the war, after all, and they were broke.

I was in Taibei during that period, building and repairing houses. I had lost savings, but managed to make a living. Some people with tea and rice to sell did well.

All kinds of sharp dealings were going on in the late forties. Two private mainland banks with very large capitals began to offer high interest to their customers—a thousand a month interest on a ten thousand deposit, ten thousand on a hundred thousand, and so on. People, greedy to get the interest sold land, rice fields, and houses to put money in these banks. They thought they'd just sit and live on the interest without having to work. But the inflation had already begun. A sack of rice cost 100,000 Old Taiwan Dollars today and 150,000 tomorrow. Money was worth less and less. Then the banks broke, and people couldn't get even their capital back, let alone the promised interest. Public banks gave you a check for your money; private ones nothing. I had put over five million in a private bank, and lost it all. Where the bankers went with it, I never learned.

As I built and repaired houses, everything cost more each day. It was hard to figure how much to charge in order to make a profit. Today I paid a wage worker OT$500, tomorrow OT$700, the next day OT$800. I was sure that the government would solve the problem sooner or later, so I stopped working as a builder for six or seven months rather than lose money at it. Then Mr. Chen Cheng came, in 1949. He called in the Old Taiwan Dollar currency and issued New Taiwan Dollars at a rate of OT$40,000 to NT$1. The worst of the inflation lasted three or four years, but the currency became stable only by the mid-1950s.

When the Chinese came, there was a high rate of tenancy in Taiwan. Some landlords just sat and waited for the harvest, while their tenants had to struggle to survive. After paying rent to the landlords and tax to the government, they had nothing left for themselves.

Mr. Chen Cheng reformed the tenancy situation with the "three-seven-five" law under which landlords could receive no more than 37.5 percent of the harvest. Later, the government bought up tenanted land in excess of three *jia*[9] from landlords and sold it to the tenants. The landlords were

9. Three *jia* equal approximately 7.2 acres.

angry about the land reform, but what could they do about it? No one dared oppose the government after the events of 2:28. The reform was peaceful, and within ten years the government paid the landlords off, though at a price much below what the land was actually worth. So the landlords all lost out, despite what they were paid—a real reversal, since they formerly had been so greedy.

My fields in Xindian had long been cultivated by my relatives, so the government considered this family land, not tenancy, and left us alone. Even now, my nephews work that land and give me whatever share of the harvest they wish. I'm glad I kept the land rather than selling it to get capital for my business. It's been a small source of income, and I've been able to help my relatives make a living, too.

I've been in the construction business ever since the early fifties, and members of my family have always kept a shop. My wife managed that for years—it was her shop, really. After she died three years ago, my eldest daughter-in-law took over. She's away now, touring southeast Asia, so things are in a bit of a muddle.

Some years have been better than others in the building business. There's a lot of red tape in land transactions because the government doesn't want good agricultural land sold off at random any more for construction. Four men were tried and executed this summer for illegally rezoning land. In the sixties it was easier because the loss of agricultural land wasn't seen as such a problem then. The economy was really beginning to do well, too, and people needed houses. I built a lot then—employed dozens of laborers all the time, and earned enough to keep my family and educate my children. There were heavy expenses, too, though. Labor got dearer, the cost of cement went way up during the Vietnam war, because we were selling it to the Americans and South Vietnamese. A contractor has to give a lot of expensive banquets to keep building inspectors and officials who grant various licenses on good terms with him. So I never became rich.

By the time I reached my sixtieth birthday, in 1970, I decided to retire. My son was grown and capable, with a good job in a chemical company; my son-in-law had his own construction firm in Taizhong. I wanted to devote more time to studying our religion. I kept my hand in—I built this building just five years ago, on the site of our old house—but I slowed down.

Now I have time to observe life in a relaxed way. People come to see me, and sometimes I can help them by getting them a job, introducing them to someone, lending them a little money, giving some advice. The local people have elected me Neighborhood Head for many years now, and I have the responsibility of informing them of government and party directives, of holding citizens' meetings, and of making sure the neighborhood people keep their household registration records up to date.

When the central government of China left the mainland in 1949, they planned to establish a model province here. In recent years, this has begun to come true as life gradually becomes easier. At the beginning, though, we often regretted losing our place in the Japanese empire. Each nation has its fate, just like a person—sometimes good, sometimes bad. I have seen many changes in Taiwan during my lifetime. Education is more widespread but less effective now. People generally are less disciplined, both those above and those below. But some things have remained the same. Under the Japanese, we Taiwanese could form businesses as we liked, but we were not allowed to get into politics. Under the Chinese government, we have done very well in business, but we are still not very active in politics. We are free to do so now, but, for myself, I am too old. It is the young men's turn now.

[9]

Education, the Great Escape

While state power and the national economy affect indirectly even intimate family and community institutions in Taiwan, some institutions and patterns of life are very directly shaped by the forces "out in society." Education is one of the strongest of these forces, making itself felt in every family in Taiwan. Chinese people take education very seriously; it has for centuries offered an escape from poverty and manual work in a preindustrial society where nearly everyone but a tiny class of official academic degree-holders farmed or labored for a living.

Learning is a sign of wealth, ease and security, and in the past only those with these advantages could afford to be learned. Traditional education stressed literacy in a difficult written language, an understanding of early forms of Chinese (comparable to learning the English of Chaucer or Beowulf), and familiarity with a body of classical texts whose relevance to practical daily matters was extremely limited. The learned were expected to use these language skills creatively, writing poetry as a pastime or at least inscribing documents, calling cards, and gift messages with the graceful calligraphy that indicates self-cultivation.

These traditions were taught to boys in the last century mostly in private academies or by home tutors. The Japanese initiated more modern schooling that retained many traditional elements while also incorporating parts of the Western curriculum. Education was far from universal even for the elementary-school population for whom it was primarily intended, but it was, surprisingly, coeducational. By the twenties, when Mr. Kho and Mrs. Lim (this chapter) were beginning their schooling, Taiwanese children could train as schoolteachers, technicians, and doctors. To succeed meant competition in the Japanese language with more and generally better-trained Japanese children (see Tsurumi 1977). It is no wonder that many children, like Guo A Gui (Chapter 5), found their lessons too much trouble to pursue.

The Nationalists built on and expanded the Japanese system using retrained Taiwanese and Mandarin-speaking Mainlander refugees as teachers. Over the years, higher education based on Japanese beginnings and transplanted colleges from the mainland greatly increased the scope of occupational aspiration as well as Taiwan's industrial research capacity. In the fifties, the Nationalists pressured even skeptical rural folk to send all children to elementary school (Diamond 1969:77–79), apparently both because government officials shared the Chinese respect for learning, and because schooling seemed the most direct way to return the Japanized population to Chinese cultural orthodoxy and Nationalist sympathies. By 1970, demanding sixth-year exams that filtered many elementary graduates out of the system were abandoned so that many more children at least began junior high school. Substantial tuition fees for middle schools continued in force for another decade, and they are still required of senior high students, a factor that discourages many poorer families from maintaining their children in high school.

Very early in my first stay in Taiwan, I passed a large, grim building with barred windows, out of which peered the wistful faces of a group of adolescent boys. Their heads were shaved nearly bald, and they wore plain khaki uniforms with numbers on the pockets.

"A juvenile prison," I thought, "and what a big one!" When I reached the entrance to the building, however, I realized my mistake. It was a senior high school—and, as I later learned, one of the best on the island. I soon came to take for granted the military-looking adolescents—boys in khaki, girls in various baggy skirt and blouse combinations of dark green, navy, khaki, and white. Until the last year of senior high, girls wore their hair cut straight off from earlobe to earlobe, and held away from the face with plain bobby pins. Younger children in elementary school wore similar uniforms topped off with bright yellow caps, so they would be easier to spot in traffic.

These outfits—cheap, practical, and reminiscent of the military uniforms then ubiquitous in Taiwan, summed up an important attitude toward education. Learning is hard, important work, a child's job in the same sense that carrying bricks or making noodles may be an adult's job: serious and, in a sense, official business.

Education takes the child, at the age of seven or so (the schools use Western birthdays to calculate age for this purpose), "out into society" under the direct influence of the state. The state requires universal schooling so that the young will grow up as disciplined, literate, and skilled workers in society, and as citizens who have been well instructed in the Nationalists' ideals and goals, including defense of the island and eventual reconquest of the mainland. Schools are not seen primarily as places for children to explore their capacities or develop socially (although these things also happen), but as training grounds for hard-working and loyal adults. Girls and boys should not distract each other when they reach puberty, so the separate girls' and boys' junior and senior high schools enforce an intentionally ugly, plain style of dress and grooming. Physical toughening is part of the school regime, through exercise, military drills, and drafty, unheated classrooms. Girls and the younger boys, who wear shorts, especially complain of the cold after sitting still for hours on raw winter days.

The style of learning in these schools also emphasizes discipline. The complex forms of the written Chinese characters that all children must learn bear only a limited relationship to the way they are pronounced, so learning each character demands a separate act of rote memorization. Children learn about two thousand characters in the six years of elementary school, and another four or five thousand by the end of senior high. After that, the high school graduate only occasionally needs to check a dictionary to read a newspaper, though a student studying college subjects must acquire a large new specialist's vocabulary, just as American college students do. Little children, just beginning this task, are usually assigned to write and review characters dozens of times as part of an evening's homework. At the same time, they learn to proportion each character within the conventions that make Chinese script an art form as well as a means of communication. English is taught in middle schools, and many college textbooks must be read in that language, adding to the burden of study. Coaching by an educated mother with plenty of time to spare helps enormously in keeping young children up to the mark (Diamond 1973).

Other subjects, too, stress the memorization of facts and, in vocational schools, of such specialized skills as calculating on an abacus or operating a massive Chinese typewriter—with keyboards of hundreds of keys. Chinese history and literature are naturally stressed, as are mathematics and science.

In place of the United States-oriented social studies and civics lessons American teenagers receive, Taiwan's young people study Chinese history from the Nationalist point of view and the political writings of Sun Yat-sen, the "father of the nation," who became its first president in 1911. Every school day begins with bowing to Sun's portrait, which hangs at the front of all classrooms. In political-study class, current Nationalist party materials are also discussed, sometimes under the leadership of one of the party cadres assigned to maintain political orthodoxy in each school. These classes are important. If a child expresses unorthodox ideas on political subjects, the views and loyalty of her family may be investigated by the party or even the dreaded Garrison Command—the island's semisecret headquarters of martial law. Young people quickly learn to give the required responses on sensitive subjects, to show enough patriotism and to avoid conspicuousness. Some young people—in my experience, usually Mainlanders whose parents are strongly committed to the Nationalist government—are genuinely inspired by these sessions; most students find political study boring; children of convicted political criminals, I have heard, find them absolutely terrifying.

The discomfort, discipline, and hard work of education are not simply imposed by the state and accepted unwillingly by the students. Many Chinese schoolchildren take their "job" seriously and work hard, although the life histories also reveal many examples of children who found schooling too boring, too difficult, or too expensive to continue. Those who struggle to succeed at school do so because society, their families, and a long tradition of Chinese respect for education urge them on, but they also do it because their educational goals are clear and, for many, attainable. Education is the ladder of success, the path to riches, the great escape from manual work.

High-paying, high-status jobs in government and business require educational credentials from their applicants. Although graduating from college does not guarantee anyone such a job, not doing so dooms the attempt to rise to these positions. Entry into college is likely only for students who have climbed the educational ladder astutely, doing well at every level. A career as an engineer or business executive must begin almost in infancy.

Children take their first step toward success when they learn to speak. A child from Mandarin-speaking households and neighborhoods, growing up with the "national language," will enter the Mandarin-speaking school system more easily than one who speaks only Taiwanese. These days, assisted by many hours of Mandarin-language television programing, even Taiwanese children learn quickly in school from their Mandarin-speaking teachers. Until the mid-sixties, however, this was not so; Taiwanese, Hakka, and Aboriginal children began school with a pronounced language handicap. These days, education-conscious parents may decide to speak only Mandarin to their children, whatever their own first language is, while some even teach their children a little English, as well. This situation parallels perfectly the pattern of language use under the Japanese, when that language was required for academic success. As the following life history records, Mrs. Lim's unusual educational achievements owed much to her parent's coaching in Japanese, and she raised her own children to speak Mandarin as well as Taiwanese.

Families can also help their children do well scholastically by sending them to the best schools they can afford. Taibei has better schools than those in smaller cities, which in turn outperform rural ones. But even in Taibei, some elementary schools have higher academic traditions than others. An ambitious parent will reregister a child's residence with relatives who live in a good school district. This may mean a long commute on crowded buses, or the child may actually leave her rural home to live with urban relatives. Similar reshufflings may occur when the child moves up to junior high school; these, too, have differing standards.

At the end of junior high, students take exams that allocate them to variously ranked academic or vocational high schools. This is a critical sorting, for once tracked out of the relatively few schools that lead to college, it is nearly impossible to attain higher education. The few best girls' and boys' senior high schools in the major cities produce the majority of the students who are properly prepared to take the all-important college entrance examinations. Students may take these exams over again for several years if they fail, as Miss Ong's husband did. Based on their exam scores, high-school graduates are assigned to universities and to the academic areas they will study.

Young people take the college entrance exams for the main universities in an atmosphere of great solemnity and extreme anxiety. The candidates are sealed into the testing rooms with officially stamped strips of paper pasted across the doors, and great care is taken to prevent cheating or breaches of the anonymity under which the papers will be graded to ensure fairness. Families often escort their children to the examination and wait, anxiously burning incense and picnicking on the campus lawns, until they emerge from the ordeal. Weeks later, when exam results are posted, the campuses are jammed with young people searching the lists with carefully controlled faces.

For most people it is extremely difficult to get government permission to attend undergraduate school outside of Taiwan, and men cannot obtain it until they have completed military training. In the seventies and eighties, however, rich families have obtained citizenship either in the United States or in countries such as Costa Rica so they may send their children to American preparatory schools and universities—and so that they will have a refuge for themselves and their capital should Taiwan be taken over by the People's Republic.

For a very few students, beyond receiving a bachelor's degree from a Taiwan university lies graduate school at home or abroad. Many graduates come each year to American universities to pursue advanced degrees. Since this pattern began in the fifties, over 90 percent of Taiwan graduate students have remained in the United States as engineers, chemists, and other professionals. After becoming permanent residents, many Mainlanders bring over their parents and other relatives. Taiwanese, initially disadvantaged by language and subtle discrimination, were once less likely to go abroad for advanced study and less likely to remain there, but this has changed. Wealthy Taiwanese are now as anxious about the future of the island as Mainlanders, and they are nearly as willing to emigrate.

Most young Taiwanese, of course, do not get American Ph.D.'s and leave the island; indeed, only about 10 percent receive some higher education. Senior high graduation is still an important educational achievement, with many young people, especially girls, getting along with less. But the ladder from kindergarten to doctorate is well known as a clear-cut, honorable, highly prestigious road to security and comparative wealth. People often contrast the harsh physical conditions of manual labor, or the necessary but "crooked" trickiness of running one's own small business, with the apparent simplicity and dignity of moving from grade to grade in an academic and then a bureaucratic hierarchy. Except for some built-in handicaps for more rural Taiwanese, the educational process now operates with admirable fairness in Taiwan. Those who fail to go far in it can hope that hard work and innate talent will carry their children or younger siblings a little farther than they themselves were able to go.

Schooling in Taiwan also develops a strong sense of the value of membership in a group (Wilson 1970), a cultural pattern of great significance in Chinese society. Although children enter school with something of this sense from their experience of family life, the schools expand the students' identification by constantly reminding them of their responsibilities to their classmates, their school, their society, and their country—which includes mainland China. Practice starts with the smallest entity, the class, which elects a leader, undertakes projects, and is collectively rewarded or punished for the behavior of any of its members. Once, when I scolded some members of a college English-language class for their poor preparation, the class head came up to me, white and trembling, to apologize on behalf of the seventy-odd students and to ask what punishment I intended for the class. (He looked mightily relieved when I told him only to get the slackers to do their homework, which he did.)

The emphasis on group unity is an important element in Chinese society, but it contrasts sharply with the devil-take-the-hindmost attitude that Taiwan's economic life fosters, and that many working-class folk I know express. Chinese educators appear to believe that such group-consciousness has to be rigorously trained into children and that it is not, as Americans often assume, a cultural attribute that Chinese youngsters absorb automatically from their surroundings.

One question that is rarely asked of an educational system is, "What do people actually learn from it?" Schools in Taiwan strive not simply to impart literacy, numeracy, and technical information, but also to mold disciplined and group-oriented characters and to create a nationalistic world view. Although the success of this attempt would be very difficult to measure, it has a powerful effect. The Japanese educational system had much the same general influence (minus the sinocentrism) on an earlier generation as Nationalist education does at present.

People who have spent many years being taught an elite view of what it means culturally to be Chinese, who have learned to accept the discipline of a hierarchically structured school system, and who have taken to heart the Confucian moral values of filial piety and loyalty differ subtly from those with minimal formal education. People who have been working class all their lives—unlike Mrs. Lim and Mr. Kho—have not been as thoroughly instructed by the state in what their cultural identity should be. To me, they seem more open to new ideas (Taiwanese working-class entrepreneurial skill attests to this), more likely to break with custom to follow their own interests, and more unconstrained in their personal relationships than long-educated Chinese. Such openness, individualism, and unconstraint are precisely the characteristics that formal education aims to replace with conformity, group orientation, and tight emotional control. Unless education through high school or college becomes universal, which is unlikely to happen, we can expect a persistence of this difference in personal style between working-class people and Taiwan's elite.

Education has made upward social mobility a possibility in Chinese society for a very long time. For large numbers of people actually to achieve such mobility, however, requires that the economy expand, as it did slowly in the late Qing, rapidly under the Japanese, and explosively since the sixties. Taiwan's people have reason for their strong faith in education; as long as economic expansion continues, the faith in study that engenders sacrifices by parents like Mrs. Zhang, and hard work by children like Lim Fumiko, will be rewarded for a significant part of the population.

Lim Fumiko: Japanese Girl, Chinese Woman

Lim Fumiko is a Taiwanese woman in her mid-fifties who remembers the Japanese period vividly, and still quietly mourns its passing. Under the

[211]

Japanese, Mrs. Lim was one of the rare, well-educated Taiwanese women—
a graduate of a normal school and a schoolteacher herself. The strong code
of submissiveness expected of Japanized women reinforced Chinese ideals
so strongly that, after graduation, she meekly married her adopted brother
and remained as a filial adopted daughter-in-law in the Lim family. Her
experience as a *simpua* (adopted daughter-in-law) is highly atypical, however. The Lims treated her well, and she retained strong ties to her birth
parents until their deaths. Unlike the marriages of many simpua, hers has
been a fairly successful one, resulting in a large family of sons and daughters—none of whom was given away in adoption. Mrs. Lim now keeps a
small shop and offers us a typical example of the movement of the Japanized
Taiwan intelligentsia into small business enterprises after the Nationalist
takeover. Such people continue to flavor working-class Taiwanese life with
deep respect and admiration for Japan's culture and achievements, and with
a sense of having lost membership in a progressive and respected nation
only by historical accident.

Mrs. Lim, surely a beauty in her youth, is still beautiful, still graceful,
slender, and unlined. In a street where many women her age are plump
and careless about daily dress, Mrs. Lim's appearance is all disciplined
femininity. Her taste, formed in more prosperous circumstances, is out of
keeping with that of her neighbors, though there are richer Taiwanese
neighborhoods where her Japanese-adapted Western style is the usual
mode. Her way with the give-and-take of verbal etiquette is refined as well,
the constant small courtesies of Chinese social relations flowing easily and
naturally—delicately flattering to her listener and subtly displaying her
skills in politesse.

Her high standards leave their mark, however, only on her own person.
Her husband and children have no trace of Mrs. Lim's nicety. They dress,
speak, and live like their neighbors: not badly, but with no grace. The
difficulty of the struggle for cleanliness and order showed especially in their
former house, where nearly forty people (and a shop!) shared less than 250
square meters of space, three taps of cold water, and a constant in-draft of
diesel smoke from the eight-lane highway on its doorstep. The rebuilt
house the family has occupied since 1980 suits her better, carrying some
imprint of her tasteful choices.

She sat with me to reminisce about her life in her house-front shop where
she helps run a fruit-and-ice parlor. Such shops are common in Taibei City,
selling chilled slices and chunks of semitropical Taiwan's luscious fruits—
pineapple, mango, watermelon, and papaya—drinks made of pureed fruit,
sugar, milk and ice, and dishes of shaved ice topped with sweet bean sauce.
In the short but raw winters when these cooling dishes are thought un-

healthy, Mrs. Lim sells hot sweet bean and millet soups instead. Her clientele consists mostly of undergraduates from the nearby university and uniformed middle school students who drop in between legs of their bus journeys home—impersonal spenders of small sums who require little attention or service beyond the preparation and dishing out of the desired treat. Mrs. Lim can tend the customers and still give most of her attention to visitors, her husband, and her children, or to the large color television set on the wall.

As the family uses the shop for its living room, there is usually a Lim son or daughter about, watching a program, giving a hand at busy times or just loafing. Except on very hot nights, there is little business in the later evenings, so the Lims have the room to themselves at the end of the day. Up and down the street, all over the city, indeed, throughout the island, half the people live in households in which some of the family's income comes from work done in their homes, and the separation between "work" and "home life" that most Americans take for granted never emerges.

Mrs. Lim is a good neighbor, meticulously responding to the births and deaths of nearby acquaintances with small but appropriate gifts of money in red envelopes for happy events, or in white ones for bereavements. She has not sought out friendships among them, however, for, disliking gossip, she has always preferred to mind her own affairs. As the oldest neighboring families slowly move away from the street, she makes less effort to keep track of the other households' doings.

A wish to get on with and to be thought well of by their more established neighbors used to oblige the Lims to participate in three community religious festivals each year. Each household contributes money for opera performances and protective rituals and invites dozens of guests to dinner. Mingling with the crowds of soon-tipsy guests, gorging on the lavish feasts, and following the noisy, colorful operas used to be nearly the only entertainments for the people of this frugal, hard-working community—before television.

Mrs. Lim has never really approved of these celebrations. They cost too much and, she privately believes, are based on mere superstition. She is an educated woman, not interested in the gods, ghosts, and spirit mediums of popular Taiwanese religion. But because everyone expected it, and her mother-in-law insisted, Mrs. Lim shopped and cooked and served and cleaned up every year for forty or fifty eager revelers—a modest number, but respectable. Now, with her mother-in-law too ill to supervise her, she no longer does so. The family contributes money for the public festivities, has an especially good meal for themselves and their married-out daughters in honor of the occasion, and lets it go at that.

[213]

By contrast, she tends to the ancestral tablets of ascending generations of Lims diligently, the scent of her daily incense to them curling up the stairs, alerting the whole house that her dinner is prepared and her filiality is perfect. The handsome, heavy altar table of carved black wood on which the tablets stand is the focal point of the neat new formal living room upstairs, as it was in the old house. When Mother-in-Law Lim joins those ancestors after death, she too will be remembered by her filial daughter-in-law through the prayers and offerings that memorialize the unrepayable debt of having received life, or at least the property to maintain it, from one's seniors. Even someone who disbelieves in spirits, as Mrs. Lim probably does, honors such a debt, which has nothing necessarily to do with the supernatural.

In a way that derives from her heavily Japanized girlhood as much as from Chinese ideals for women, Mrs. Lim has lived a life of dependent service to others. Now, in her mature years when most Taiwanese women have fought for and won control of their homes, she still looks about for guidance in managing her family. That she takes charge as much as she does seems due more to her husband's timid incompetence and her mother-in-law's recent senescence than to any taste for power. Uninterested in pilgrimages, too old for her impossible girlhood dreams, she is satisfied, though not content, with her own hearth.

I was born on Eternal Spring Street in 1925, in a family of four sisters but no brothers, and was adopted into the Lim family as a baby. Both my birth family and the Lim family took care of me as I grew up. My mother's family, surnamed Ong, had prospered with a comfortable big house in Eternal Spring Street, and nine more which they rented out. My grandparents didn't have any children, so they adopted my birth mother and father, who married after they grew up. My Ong grandparents could afford to give both my parents a good Japanese education, permitting them to study beyond high school in a teachers' training school. After graduation, my parents taught in primary school.

At that time, when Japan governed Taiwan, richer people were very interested in getting a Japanese education and in Japanese ways. My father even visited Japan once, with his high-school class, although Mother never went. So our family's customs were a mixture of Taiwanese and Japanese ones. Our house was Chinese, as was the furniture in most rooms, but our bedrooms were like Japanese ones, with tatami mats and quilts to sleep on, not bedsteads. We still sleep this way in our family, as it suits the hot climate better. Japanese household arrangements are very clean. My parents wore Japanese clothes to work, though they didn't wear them the rest of the time. I used to wear kimono at New Year. We ate Chinese food, but my father learned to eat raw fish, *sashimi*, in the Japanese way as a delicacy. We never had it at home and I have never learned to like it.

In my parents' household, and later in my adoptive family, we venerated the ancestors much as we do now. Grandmother made food offerings on the first and fifteenth day of the lunar month, celebrated ancestors' death days with special foods, and put out tea and incense on ordinary days. There are some other special days during the year when ancestors are particularly remembered, too. In addition, by order of the Japanese government, we worshipped the founding god of Japan. This was just a piece of wood with the god's name on it which every household had to have. The Japanese used to have sanitary inspections of all houses, so they could check on things like that. We burned it[1] after Retrocession.

My school naturally had only Japanese holidays. Before Retrocession, Father and Mother used to read Japanese newspapers; there weren't any Chinese ones. At home and at school we spoke only Japanese. I had close relations with Japanese fellow students and later spoke Japanese with my colleagues at work, so it was my mother tongue. I learned Taiwanese too, of course, from my surroundings, but I didn't begin to learn the Chinese national language until after Retrocession. My adoptive family, the Lims, were not as Japanese-influenced. They spoke Taiwanese at home, and the old people didn't wear Japanese clothes.

Father stopped teaching and went to the mainland, to Hangzhou City, for a while, where he went into business trying to make his fortune, when I was thirteen. He came back because of bad health. He went to the Taiwan University Hospital to recover, then went back to Hangzhou when I was sixteen. He never came back and probably died there. Mother retired from teaching at fifty.

As Mother had to work, my two elder sisters were brought up by wet-nurses till they were six or seven years old. Grandmother said, "If anybody wants these two, then we'll give them away," because they were always crying. Mother couldn't spare the time to take care of me, and heard from my relatives that some old lady wanted a girl. I was brought to her when I was fifty days old. My adoptive father and mother had had seven daughters, several of whom were adopted out. She finally adopted a three-year-old boy to care for her and her husband in their old age. I was adopted to be his wife, so I am an "adopted daughter-in-law." My father-in-law mined coal, going to the mine twice a day and delivering it to the professors at National Taiwan University, down the road. It was a hard job, but the money wasn't bad. Though he had seven daughters, there were no sons to help him.

My husband was one of four sons born to a family, related to mine, that

---

1. A respectful way of disposing of ritual objects.

lives across the river. His father died of a very expensive illness when he was a baby, and all his money was spent for hospital bills. Because they needed money and had many sons, his family allowed my husband to be adopted when he was about three years old. He was adopted about the same time I was and is three or four years older than I am. His life in this family has been different from mine. The old lady breast-fed me just like her own daughter, but because of his age she didn't nurse him, so he was never as dear to her as I have been. Nevertheless, he is still very filial to his adopted mother, very nice to her. The old lady has lived here for eighty years; she was adopted, too.

Both families liked me very much. Over here, in my adopted family, they gave me lots of pocket money, gave me lots of good things to eat, and didn't make me do any housework. They treated me even better than their own daughters because they wanted me to stay to serve them. I really had a comfortable childhood; in my mother's family, I was treated like a guest. If I wanted money, they gave it to me. It was really nice at Mother's. I got along very well with my classmates, and teachers, too. I was happy when I was young. My adopted sisters didn't treat me badly. The eldest two stayed in the family, but the others were all given away while they were small.

We had no toys, although we played cards during the New Year. Mother was strict about our studying, insisting we really use all our energy for it, as otherwise we'd never pass the exams. We wanted to play, but she wouldn't let us. In those days, there was a little stream (which is now covered by buildings) where we would go to play and to pick fruit. The university has built over that now. We went to the Xindian River sometimes, too, to play hide-and-seek. Once, just after entering first grade, I came home almost an hour late because I was playing. So they beat me. After being beaten once, I knew it was not a good idea to worry people.

Because the distance to a good school from Mother's house was shorter, I lived there during my elementary education and went to my mother-in-law's on Saturdays and Sundays. After sixth grade, Mother suggested that I go further in school, but my mother-in-law disagreed; her own daughters had not gone to middle school. Her eldest daughter's husband and my mother pointed out I always did well in school, so they let me try. If I couldn't pass the exam, then I wouldn't go on. My teachers really helped me, and Mother coached me too. The examination was harder than university entrance examinations are these days, and the quota for us Taiwanese was small.

Taipei only had three upper-level schools. The first and second were for Japanese, and in our school, only half were Taiwanese. Students from the whole province tried to get into that school. I *really* worked, and I passed the entrance exam. The old lady paid my tuition, and my mother's family paid the rest of the school expenses. While I was in school, I continued to live in my mother's family.

We were forbidden to speak Taiwanese in school. We read Japanese, and that's what the teacher spoke. Even at the beginning, we couldn't use Taiwanese in school; the teachers weren't Taiwanese and didn't speak Taiwanese. It wasn't a case of speaking a little Taiwanese together with a little Japanese. From the beginning, we just slowly learned, and in a few months we could understand, and finally we were able to use it. Although I hadn't been to kindergarten, my mother's family all spoke Japanese, and so I learned quicker than most.

There were sixty students in class, and later about seventy. We went to school at 7:30 in the morning, finished at 4:00 in the afternoon. The fifth and sixth grades had to stay after class to prepare for the examinations. The school had to turn the lights on in the classroom so we could see in the evenings. We went home at dinnertime. This was a four-year girls' middle school—there was no division between junior and senior middle school then.

Because I only studied at that time, I wasn't very good at housework. Mother-in-law was good to me, and didn't give me any to do. Her daughters did it. She just wanted me to study hard.

After four years of middle school, I was graduated at eighteen. I didn't marry immediately but went to normal school for half a year. I had a classmate who wanted to teach, so the two of us went to study at normal school. It wasn't necessary to take an exam—if you'd graduated from middle school, you could enter. I then took a qualification examination to be an elementary-school teacher. I went to Jingmei elementary school to teach because the principal there was my mother's former colleague, and stayed for six years. I liked teaching because I like children—I'm good with them. Some teachers seem to like to get angry and hit children, but I don't. I was very popular in that school.

At that time, my beginning salary was thirty-eight yen, enough to support one person. It wouldn't be enough to support a wife on, but most teachers were female, because of the war. The men went as soldiers, leaving only a few older men teachers, and the rest, women.

Taiwan was returned to China when I was twenty. Because I couldn't speak Mandarin, I thought I would have to retire. However, the principal said we should study Mandarin as the students were doing, so we started. The school got teachers and we went to night school to learn the national Chinese language. At the same time, we kept on teaching. They said we could teach if we learned the national language. I wasn't afraid of losing my job, because nobody spoke the national language, and it would have been impossible to fire all of us. The whole island was Taiwanese, and nobody could speak the national language. I became quite fluent in it. If my daughter had not become seriously ill when she was about two, so that I had to quit work to take care of her, I might have worked right on till retirement.

Schools didn't stop because of Retrocession, and the men who had gone to war came back to teach again. There wasn't much change in my school at that time. However school became disorderly because of too much freedom; students didn't show as much respect to teachers as they had. After Retrocession, people talked rather wildly about freedom, for some believed that we would now govern ourselves. School became much less orderly, as students rebelled against the strict Japanese ways. Students didn't have any formal meetings to discuss the new change; they just talked among themselves. This went on for over a year, then it slowly settled down. I still have this feeling that present-day students think that teaching is just like any other occupation. To be a teacher was a very special responsibility then.

Our Japanese teachers had to go back to Japan, and that was sad. I remember the day when the principal heard on the radio that Japan had surrendered. He burst out crying. He felt terrible for a month. I had had a Japanese education, so I didn't know what to do; I was as sad as the Japanese. Gradually, anyway, I came to feel that everyone is Chinese, and now, everything is better than in the Japanese period.

Right after Japanese rule ceased, we were still paid—that didn't stop— and my salary was much higher than others' because I had passed the qualification examination. At that time, many teachers' salaries were very low.

In general, at that time Taiwan's economy was not at all good. The value of money saved in banks during the Japanese period dwindled to nothing. My husband and I didn't have any bank savings, because we had just begun to work. But I had been buying insurance during the Japanese period. At school, every month you had to buy some. It wasn't much, but we lost it. Mother-in-law lost a great deal, however. She had money in the bank, but didn't buy houses or land or trade with it, she just saved it. After a while, with the continuing inflation, the money was useless.

At that time many goods, such as medicine, were unavailable. My eldest daughter's serious illness required so much money that in one week I spent three months' pay on medicine. Penicillin was expensive but she needed it. Thanks to my husband's business, we got through it. What we spent on her could have bought three houses, so she is now very filial, and gives me big red envelopes at New Year.

I was married when I was nearly twenty years old, on December 28, 1944, and had my first daughter when I was nearly twenty-two. After one month, my husband went into the Imperial Japanese Army. He served about a year, always on this island, stationed on the east coast and several other places, but he never had to fight. He came home in 1946. If it had not been the end of the war, he would have been sent abroad. That was a terrible time. When my husband came home, he had no job, so he went to work with his brother who lived with their real mother in Jilong Harbor. I had already left my job, so I went with him. During the six or seven years we lived there, I didn't work, only took care of the children, and began to learn cooking and housework.

My husband was an accounting clerk at Jilong Harbor. For a while this wasn't a bad job. The pay was good, and people made extra money smuggling in foreign goods. But when the place he worked became part of the official harbor affairs organization, the pay and other opportunities became much less.

We began to think of moving because of the low salary but also because we were getting very tired of living in Jilong. The weather there is simply terrible: it rains constantly, and the wind blows. Because of this my bones hurt, I was always cold, and I wanted to go back to Taibei. At first we lived by ourselves over by the university, but when Father-in-law died and Mother-in-law began to fail in 1966, we moved in here with her.

It wasn't easy for my husband to find a job, however. It was around 1951, when conditions were just dreadful. My husband was educated in a private high school, but his education was not the best. He has poor health, so he can't do heavy work, and he has no head for business. He was best at office work. All he could get then was a clerical job in an iron factory where he was introduced by my sister's husband. He worked there until about ten years ago, then changed to his present job.

He works now in the packing department of an export clothing factory in the town across the river from where he was born. He's not an office worker anymore, just a manual worker. He earns NT$10,000 (U.S.$250) each month, more if there is overtime. He also gets one month's pay as a bonus at New Year. There are no fringe benefits, really. His labor insurance only covers himself, so our family must pay everything for our medical expenses. Taiwan's prosperity hasn't done much for my family.

You can see that with our large family, it hasn't been easy. In recent years, living with Mother-in-law, with the children nearly all grown, you'd think it would get better. My mother-in-law is rich, but she's also very close with her money. And right now, for example, none of the grown children still at home has a full-time job! It has often been very difficult to manage with all our children. A few years ago, when Taiwan's economy turned bad again for a while, we really suffered. Only my husband had work, so I was forced to take on the job of caring for a one-year-old girl whose mother worked in a bank. She paid me NT$1,000 (U.S.$25) each month. Lulu came to us Monday morning and stayed till noon on Saturday. She was very cute, but just at the worst age. She wanted to walk, but a baby that age can pull down a gas burner, or fall into the toilet, or have some other accident. The old house was so dirty and the traffic so near the door that I never dared to put her down. I had to carry her on my back all the time as I did the housework for this large family. I was always tired that year.

We have eight children. At first, I had four daughters in succession, and finally two boys. I decided to have an operation so I would stop having children, but my mother-in-law refused to allow this. She thought my health was too poor to stand an operation, so I had two more daughters. Eight altogether. Having so many children has not been good for their education or my health. I've had bad luck. Formerly, women had to have *so* many children. I agree with today's family-planning policy; two are just enough. I wanted to abort my eighth child, but the doctor refused because the operation was dangerous. Since I already had seven, another wouldn't make much difference, he thought. I didn't have the strength to push out the eighth baby. It took several hours. I was thirty-nine then so I decided not to give birth anymore. My husband began to sleep in one bedroom with the boys and I slept in another with my two younger girls.

My eldest daughter is the one who's caused us the most difficulty, even though she's really a good girl, always helping me. When she was nineteen, she liked to dance, and she met a young man at a party. They decided they wanted to marry. Well, there were problems. For one thing, the young man was a Mainlander whom we didn't know. The old lady naturally preferred her to marry someone more familiar. But—and this is much worse—our family had already planned a marriage for her, which my daughter had never objected to.

The man we wanted her to marry is our Mr. Su, who lives with us and manages the fruit-and-ice shop. Mr. Su has a bad fate, surely. He was a soldier from north China who came here in 1949 with the government forces, but he was demobilized after a few years because his health was so poor. He says he nearly died from years of bad army food and from getting almost no food after the army came to Taiwan. When they demobilized him, they just turned him loose with not enough to live on, and no job. He was living in a little room across the street twenty years ago when we got to know him. He rented a room in our house and began to eat meals with us. He was a taxi driver then. At one time, when my husband was earning only a few hundred New Taiwan dollars a month, we still gave it all to Mother-in-law, who gave us NT$30 (U.S.$0.75) a day for food. It was impossible to feed the family on that. Mr. Su gave us NT$40 (U.S.$1) a day to eat with us, so we can say that he helped to rear our children. I told the children to be nice to him, and he seemed more and more like one of the family.

He had never been married and naturally wanted to have his own family. He asked us about our daughter when she was still quite young. They seemed to get along well, and we knew he had a good character, so we began to treat him as a kind of son-in-law. He opened an electrical appliance repair shop in our house. My mother-in-law was very pleased that my daughter would be marrying him so she could remain at home and help in the business.

Then my daughter met her future husband. She argued that Mr. Su was too old for her—fifteen years older. Besides, she wanted the other one. The old lady was very angry, refusing to do anything for them. So they went to court and got married in a civil ceremony and now Mother-in-law won't let my daughter in the house. It's been five or six years, and she still won't have her back. She's very stubborn.

The old lady took her anger out on me. Though she had always been so good to me, she now scolds me constantly. I was wretched when this all happened and cried a great deal. This was the biggest conflict between the generations that we have had.

I was disappointed at my daughter's decision, but I decided not to interfere. I remember so well the day I was to be married. Suddenly, I felt I just could not go through with it. I wanted to die. My husband and I have never been close. My sisters came to persuade me that it was my duty to marry him. Everything was arranged by all of our relatives; it would be very improper for me to oppose their will. I married, but could never force my daughter to marry against her wishes. Both my older daughters have chosen husbands for themselves.

That marriage turned out well. My daughter's parents-in-law and husband are good to her. Her father-in-law is a general who works in a government bureau, her mother-in-law used to be a teacher, like me. Though her husband had been a bit of a playboy who liked to drink and dance, after they married, he went to university. He became a good man and a good husband for her. Her parents-in-law have said to me, "We didn't bring our son up properly; now your daughter is doing it for us." It's my daughter's good destiny.

I really pity Mr. Su, though. He can't bear to be near my daughter now because he loved her deeply. It is very sad for these old soldiers with no family and friends to help them. He should keep trying to get a wife.

[221]

Though he has been introduced to some prospects, they've all turned him down. He sometimes talks of going back to the mainland to look for his brothers. They were educated people; one of his brothers became a university professor. There's no political motive, he just wanted to find his family. But my daughter warned him, "If you go, you won't be able to get back." He still lives with us, running the fruit-and-ice store, and helped a great deal when we were having the house rebuilt last year.

Our second daughter married years ago and has two children. I don't worry about her. The boys, now twenty-one and twenty-two, were not good students, never wanting to study. Each of them has done his two years of military service in the army, but neither has a job yet. The older may be working in a munitions factory soon. Though that is not much of a job, it may be the best he can do for the present. My husband's brother just last night suggested that if we think the younger boy can learn to make bread, he can find someone whom we can hire to teach him how to bake. It's not a bad idea, selling bread from our new shop. He is willing to learn. It's hard work, so it will have to be up to him. I have never pushed and forced my children to do things.

My third and fourth daughters weren't good students, but they are very dutiful. They have had different jobs since graduation from senior high school, always part-time office work that pays each of them only five or six thousand a month. They are very shy girls, so they still are not thinking of marriage, although they are in their late twenties. I worry about that. They should marry and get established before the boys marry. Already, we have found a young woman who works at my husband's factory who might suit our oldest son well. We'll have to wait and see about that. When the boys are earning money and our business is prosperous—that will be time enough.

Of all my relatives, I have the greatest obligation to my adopted mother-in-law. Her daughters have all moved away. My husband's original family has his brother to rely on, and my mother died a few years ago. So old Mrs. Lim needs me most. She raised me so that I would take care of her when she became old. Now she's bedridden, and often can't understand anything, but my husband and I try to take care of her, to cherish her.

My mother-in-law has never had good luck or good judgment with money. In the early 1960s she bought some land, and it was taken by the government to build a sports field for the university. There was compensation, but not what the land was worth. We didn't get into the trouble of land reform as did people who owned substantial land; we only own this house, while another is in her daughter's name. In recent years, the old lady put all her money out at interest, some in rotating credit associations, but mostly to individuals for interest. She has had some big losses—a couple of people just absconded. We lost enough to buy another house like this one.

The Lims have lived in a house on this spot for five generations. This little neighborhood, Prosperity Settlement, was always a small commercial district, not a farming village. The houses were built of brick along the road, as they are now, as long as I have known the place. The Japanese built a railroad right behind our house in the 1920s, but it was taken out and the main motor road that runs past the front of the house was widened and concrete-surfaced after the Nationalist government came here. It was named Roosevelt Road then, to honor the American president who helped Taiwan to reconstruct after the war. We lost a small amount of land at the front of our house when the road was widened, and had to rebuild the front part of the house. Roosevelt Road was widened again in 1971, but it didn't affect our house, except to make this a busier commercial district. It's been good for business.

To make up for what we lost in the front, we extended our house backward over the old railroad bed. That was not exactly legal because the land is the government's. But there has never been any trouble about it. Every house in the Prosperity Settlement did the same thing. We also raised the house higher, so that we had three stories. The upper floors were rented out—two families to each floor, each with two rooms, sharing kitchen and bathroom. We put running water up to each floor so it was very convenient, even though when a downstairs family was using the water, the upstairs family didn't get any.

My mother-in-law earned quite a bit of money from the rentals, which we needed, but we also began to feel very crowded. Behind the appliance shop was the bedroom that my husband shared with our sons, then one for me and my middle two daughters. Mother-in-law slept in a small room out behind the kitchen. Sometimes the two little girls slept with her, sometimes with Mr. Su upstairs. The rooms are not large, and when the girls began to have more clothes, we felt very cramped. Sometimes our tenants were not very clean or had fights in their families. There were always more than thirty people in this house.

Three years ago, we decided to rebuild the house completely. It was a good time to do it because the Taibei City government was altering Roosevelt Road again to build a bridge across the river. Although the changes would not affect us directly, the value of the property would increase a lot, and so would the taxes. The rents we got were not enough, we thought. Also, many of our neighbors would be directly affected by the road widening and started to tear down their small old brick houses to replace them with modern four- and five-story ones. We thought it would look bad if we did not do the same. My mother-in-law approved, because she thought we could earn a lot of money from rents.

It is easy to get building work done in Prosperity Settlement, where many men are construction workers. They know the trustworthy contractors, and we cooperated with our neighbors in a unified design. It was a mess for a while, but we are very satisfied with the house now. Mr. Su's and my fruit-and-ice shop and our kitchen are downstairs, along with one bedroom for Mother-in-law. The rest of us have larger bedrooms on the second floor, and the bathrooms are modern ones with Japanese-style flush toilets.[2] It's much cleaner. We rent out the third floor for four thousand and hope to rent the fourth very quickly. The whole thing cost NT$180,000 (U.S.$4,500), of which we had to borrow NT$80,000 (U.S.$2,000) through a rotating credit club.

Recently, I've been thinking about the Japanese times again, because I saw two Japanese films at the Golden Horse Film Festival last week. It was the first time I'd seen Japanese life in many years, and I felt very strange. When I was a child, I didn't like to go to movies because the theaters were crowded and smelly. But now Japanese movies seem more artistic and moving than Chinese ones. Most present-day Chinese films are just made to make money, so I rarely go. I used to go to see Japanese ones, which were shown up to about fifteen years ago. Then they were banned, so I hadn't seen one until this foreign film festival. My older son stood in line for about five hours to get me the tickets! They were very popular.

My whole early life was lived in the Japanese period, which is why I thought of myself as Japanese and never considered that I was Chinese. At Retrocession, my feelings were strange, I was puzzled. What would things be like? What were we going to *be?* The principal of the school I worked in cried for a whole month and didn't speak to anyone during that time. Later, we became Chinese gradually, and now I feel it's good to be a Taiwanese, though the Japanese did not treat us badly.

Because I get together with my old classmates twice a year for reunion dinners, I still can speak Japanese quite well. Consequently, some of the neighbors have asked me to teach a class to their daughters. Because there are many Japanese tourists and businessmen in Taipei, many girls would like to learn Japanese to help them get a job. But I have many responsibilities at home, so I can't go out to work. It is a long time since I was a teacher. I'm too old to start something new.

2. "Squat" toilets, with the bowl set into the floor.

Postscript, 1985

When I dropped in on them unexpectedly on the last day of 1985 during a brief visit to Taiwan, the Lims hospitably insisted I stay for dinner. During the delicious Taiwan-style hotpot meal, I caught up on family news that our infrequent correspondence had only incompletely described.

Mother-in-law Lim died three years ago, and Lim Fumiko herself has become a mother-in-law to her older son's wife. The son, his wife, and little boy live upstairs, as do the Lims' third and fourth daughters, now married. Number Four, A Bi, has a three-year-old daughter with all her mother's charm but none of her shyness. Number Three, A Gu, is as silent as ever, but glows like a camellia with her first pregnancy. Daughter Number Eight studies hard at college, hoping to go to the United States for graduate school. The other son and daughter work full-time, looking forward to marriage.

The house is full of family, but there are renters, too. Mr. Su, who now corresponds, cautiously, with his professor brother on the mainland, shares a room with an Aborigine boy who needs to live in town to attend high school. The Lims patronize this ethnic outsider a little, but kindly, as they treated me when I too was a cultural alien in their home.

Mrs. Lim has aged with the strain of caring for her adopted mother in her last years of illness. Always demanding, she became nearly unbearably fractious toward the end. The struggle to keep the old lady clean, to tempt her appetite, and to massage aching old bones into comfort shows on her face; lovely Lim Fumiko is now an old lady herself.

But her ideas have not changed, as I gathered from hearing her daughters discuss the shop's business. Mrs. Lim and Mr. Su have expanded into simple noodle dishes and other fast-food take-out meals. Although there are plenty of customers, the daughters complain, the shop doesn't earn much because Mrs. Lim insists on the same high standards of raw materials and preparation for these cheap meals as she does for her own family.

"I couldn't cheat people by giving them bad food!" says Lim Fumiko.

"How will we ever get ahead that way! Business is business!" says A Bi.

But this disagreement, like A Gu's momentary grumpiness toward her sister over the baby's plasticine mess on the table top, is not disagreeable. Theirs is a loving home, where a strong sense of duty helps keep people doing right by each other when affection fails, as it sometimes must. Mrs. Lim's principles, drawn from the best of her Chinese and Japanese heritages, live on in her filial children, giving them both a strong family bond and a sense of decency and kindliness that reaches beyond the kinship circle.

[10]

Conclusions

The Chinese urban working-class people whose voices we have heard here are not extraordinary. They represent fairly well most of Taiwan's nonfarm population, unlike the much smaller educated elite that Americans usually meet through diplomatic, journalistic, business, and academic contacts. They are not especially poor or burdened with troubles, compared with people in many countries. Taiwan, after all, has few beggars, no one dies of malnutrition, and unlike many of their seniors, most young folks today can reasonably expect both work and family life as assured elements of their futures.

But, for every prospering small-business family whose sons and daughters attend college and whose thriving shops and factories line the main streets, there are dozens of households whose economic and educational struggles are less well rewarded living in the back alleys. For every Taibei family with access to a large job market, good schools for the next generation, and some of the amenities of urban life, there are several who inhabit such grubby and discouraging cities as Gaoxiong, Sancheng, and Jilong, or rural backwaters like the place Stevan Harrell calls "Mountainside" (1982), where the roads are so bad that a refrigerator cannot be delivered, and people must leave permanently to find work. And then, there are the Aborigines.

Our subjects and their families represent "average people" as much as a few dozen people *can* represent millions. It is people like these who teach us what economic expansion means and does not mean, when it is not accompanied by a political commitment to equality.

Taiwan's working class comprises about three-quarters of its population if we include owners of small businesses and farms and the aging, low-ranked veterans of Jiang's mainland armies along with farm and other manual laborers, service workers, and those who hire out to big industries. Different historical experiences and regional loyalties divide the older people of this class into Taiwanese and Mainlander ethnic groups; in some parts of the island, Hakka and Aborigine ethnic identities also remain strong. Taiwanese rather than Mainlander culture dominates the working class, although the views of the heavily Mainlander elite are stronger in the schools, in the media, and in the world of officials.

Social power is now more evenly divided between Taiwanese and Mainlander than it was in the forties, fifties, and sixties as Taiwanese numbers and success in business balance Mainlander domination of the political and economic center. One result of this shift is the clearer emergence of class as a factor in the workings of the socioeconomic system. Being a Mainlander, if one is working class, is hardly a striking advantage to Mr. Kang, as compared with earlier times when Miss Guo and Mrs. Lo were grateful simply for the regular food a soldier-husband could provide. While rich Taiwanese and Mainlanders entertain each other at expensive business dinners, poor ones, along with Aborigines, marry, share kitchens with other renters, and gingerly make friends despite those among their relatives who still despise the "others." Working-class children of mixed marriages draw away from these distinctions, from which they can gain little advantage. The government, too, seems to have learned that under current conditions, it gains less and loses more by fostering ethnic divisions. If its representatives could learn also to accept regional cultures as valuable rather than substandard versions of Chineseness, the ethnicity issue would fade further still.

Working-class culture in Taiwan is reproduced more and more from the workings of present rather than past realities—realities that include an economy that demands both reasonably skilled and reasonably inexpensive labor to maintain its world trade. These realities also include a living heritage of skill in small-business practice, which inexpensively meets many of the island's consumer and export requirements, a complex but flexible kinship system that socializes women and the young to accept discipline and firm social control, and a folk religious tradition that teaches both submission to authority and the value of household integration into relatively egalitarian and self-reliant communities.

These influences shape relations between women and men, young and old in the working class so that farms and small businesses provide a steady stream of young, cheap workers who add value to export products for a few years before typically moving into small businesses of their own. There is no real division between Taiwan's industrious small-business people and its industrial workers, for by and large, the latter are the children of the former, temporarily earning cash for family expansion.

The preservation of working-class culture requires the continuation of patterns of kinship behavior and belief, of community stability, and of informal education in work and business practices that have evolved over the long period of capitalist development of this frontier island. Some of these patterns, such as the strong control of parents over their children, have lessened in this century, particularly in the families of poor Mainlanders who own no property on which sons might found a future. As long as Americans buy Taiwan's shirts and shoes and silicon chips, however, even these young folks may find a way to purchase a truck to start a transport business, to take over their parents' dumpling restaurant, or to use a powerful fellow-provincial contact to enter the export-import market. Informal sources of capital, business expertise, and contacts abound for those who know how to use them. A Mainlander lad who speaks Taiwanese well and practices the common etiquette of giving and receiving gifts, favors, and banquets that solidifies friendships will find as much success, I believe, as a Taiwanese.

The educational system imposed and controlled by those whom the working class cannot easily influence remains a safety valve for the strong pressures for a better life that motivate young and old alike. By preserving the integrity of the education and examination processes, the government encourages young people to learn what it chooses for them, or, should they fail in schooling, to transfer their hopes of rising from the working class to the next generation. In addition to its other functions, the educational system thus reinforces the old ideal of family continuity.

Influences from outside the island, too, are part of the realities of everyday life. Their immediacy is obscured by the lack of free access to information that the tightly controlled schools and press ensure; world politics and intellectual currents arrive in carefully filtered versions. The working class still remembers the Japanese, either as friends or as enemies. But, except for prostitutes and others in the tourist business, its members rarely encounter the thick network of relationships that tie the Taiwanese elite to Japan's corporate world. American culture makes fewer inroads here than many might suppose—even rock music is not really popular—and it was rare for me to meet a working-class Chinese, unless a servant, who had ever conversed with an American. Except for American movies and a vague sense of the "Communist menace" from the mainland, only the way economic trends affect business draws much Taiwanese comment on the rest of the world.

In many ways, my subjects are like most of us in complex societies: excluded from participating in the major political and economic decisions that shape the wider society, we concentrate on work, family, religion, and amusement—things we can control. In societies with inherent hierarchies of class, ethnicity, and gender, we learn early to admire the "rich" or "educated" who are "above" us, and to concentrate our efforts on reaching a higher social place than that in which we were born. In Taiwan, such striving encourages hard work and produces modest comfort for workers, along with very considerable wealth for those who control the products of that work.

Taiwan's working class has escaped the impoverished fate of many Third World countries from whose labor, minerals, and agricultural products only outsiders have profited. Working-class people have contributed many of the technical, entrepreneurial, and organizational skills that have kept the island's economy afloat in hard times and made it enormously productive in good ones. Theirs is a culture with considerable power and resilience, as history shows. In any foreseeable future, I believe that, one way or another, people like Mrs. Zhang, Miss Ong, and the rest will somehow get by.

Source Materials on Taiwan

The written sources from which we can learn about Taiwan's culture were produced in specific historical contexts and in response to the varying intellectual, political, and economic pressures that made events on this small island worthy of recording. Because of its strategic significance to sixteenth-century Fujianese merchants, Dutch mercantilists, Japanese imperialists, and Nationalist irredentists, Taiwan has had an importance far greater than its size and peripherality to the Chinese world would suggest. As a result of these historical accidents and of the way in which knowledge is produced in societies such as our own, the social-science literature on Taiwan is now probably higher in quality and quantity than that for any other part of China. We are easily tempted, therefore, to use Taiwan as a microcosm of the harder-to-study China of the past and present, while at the same time the unusual circumstances that prompted so much scholarship argue for the special nature of the Taiwan case. We know far less about China's cultural variations and unities than we must if we are to give Taiwan its proper place in Chinese and in comparative studies.

Far removed by distance and politics from the dynamics of nineteenth- and twentieth-century change on the mainland, the island has especially interested Japanese and Americans. Since the Japanese conquest in 1895, therefore, support has been available, and permission readily obtained, for Japanese researchers (before the Pacific War) and American ones (after it) to study its social relations and cultural patterns. Since about 1970, as economic success and continued political autonomy prompted concern for and pride in Taiwan itself, the Nationalist authorities, too, have supported Chinese researchers in growing numbers. Scholars from countries without special political and economic interests in the island have been few.

[231]

The anthropological literature, created largely by American scholars after 1960, although generally of a high standard, contains a marked bias toward seeing Taiwan as a sample of an essentially homogeneous Chinese whole. Although much of this literature describes the "ethnographic present" accurately, its data and conclusions have frequently been held to stand for an "ethnographic past" as well. Those who have studied Taiwan's farmers and urban poor have sometimes assumed that they were uncovering Chinese traditions that would reveal the past, both in Taiwan itself and in the wider Chinese world. My study of Taiwan's working class often does precisely this, as when I assume, in Chapter 3, that contemporary views of gods, ghosts, and ancestors reflect nineteenth-century (or earlier) popular perceptions of significant social categories.

Although there clearly *are* continuities between Taiwan's present and China's past, precisely what is continuous, especially in the slippery and shifting realm of meaning, is always open to question. We must demonstrate these continuities, not assume them, for recent researches into the Chinese past increasingly undermine the sometimes unarticulated assumption of an unchanging Chinese past in favor of a search for the processes and particularities of its evolution (P. Cohen 1984). Over time, important pressures have reshaped and adapted Chinese ideologies and practices of kinship, class, economy, and power. Primary among these pressures are the competition of ethnically non-Han regional substrates with Han culture; the differential impact of China's indigenous commercialization in, for example, the southeast coast versus the northwest interior; the unequal penetration into regions and social strata of European imperialist capitalism since the mid-nineteenth century; and the political and economic divergence of Taiwan from China for nearly one hundred years. When we consider these potent sources of cultural variation, it becomes easier to guard against assuming the universality of a pan-Chinese cultural coherence. Although Chinese states consciously foster a belief in such coherence and the relative ignorance of Westerners unconsciously supports that belief, the unity or variability of Chinese culture remains an open question both for empirical examination and for political interpretation.

The unity of Taiwan society with China's, as well as its essential Chineseness, has by no means been a politically neutral issue to many who have an interest in the society: to the Qing authorities, beset with foreign imperialist attacks on its outlying province; to the Japanese, who wished to Japanize the Taiwanese while at the same time feeling superior to them; to the Nationalists, struggling to maintain their legitimacy at home and abroad; to the government of the P.R.C., which, like Qing rulers, is uneasy with foreign influences so near its shores; and to American military and industrial interests, eager for allies and exploitable labor in the Pacific. As assumptions about Chinese unity frequently underlie the anthropology carried out on Taiwan, the written sources on which that anthropology draws should be read with particular attention to the social contexts and viewpoints of their writers.

The reader of this volume who wishes to pursue Taiwan studies further will receive some guidance in locating important sources of information from the list of citations on the following pages. It may also be useful to know something about other sources that, although not cited directly in this study, have formed opinion about Taiwan. This brief addendum, then, is meant to expand and give intellectual context to that list. I will briefly consider sources deriving from Western writers about pre-twentieth-century Taiwan, certain Chinese historical and popular culture genres, and Japanese scholarly and administrative writings about its colony before turning to the main body of English- and Chinese-language analyses and interpretations that have appeared since the late 1950s. This book is based primarily on these works, along with my own field notes. The emphasis in the following is on English-language materials as much as possible, for I assume that specialists will already know their way into this scholarly thicket, even if they have not yet found their way out.

Among the Western-language sources on Taiwan as it was prior to the nineteenth century, William Campbell's *Formosa under the Dutch* (1972 [1903]) is especially useful in summing up the Dutch experience and Aboriginal cultures of that time. Campbell draws on contemporary Dutch and Chinese accounts, as well as on later scholarship. In the nineteenth century, relatively few of the Westerners, mostly merchants, who traveled to Taiwan published descriptions of Chinese life there. An important exception, and still a folk hero in Taiwan to some, was George Mackay, a Canadian Presbyterian medical missionary. Mackay's *From Far Formosa* (1895) contains more than the usual missionary quotient of observations from his professional travels. A second important late-nineteenth-century source is James W. Davidson's *The Island of Formosa* (1967 [1903]), a valuable study of the early Japanese period and its economy. Though utterly unimpressed with the Chinese elite of the time and transparently biased in favor of the Japanese government that made use of his talents as a journalist, Davidson shows much sympathy for the life, work, and character of ordinary Chinese.

These descriptions of Taiwan life may be cautiously supplemented with those from the pens of the many Westerners living in southern China, especially Fujian, during the nineteenth and first half of the twentieth centuries. The extensive studies of Chinese popular religion by Justus

Doolittle (1966 [1865]) and J. J. M. de Groot (1969 [1882]) are especially valuable, since they are based in large part on the regional culture from which Taiwan's derives, and with which it was complexly connected at the time.

Early Western observers often distinguished sharply among the social classes and paid particular attention to regional differences and local peculiarities in order to proselytize or make use of local resources. But they also often assumed a fundamental cultural unity, using elite Chinese culture as the standard for the entire society.

We necessarily supplement writings by Westerners with the vast store of materials that the Chinese published for themselves. Most important are the "gazetteers," or local histories, which imperial officials regularly compiled as part of their duties. These documents, intended for court use, detail not only history in a strict sense, but also economic activity, unusual phenomena or weather, local customs, and a myriad of other facts. Centuries' worth of these documents—some insightful and apparently accurate, others rather less so—exist in archives, libraries, and microfilm collections in numbers that intimidate as much as they inspire. Taiwan's *xianzhi,* as they are called, have proven a treasure trove of information about the locations and nature of economic resources and industries (for example see Harrell 1982), community rituals (for example, Weller 1985), and Chinese/Aborigine relations (for example, Shepherd 1985), to name only a few. Such materials, although they are richly informative about local variation, were written at the behest of the state to assist in the administrative tasks of unifying and ruling.

Also useful to contemporary scholars are the writings of literate Chinese who used writing in the course of their occupations, such as merchants (for example, Eberhard 1967); for religious purposes, such as Daoist or Buddhist ritual specialists (for example, Schipper 1974); or as a medium for folk art, such as the often anonymous balladeers whose broadsheet poems were sold in Taiwan's streets well into this century) (for example, Eberhard 1972; and see also Johnson et al. 1985). Such materials, preserved more rarely than official documents, are particularly precious because they reveal viewpoints of the common folk in all their variety and unexpectedness.

Under Japanese rule, administrators and scholars also gathered written materials for administrative or academic purposes. Many of these now provide invaluable data for different kinds of analyses. Although many historians, folklorists, and legal scholars (such as Oyamatsu 1901) explored local traditions and customs, the administrators' documents, carefully compiled over decades, constitute the greatest Japanese contribution to our knowledge of Taiwan society. Their system of household registers, described fully in Wolf and Huang (1980:16–33), still maintained by the Nationalist authorities, provides demographic, social-organizational, and cultural data on a scale and of a thoroughness unparalleled anywhere but in Japan itself. Further reference will be made below to the uses to which contemporary anthropologists have put these data. For those with linguistic access to Japanese materials, a valuable resource, in either Chinese or Japanese, is the dissident (and pseudonymous) Taiwan historian Shi Ming's enormous *Four Hundred Years of Taiwan People's History* (1979), which cites copiously from Japanese-language sources, many of them in government archives. To Japanese administrators, gaining a detailed knowledge of local cultural variation was less important than defining a simple framework of Taiwanese culture on which to build the changes that their goals for the island required.

We know the Japanese period, too, from some important English-language sources written because of the American concern for Japan's expanding Pacific empire. Andrew J. Grajdanzev's *Formosa Today* (1942) is especially strong on the island's colonial economic development. George W. Barclay's *Colonial Development and Population in Taiwan* (1954) retrospectively laid the groundwork for later demographic work.

From 1945 to the late 1950s, Chinese archaeologists from the transplanted Academia Sinica continued work begun on the mainland, and ethnologists in the Department of Archaeology and Ethnology of National Taiwan University pursued their studies of Aborigines. But Western cultural anthropologists who might have studied contemporary Han culture had little access to Taiwan in those turbulent years, and probably little interest in the island. For although some China scholarship, under McCarthyist attacks, retreated into an emphasis on the past, many of those who still focused on the present were more interested in the dramatic events unfolding on China's mainland than on a Taiwan that might "fall" at any time. But precisely because of the island's political and military significance, various American advisers and diplomats studied Taiwan in its first two postwar decades, generally as a part of the U.S. mission to help the Nationalists create a capitalist democracy there. Fred W. Riggs (1952), Arthur Raper (1953), Neil Jacoby (1967), George Kerr (1965), and Mark Mancall, as editor (1964), have left especially valuable volumes examining, respectively, early Nationalist rule, rural conditions, U.S. aid to Taiwan, the U.S. betrayal of Taiwanese hopes for postwar independence, and, in a collection of papers by various authors, a range of topics from literature to the state of the military.

These and other similar sources on the early Nationalist years were supplemented by a vigorous anti-Nationalist literature in Japanese and

English by émigré Taiwanese (for example, J. Liao 1950; T. Liao 1960). Chinese-language newspapers and magazines in Taiwan, especially *Ziyou Zhongguo (Free China)*, escaped press censorship long enough to criticize the building of a Jiang dynasty, the treatment of Mainlander soldiers, the endless and corrupt wartime economy, and many other aspects of Nationalist governance. The Nationalist government published a torrent of often unjustifiably optimistic material on the state of the economy in such periodicals as *Industry of Free China* and in annual statistical data books (for example, DGBAS, *Statistical Abstracts of the Republic of China*). Often writing in English, and clearly for an American audience, Nationalist supporters in Taiwan and the United States based many of their arguments on the premise that Taiwan was an integral part of China, and its people were wholly and essentially Chinese. In opposition, various anti-Jiang groups hotly insisted that the island had evolved so differently that its people deserved the right to choose their own government.

By the late 1950s it was clear that American anthropological fieldworkers would not be welcome in the People's Republic of China in the foreseeable future. It was beginning to appear too that the McCarthyist destruction of China scholarship in the United States was hampering the American ability to understand events in China proper. Support emerged for anthropological investigation of everyday Chinese life in Taiwan, where, it was assumed, traditional Chinese culture had been preserved from the changes set in motion by the Communist revolution. The postwar assumption of superiority to the Japanese by both Chinese and Americans led them to underestimate the impact of Japan's fifty years of control, while the Nationalist need for legitimacy caused them to emphasize cultural continuities with China. American fieldworkers began to arrive, led in 1956 by Bernard Gallin and Rita Gallin, and followed in 1957 by Arthur Wolf and Margery Wolf and in 1960 by Norma Diamond, all based at Cornell University.

These academic siblings and their students have trained the great majority of American anthropologists who have worked in Taiwan, although Morton Fried and his students Myron Cohen and Burton Pasternak of Columbia University have also played major roles in Taiwan anthropological production. In 1971 the center of gravity of Taiwan studies shifted with Arthur and Margery Wolf's move to Stanford University.

The most productive of these scholarly foci, the Stanford/Cornell group, has been primarily influenced by three areas of theoretical concern: the application of British Africanist kinship studies as developed for Chinese studies by Maurice Freedman, especially in his *Lineage Organization in Southeastern China* (1958) and *Chinese Lineage and Society: Fukien and Kwangtung* (1966); the macroscopic vision of central-place theory as applied to the Chinese case by G. William Skinner, set forth in his three-part article "Marketing and Chinese Rural Social Structure" in the *Journal of Asian Studies* (1964, 1965a, and 1965b) and further developed in the essay "Cities and the Hierarchy of Local Systems," along with his other contributions to his edited volume *The City in Late Imperial China* (1977); and on Arthur Wolf's use of Taiwan's household registers to test sensitive hypotheses about Chinese kinship patterns and the cultural effects of family dynamics. Detailed and perceptive analyses of Taiwanese folk religion as behavior that reflects, supports, and reproduces island working-class life have been an important result of anthropological research done against this theoretical background (for example, Ahern 1973, 1981a, 1981b, and Sangren, in press).

Using a sophisticated mix of field interviews, archival research, and the manipulation of an immense body of household-register data, Arthur Wolf has explored one of anthropology's fundamental questions—the origins of the incest taboo and its effects on fertility (1966, 1970a, 1976). With Huang Chieh-shan (1980), he has examined an unorthodox pattern of Chinese marriage and adoption, uniting the study of Chinese kinship with demography. Wolf's concentration of his own and his students' research in Haishan, an area of northern Taiwan, has resulted in a profusion of fine work informed by the theoretical frameworks with which he, Freedman, and Skinner began. A helpful bibliography of studies of Haishan is supplied by Wolf and Huang (1980: 381–86).

Whereas the Stanford/Cornell scholars have been preoccupied with the continuities in Taiwan of patterns that Freedman and Skinner had found in China proper, an emphasis on change surfaced in the work of Bernard Gallin and Rita Gallin. These scholars brought the economic change, industrialism, and urban migration that were changing Taiwan so rapidly during the 1960s into Taiwan anthropology's mainstream (for example, B. Gallin 1963, and B. Gallin and R. Gallin 1974, 1982a, 1982b). Both Bernard Gallin and Diamond produced baseline ethnographies of village life, *Hsin Hsing: A Chinese Village in Change* (1966) and *K'un Shen: A Taiwanese Fishing Village* (1969), respectively, against which to measure this change. Margery Wolf's vivid description of a rural family, *The House of Lim* (1968), and Myron Cohen's account of a Hakka community, *House United, House Divided* (1976), are other such baseline studies.

Burton Pasternak introduced the perspective of cultural ecology in his *Kinship and Community in Two Chinese Villages* (1972), and has shared Arthur Wolf's demographic interests in subsequent work, notably *Guests in the Dragon* (1983).

Important contributions to the newly emerging anthropology of women

[237]

were made by Margery Wolf in her *Women and the Family in Rural Taiwan* (1972) and in other publications (for example, 1974, 1975), and by Norma Diamond (1973, 1975, 1979), Emily Martin [Ahern] (1975), and many of their students, notably Lydia Kung (1983), who has studied women factory workers. Arthur Wolf's previously cited work has obvious implications for women's studies, and Rita Gallin has written on women in industrialization (1984a, 1984b). Taiwan anthropology has had a valuable influence on the rest of the discipline through these early contributions to the belated development of an anthropology of women.

During the later 1960s and 1970s, when the early Taiwan anthropologists were establishing their own careers and placing students in Taiwan field sites, a series of six important and academically fruitful conferences on Chinese society was administered by the American Council of Learned Societies and the Social Science Research Council. Five of these included Taiwan as a research area. These prestigious meetings defined the central intellectual issues for Taiwan anthropology at that time, and their impact remains strong (see Marks 1985 on the agenda-setting roles of such events in the China field).

Not all the participants were Taiwan anthropologists. The organizers invited historians, political scientists, sociologists, and others, many of whom studied other regions of China and time periods ranging back through the whole of late imperial China. The conferences supported the traditional inclination of Chinese social scientists toward history, thus encouraging the growing alliance between history and anthropology which has enriched both disciplines in the past two decades. In this, China specialists may have been somewhat in advance of anthropologists as a whole. At the same time, however, the conferences fostered a generally conservative tendency to assume Chinese continuities over time and space more than it encouraged equally valid tendencies to look for variation and change among Taiwan and mainland regionalisms.

The conferences resulted in six volumes of essays, many of which bear on Taiwan studies: *Family and Kinship in Chinese Society*, edited by Maurice Freedman (1971); *Economic Organization in Chinese Society*, edited by W. E. Willmott (1972); *The Chinese City between Two Worlds*, edited by Mark Elvin and G. William Skinner (1974); *Religion and Ritual in Chinese Society*, edited by Arthur P. Wolf (1974); *Women in Chinese Society*, edited by Margery Wolf and Roxane Witke (1975); and *The City in Late Imperial China*, edited by G. William Skinner (1977). They contain over two dozen articles based largely on Taiwan fieldwork, which together constitute a necessary background for any researcher in this area. A similar conference held in 1976, resulting in the volume *The Anthropology of Taiwanese*

[238]

Society (Ahern and Gates 1981), attempted to sum up research focused on the island up to that time.

These conferences drew more Chinese anthropologists into the still largely anglophone tradition of studying Han culture in Taiwan. Their publications in the *Journal of the Institute of Ethnology, Academia Sinica,* and National Taiwan University's Anthropology Department *Bulletin* helped disseminate the ideas of current American anthropology in the Chinese scholarly community, where the emphases on historical anthropology, kinship studies, and traditionalism were easily accepted. The volume *The Chinese Family and Its Ritual Behavior,* edited by Hsieh Jih-chang and Chuang Ying-chang (1985), itself a result of a 1982 conference in Taiwan, exemplifies this merging of Chinese and American scholarly interests. In late 1985 the two major institutions for the study of anthropology in Taiwan cosponsored another international conference on accomplishments and prospects. From this conference may soon emerge another English-language collection, edited by Kwang-chih Chang, Arthur Wolf, and Alexander Chien-chung Yin, which will emphasize mainstream archaeological, historical, and kinship topics.

Chinese anthropologists (and sociologists) in recent decades have turned also to studies of urban life (notably T'ang Mei-chun [1978], Alexander Chien-chung Yin [1981, 1985] and Susan Greenhalgh [1984]) and to aspects of social change that can be discussed without implying serious criticism of official social, economic, or political policy. Research into controversial matters—poverty or the detrimental consequences of industrialization—is not yet well incorporated into the expanding Taiwan anthropological tradition, just as it has not been by American anthropologists. A monograph is being prepared, however, on the emerging issue of Aborigine rights by Hsieh Shih-chung; Huang Shu-min has written of agricultural degradation in Taiwan (1981), and Linda Gail Arrigo has written of the plight of women workers (1984, 1985).

Although anthropologists have conducted many studies of microeconomic processes (for example, Silin's 1976 examination of a major Taiwan corporation), analyses of economic and political change have come largely from outside of anthropology. Many of these writers begin from uncritically pro-Nationalist and pro-capitalist premises that limit the value of their conclusions. Others fail to place economic change in its political and social context. The work of economists such as Samuel P. S. Ho (1978), that appearing in *The Experience of Rapid Industrialization in Taiwan,* edited by Walter Galenson (1979), and the prolific work of Gustave Ranis, John Fei, and Shirley W. Y. Kuo (for example, Fei et al. 1979; Kuo et al. 1981), however, have made available important data and insights from which a

[239]

variety of conclusions can be drawn. Some of the political context for interpreting Taiwan's economic change comes from the work of relatively critical American scholars such as George Kerr (1965); Mark Mancall, who edited a collection of outspoken papers in 1964; Douglas Mendel, who wrote on *The Politics of Formosan Nationalism* (1970); and Lloyd Eastman, who is a strong critic of the Nationalists in their pre-Taiwan period (1974, 1984). Dissidents such as P'eng Ming-min in his 1972 autobiography; the historian Mab Huang, describing *Intellectual Ferment for Political Reforms in Taiwan, 1971–1973* (1976); and a wide variety of publications by pro-independence Taiwanese at home and abroad (for example, the documents of the Formosan Association for Human Rights, magazines such as Formosa *[Meili Dao], The Independent Formosa, Mayflower [Wang Chun Fong],* and *Taiwan Wenzhai* and even testimony before the U.S. Congress on human rights [Committee on International Relations, U.S. House of Representatives, 1977]) balance the bland superficialities of official Nationalist publications.

China anthropology, despite the hopes expressed for its future significance by Maurice Freedman in an essay titled "A Chinese Phase in Social Anthropology" (1963), seems often to lag behind the rest of the discipline in its theoretical development. Where we can do fieldwork, our researches are constrained by tight governmental limits on the pursuit of topics that might undermine national policy. Where we cannot do fieldwork, we can do anthropology only on the safely dead. Intellectual issues thus come to be defined conservatively, and research topics become studies in the art of the possible. Although since the late 1960s American anthropology has absorbed and been revitalized by the exploration of various versions of Marxism, dependency theory, and other such "critical" approaches, Taiwan specialists have been slow to adopt them, although articles rebutting such approaches are smuggling them into the field nonetheless (for example, Amsden 1979; Barrett 1982; and Greenhalgh 1985a, 1985b).

Intellectual ties among American anthropologists and those in other disciplines who bring a critical and/or Marxist viewpoint to Taiwan studies have had little institutional support thus far, although the journal *Modern China* has become an outlet for such work (see the special issue on Taiwan of July 1979, and many other issues). Also, the Circle for Taiwan Studies at the University of Chicago began a series of annual conferences in July 1985 which have focused sharply, and sometimes critically, on the consequences of a changing political economy. The resulting volumes of papers may express a broader vision of anthropology for Taiwan than we have seen heretofore.

Curiously, the Chinese of the P.R.C. have published very little on Taiwan

[240]

society, although at least one Taiwan Research Institute exists, at Xiamen University in Fujian Province. This lack of interest is doubtless largely due to the underdeveloped state of the social sciences in China at present (see Thurston and Parker, eds. 1980), and to the unwillingness to emphasize regional tendencies that often counter central government policies. But it is a result too, I suspect, of the reality that Taiwan in and of itself matters far less to the mainland than the mainland matters to Taiwan.

Whether they "belong" to the China mainland or not is a question that has long shaped the identity of Taiwan's people. Arguments for the inalienable unity of Chinese culture can always be used, whatever the motives of the writer, as weapons in the struggle that Chinese states must engage in to control their people, and to keep outsiders from weakening that control. Arguments for diversity, for separate origins, institutions, and sentiments within the Chinese world, can be used by those dissatisfied with state control to set up their own kingdoms, as rebellious Chinese have so often done. All students of Taiwan in this century will find that their work has political weight, and will be weighed politically by those whose interests in the island are not academic, but life and death matters. Readers must be alert, then, to the intellectual and political complexities that lie behind any piece of writing on Taiwan. For these, after all, are what scholarship is really about.

References

Ahern, Emily Martin. 1973. *The Cult of the Dead in Ch'inan*. Stanford: Stanford University Press.

———. 1974. "Affines and Rituals of Kinship." In Arthur P. Wolf, ed., *Religion and Ritual in Chinese Society*, pp. 279–307. Stanford: Stanford University Press.

———. 1975. "The Power and Pollution of Chinese Women." In Margery Wolf and Roxane Witke, eds., *Women in Chinese Society*, pp. 193–214. Stanford: Stanford University Press.

———. 1981a. "The Thai Ti Kong Festival." In Emily Martin Ahern and Hill Gates, eds., *The Anthropology of Taiwanese Society*, pp. 397–425. Stanford: Stanford University Press.

———. 1981b. *Chinese Ritual and Politics*. Cambridge: Cambridge University Press.

——— and Hill Gates, eds. 1981. *The Anthropology of Taiwanese Society*. Stanford: Stanford University Press.

[American Embassy Staff?], [1973?], *The R.O.C.'s Top 100 Industrial Corporations*. [Taibei?]: Ms.

Amsden, Alice. 1979. "Taiwan's Economic History: A Case of Etatisme and a Challenge to Dependency Theory." *Modern China* 5, 3:341–79.

Anderson, Eugene N., Jr. 1983. "Why Does Humoral Medicine Work So Well?" Mimeo.

Arrigo, Linda Gail. 1980. "The Industrial Work Force of Young Women in Taiwan." *Bulletin of Concerned Asian Scholars* 12, 2:25–38.

———. 1984. "Taiwan Electronics Workers." In Mary Sheridan and Janet W. Salaff, eds., *Lives: Chinese Working Women*. Bloomington: Indiana University Press.

———. 1985. "Control of Women Workers in Taiwan." *Contemporary Marxism* 11:77–95.

Barclay, George W. 1954. *Colonial Development and Population in Taiwan*. Pt. Washington, N.Y.: Kennikat Press.

Barrett, Richard (with Martin King Whyte). 1982. "Dependency Theory and Taiwan: A Deviant Case Analysis." *American Journal of Sociology* 87:1064–89.

Black, Alison H. 1986. "Gender and Cosmology in Chinese Correlative Thinking."

In Caroline W. Bynum et al., eds., *Gender and Religion: On the Complexity of Symbols*, pp. 166–95. Boston: Beacon Press.

Bodley, John H. 1982. *Victims of Progress*. Palo Alto, Calif.: Mayfield.

Bodman, Nicholas C. 1955. *Spoken Amoy Hokkien*. Kuala Lumpur.

Burchett, Wilfred, with Rewi Alley. 1976. *China: The Quality of Life*. Harmondsworth: Penguin.

Campbell, William. 1972. *Formosa under the Dutch*. Taibei: Ch'eng Wen. (First published 1903.)

Chang Kwang-chih. 1977. *The Archaeology of Ancient China*, 3d ed. New Haven: Yale University Press.

Chen Cheng. 1961. *Land Reform in Taiwan*. [Taibei]: China Publishing Co.

Chen Chuzhuan. 1977. *Wushe Shejian*. [The Wushe Incident]. Taibei: Diqiou Chubanshe.

Ch'ien Tuan-sheng. 1965. "Military Rule and Nationalist Ruin." In Pichon P.Y. Loh, ed., *The Kuomintang Debacle of 1949*, pp. 41–44. Boston: D. C. Heath.

Chu, Solomon S. P. 1969. "Family Structure and Extended Kinship in a Chinese Community." Ph.D. dissertation, University of Michigan.

Cohen, Myron. 1976. *House United, House Divided: The Chinese Family in Taiwan*. New York: Columbia University Press.

Cohen, Paul A. 1984. *Discovering History in China: American Historical Writing on the Recent Chinese Past*. New York: Columbia University Press.

Committee on International Relations, U. S. House of Representatives. 1977. *Human Rights in Taiwan*. Washington, D.C.: U.S. Government Printing Office.

Davidson, James W. [1967]. *The Island of Formosa*. [Taibei]: n.p. (Taiwan reprint of 1903 ed.)

De Beauclair, Inez. 1971. *Studies on Botel Tobago and Yap*. Taibei: Orient Cultural Service.

De Glopper, Donald R., 1979. "Artisan Work and Life in Taiwan." *Modern China* 5, 3:283–315.

De Groot, J. J. M. 1969 [1882]. *The Religious System of China*. Taibei: Ch'eng Wen.

DGBAS (Directorate-General of Budget, Accounting, and Statistics, Executive Yuan, Republic of China. Yearly. *Statistical Abstract of the Republic of China*. [Taibei].

Diamond, Norma. 1969. *K'un Shen, a Taiwanese Fishing Village*. New York: Holt, Rinehart & Winston.

——. 1973. "The Status of Women in Taiwan: One Step Forward, Two Steps Back." In Marilyn B. Young, ed., *Women in China: Studies in Social Change and Feminism*, pp. 211–42. Ann Arbor: Center for Chinese Studies, University of Michigan.

——. 1975. "Women under Kuomintang Rule: Variations on the Feminine Mystique." *Modern China* 1, 1:3–45.

——. 1979. "Women and Industry in Taiwan." *Modern China* 5, 3:317–40.

Doi Takeo. 1973. *The Anatomy of Dependence*. Tokyo: Kodansha.

Doolittle, Justus. 1966 [1865]. *Social Life of the Chinese*. Taibei: Ch'eng Wen.

Douglas, Mary. 1966. *Purity and Danger*. Harmondsworth: Penguin.

Eastman, Lloyd. 1974. *The Abortive Revolution: China under Nationalist Rule, 1927–1933*. Cambridge: Harvard University Press.

———. 1984. *Seeds of Destruction: Nationalist China in War and Revolution, 1937–1949*. Stanford: Stanford University Press.

Eberhard, Wolfram. 1967. "Social Mobility among Businessmen in a Taiwanese Town." In his *Settlement and Social Change in Asia*, pp. 178–93. Hong Kong: Hong Kong University Press.

———. 1972. *Taiwanese Ballads: A Catalogue*. Taibei: Orient Cultural Service.

Elvin, Mark, and G. William Skinner, eds. 1974. *The Chinese City between Two Worlds*. Stanford: Stanford University Press.

Fei, John C. H., Gustave Ranis, and Shirley W. Y. Kuo. 1979. *Growth with Equity: The Taiwan Case*. London: Oxford University Press.

Formosan Association for Human Rights. 1980. *Repression in Taiwan: A Look at the Kaohsiung, Rally and Trials*. New York: Asia Center.

———. 1985. *Martial Law in Taiwan*. New York: Asia Center.

Freedman, Maurice. 1958. *Lineage Organization in Southeastern China*. London: Athlone.

———. 1963. "A Chinese Phase in Social Anthropology." *British Journal of Sociology* 14, 1:1–19.

———. 1966. *Chinese Lineage and Society*. London: Athlone.

———. ed. 1971. *Family and Kinship in Chinese Society*. Stanford: Stanford University Press.

Galenson, Walter, ed. 1979. *Economic Growth and Structural Change in Taiwan*. Ithaca: Cornell University Press.

Gallin, Bernard. 1960. "Matrilateral and Affinal Relationships in a Taiwanese Village." *American Anthropologist* 62, 4:632–42.

———. 1963. "Land Reform in Taiwan: Its Effect on Rural Social Organization and Leadership." *Human Organization* 22:109–12.

———. 1966. *Hsin Hsing: A Chinese Village in Change*. Berkeley: University of California Press.

———. 1982a. "Socioeconomic Life in Rural Taiwan: Twenty Years of Development and Change." *Modern China* 8, 2:205–46.

———. 1982b. "The Chinese Joint Family in Changing Rural Taiwan." In Sydney L. Greenblatt, Richard W. Wilson, and Amy A. Wilson, eds., *Social Interaction in Chinese Society*, pp. 142–58. New York: Praeger.

———. 1985. "Matrilateral and Affinal Relationships in Changing Chinese Society." In Hsieh Jih-chang and Chuang Ying-chang, eds., *The Chinese Family and Its Ritual Behavior*, pp. 101–16. Taibei: Institute of Ethnology, Academia Sinica.

——— and Rita S. Gallin. 1974. "The Integration of Village Migrants in Taipei." In Mark Elvin and G. William Skinner, eds., *The Chinese City between Two Worlds*, pp. 331–58. Stanford: Stanford University Press.

Gallin, Rita. 1982. *The Impact of Development on Women's Work and Status: A Case Study from Taiwan*. Michigan State University, Women in International Development, Working Paper no. 09.

———. 1984a. *Rural Industrialization and Chinese Women: A Case Study from Taiwan*. Michigan State University, Women in International Development, Working Paper no. 47.

———. 1984b. "Women, Family and the Political Economy of Taiwan." *Journal of Peasant Studies* 12, 1:76–92.

[245]

——. 1984c. "The Entry of Chinese Women into the Rural Labor Force: A Case Study from Taiwan." *Signs* 9, 3:383–98.

Gates, Hill. 1979. "Dependency and the Part-time Proletariat." *Modern China* 5, 3:381–407.

——. 1981. "Social Class and Ethnicity." In Emily Martin Ahern and Hill Gates, eds., *The Anthropology of Taiwanese Society*, pp. 241–81. Stanford: Stanford University Press.

——. 1987. "Money for the Gods: The Commoditization of the Spirit." *Modern China* 13, 3.

Gluckman, M. 1955. *Custom and Conflict in Africa*. Oxford: Blackwell.

Government of Formosa. 1926. *Progressive Formosa*. [Taibei]: n.p.

Grajdanzev, Andrew J. 1942. *Formosa Today: An Analysis of the Economic Development and Strategic Importance of Japan's Tropical Colony*. New York: Institute of Pacific Relations.

Greenhalgh, Susan. 1984. "Networks and Their Nodes: Urban Society on Taiwan." *China Quarterly* 99:529–52.

——. 1985a. "Is Inequality Demographically Induced? The Family Cycle and the Distribution of Income on Taiwan." *American Anthropologist* 87, 3:571–94.

——. 1985b. "Social Causes and Consequences of Taiwan's Economic Development." Paper presented at the International Conference on Anthropological Studies of the Taiwan Area: Accomplishments and Prospects. December 25–31, Taibei.

——. 1985c. "Sexual Stratification: The Other Side of 'Growth with Equity' in East Asia," *Population Development Review* 11, 2:263–314.

Hane Mikiso. 1982. *Peasants, Rebels, and Outcasts: The Underside of Modern Japan*. New York: Pantheon.

Harrell, Stevan. 1974. "When a Ghost Becomes a God." In Arthur P. Wolf, ed., *Religion and Ritual in Chinese Society*, pp. 193–206. Stanford: Stanford University Press.

——. 1982. *Ploughshare Village: Cultural Context in Taiwan*. Seattle: University of Washington Press.

——. 1985. "Why Do the Chinese Work So Hard? Reflections on an Entrepreneurial Ethic." *Modern China* 11, 2:203–26.

——. 1986. "Men, Women, and Ghosts in Chinese Folk Religion." In Caroline W. Bynum et al., eds., *Gender and Religion*, pp. 97–116. Boston: Beacon Press.

—— and Sara A. Dickey. 1985. "Dowry Systems in Complex Societies." *Ethnology* 24, 2:105–20.

Ho, Samuel P. S. 1978. *Economic Development of Taiwan, 1860–1970*. New Haven: Yale University Press.

Hochschild, Arlie Russell. 1983. *The Managed Heart: Commercialization of Human Feeling*. Berkeley: University of California Press.

Hommel, Rudolf P. 1937. *China at Work*. New York: John Day.

Hsiao, Hsin-Huang Michael. 1981. *Government Agricultural Strategies in Taiwan and South Korea*. Nankang, Taiwan: Academia Sinica.

Hsieh Jih-chang and Chuang Ying-chang, eds. 1985. *The Chinese Family and Its Ritual Behavior*. Institute of Ethnology, Academia Sinica, Monograph Series B, no. 15.

Huang, Mab. 1976. *Internal Ferment for Political Reforms in Taiwan, 1971–1973.* Ann Arbor: Center for Chinese Studies, University of Michigan.

Huang Shu-min. 1981. *Agricultural Degradation: Changing Community System in Rural Taiwan.* Washington, D.C.: University Press of America.

Jacoby, Neil H. 1967. *U.S. Aid to Taiwan.* New York: Praeger.

Johnson, David, Andrew J. Nathan, and Evelyn S. Rawski, eds. 1985. *Popular Culture in Late Imperial China.* Berkeley: University of California Press.

Jordan, David K. 1972. *Gods, Ghosts, and Ancestors.* Berkeley: University of California Press.

———. 1982. "The Recent History of the Celestial Way: A Chinese Pietistic Association." *Modern China* 8, 3:435–62.

Kann, E. 1955. "The Great Inflation in China (1946–1949)." Pt. 1, *Far Eastern Economic Review* 18, 19:592–95; pt. 4, *Far Eastern Economic Review* 18, 22:689–90.

Kerr, George H. 1965. *Formosa Betrayed.* Boston: Houghton Mifflin.

Kung, Lydia. 1983. *Factory Women in Taiwan.* Ann Arbor: UMI Research Press.

———. 1984. "Taiwan Garment Workers." In Mary Sheridan and Janet W. Salaff, eds., *Lives: Chinese Working Women,* pp. 109–22. Bloomington: Indiana University Press.

Kuo, Shirley W. Y., Gustav Ranis, and John C. H. Fei. 1981. *The Taiwan Success Story: Rapid Growth with Improved Distribution in the Republic of China, 1952–1979.* Boulder, Colo.: Westview Press.

Lamley, Harry J. 1981. "Subethnic Rivalry in the Ch'ing Period." In Emily Martin Ahern and Hill Gates, eds., *The Anthropology of Taiwanese Society,* pp. 282–318. Stanford: Stanford University Press.

Liao, Joshua [Wen-k'uei]. 1950. *Formosa Speaks.* Hong Kong: Graphic Press.

Liao, Thomas W. I. 1960. *Inside Formosa—Formosans vs. Chinese since 1945.* 2d ed. Tokyo: Formosan Press.

Mackay, George Leslie, D.D. 1895. *From Far Formosa: The Island, Its People and Missions.* New York: Fleming H. Revell.

Mancall, Mark, ed. 1964. *Formosa Today.* New York: Praeger.

Marks, Robert. 1984. *Rural Revolution in South China: Peasants and the Making of History in Haifeng County, 1570–1930.* Madison: University of Wisconsin Press.

———. 1985. "The State of the China Field: or, the China Field and the State." *Modern China* 11, 4:461–509.

Mendel, Douglas. 1970. *The Politics of Formosan Nationalism.* Berkeley: University of California Press.

Morgan Guaranty Survey. June 1961, 1962. "Economic Development in Taiwan." In *After Seeing Free China,* pp. 43–50. [Taibei?]: n.p.

Naquin, Susan. 1976. *Millenarian Rebellion in China.* New Haven: Yale University Press.

Ng Chin-keong. 1983. *Trade and Society: The Amoy Network on the China Coast, 1683–1735.* Singapore: National University of Singapore.

Niehoff, Justin. 1987. "The Villager as Industrialist: Ideologies of Household Factories in Rural Taiwan." *Modern China* 13, 3.

Oyamatsu Santaro. 1901. *Provisional Report on Investigations of Laws and Customs in the Island of Formosa.* Kobe: Kobe Herald.

Pasternak, Burton. 1972. *Kinship and Community in Two Chinese Villages*. Stanford: Stanford University Press.

——. 1983. *Guests in the Dragon*. New York: Columbia University Press.

P'eng Ming-min. 1972. *A Taste of Freedom*. New York: Holt, Rinehart & Winston.

Population Reference Bureau. 1977. "Marrying, Divorcing, and Living Together in the United States Today." *Population Bulletin* 32. Washington, D.C.: Population Reference Bureau.

Pruitt, Ida. 1945. *A Daughter of Han*. New Haven: Yale University Press.

Raper, Arthur F. 1953. *Rural Taiwan—Problem and Promise*. Taibei: Joint Committee on Rural Reconstruction.

Riggs, Fred W. 1952. *Formosa under Nationalist Chinese Rule*. New York: Macmillan.

Rohsenow, Hill Gates. 1973. "Prosperity Settlement: The Politics of Paipai in Taipei, Taiwan." Ph.D. dissertation, University of Michigan.

Sangren, P. Steven. In press. *History and Magical Power: Chinese Order in Local Perspective*. Stanford: Stanford University Press.

Sankar, Andrea. 1984. "Spinster Sisterhoods." In Mary Sheridan and Janet W. Salaff, eds., *Lives: Chinese Working Women*, pp. 51–70. Bloomington: Indiana University Press.

Schipper, Kristofer M. 1974. "The Written Memorial in Taoist Ceremonies." In Arthur P. Wolf, ed., *Religion and Ritual in Chinese Society*, pp. 309–24. Stanford: Stanford University Press.

Seaman, Gary, 1981. "The Sexual Politics of Karmic Retribution." In Emily Martin Ahern and Hill Gates, eds., *The Anthropology of Taiwanese Society*, pp. 381–96. Stanford: Stanford University Press.

Shepherd, John. 1985. "Taiwan as a Chinese Frontier." Paper presented at the International Conference on Anthropological Studies of the Taiwan Area, December 25–31, Taibei.

Shi Ming. 1979. *Taiwan Ren Si Bai Nian Shi [Four Hundred Years of Taiwan People's History]*. San Jose: Paradise Cultural Association.

Silin, Robert H. 1976. *Leadership and Values: The Organization of Large-Scale Taiwanese Enterprises*. Cambridge: Harvard University Press.

Skinner, G. William. 1964. "Marketing and Social Structure in Rural China, Part 1." *Journal of Asian Studies* 24:3–23.

——. 1965a. "Marketing and Social Structure in Rural China, Part 2." *Journal of Asian Studies* 24:195–228.

——. 1965b. "Marketing and Social Structure in Rural China, Part 3." *Journal of Asian Studies* 24:363–99.

——. ed. 1977. *The City in Late Imperial China*. Stanford: Stanford University Press.

Stites, Richard. 1982. "Small-Scale Industry in Yingge, Taiwan." *Modern China* 8, 2:247–79.

——. 1985. "Industrial Work as an Entrepreneurial Strategy." *Modern China* 11, 2:227–46.

Stockard, Janice, 1985, "Daughters of the Canton Delta: Marriage Practices and Economic Strategies, 1860–1930." Ph.D. dissertation, Stanford University.

T'ang Mei-chun. 1978. *Urban Chinese Families*. Taibei: National Taiwan University Press.

Thurston, Anne F., and Jason H. Parker, eds. 1890. *Humanistic and Social Science Research in China: Recent History and Future Prospects*. New York: Social Science Research Council.

Topley, Marjorie. 1975. "Marriage Resistance in Rural Kwangtung." In Margery Wolf and Roxanne Witke, eds., *Women in Chinese Society*, pp. 67–88. Stanford: Stanford University Press.

Triestman, Judith. 1972. "Prehistory of the Formosan Uplands." *Science* 175:74–76.

Tsurumi, E. Patricia. 1977. *Japanese Colonial Education in Taiwan, 1895–1945*. Cambridge: Harvard University Press.

van der Sprenkel, Sybille. 1962. *Legal Institutions in Manchu China*. London: Athlone Press.

Wang Sung-hsing. 1971. "Pooling and Sharing in a Chinese Fishing Economy: Kuishan Tao." Ph.D. dissertation, Tokyo University.

———. and Raymond Apthorpe. 1974. *Rice Farming in Taiwan: Three Village Studies*. Nankang, Taiwan: Academia Sinica.

Wang, William S. Y. 1985. "Austronesian Languages in Taiwan." Paper presented in the International Conference on Anthropological Studies of the Taiwan Area. Taibei, Ms.

Weller, Robert P. 1985. "Beggars, Bandits, and Ghosts: The Failure of State Control over Religious Interpretation in Taiwan." *American Ethnologist* 12, 1:46–61.

———. 1987. "The Politics of Ritual Disguise: Repression and Response in Taiwanese Popular Religion." *Modern China* 13, 1:17–39.

White, James W. 1970. *The Sokagakkai and Mass Society*. Stanford: Stanford University Press.

Wickberg, Edgar. 1981. "Continuities in Land Tenure, 1900–1940." In Emily Martin Ahern and Hill Gates, eds., *The Anthropology of Taiwanese Society*, pp. 212–38. Stanford: Stanford University Press.

Willmott, W. E. ed. 1972. *Economic Organization in Chinese Society*. Stanford: Stanford University Press.

Wilson, Richard W. 1970. *Learning to Be Chinese: The Political Socialization of Children in Taiwan*. Cambridge: M.I.T. Press.

Wolf, Arthur P. 1966. "Childhood Association, Sexual Attraction, and the Incest Taboo: A Chinese Case." *American Anthropologist* 68, 4:883–98.

———. 1970a. "Childhood Association and Sexual Attraction: A Further Test of the Westermarck Hypothesis." *American Anthropologist* 72, 3:503–15.

———. 1970b. "Chinese Kinship and Mourning Dress." In Maurice Freedman, ed., *Family and Kinship in Chinese Society*, pp. 189–208. Stanford: Stanford University Press.

———. 1974. "Gods, Ghosts, and Ancestors." In Arthur P. Wolf, ed., *Religion and Ritual in Chinese Society*, pp. 131–82. Stanford, Calif.: Stanford University Press.

———. 1976. "Childhood Association, Sexual Attraction, and Fertility in Taiwan." In Ezra B. W. Zubrow, ed., *Demographic Anthropology: Quantitative Approaches*, pp. 227–44. Albuquerque: University of New Mexico Press.

———. ed. 1974, *Religion and Ritual in Chinese Society*. Stanford, Calif.: Stanford University Press.

——— and Huang Chieh-shan. 1980. *Marriage and Adoption in China, 1845–1945*. Stanford: Stanford University Press.

Wolf, Margery. 1968. *The House of Lim*. New York: Appleton-Century-Crofts.

——. 1970. "Child Training and the Chinese Family." In Maurice Freedman, ed., *Family and Kinship in Chinese Society*, pp. 37–62. Stanford: Stanford University Press.

——. 1972. *Women and the Family in Rural Taiwan*. Stanford: Stanford University Press.

——. 1974. "Chinese Women: Old Skills in a New Context." In Michelle Zimbalist Rosaldo and Louise Lamphere, eds. *Women, Culture, and Society*, pp. 157–72. Stanford: Stanford University Press.

——. 1975. "Women and Suicide in China." In Margery Wolf and Roxane Witke, eds., *Women in Chinese Society*, pp. 111–42. Stanford: Stanford University Press.

—— and Roxane Witke, eds. 1975. *Women in Chinese Society*. Stanford: Stanford University Press.

Yang, Martin M. C. 1970. *Socio-economic Results of Land Reform in Taiwan*. Honolulu: East-West Center Press.

Yin, Alexander Chien-chung. 1981. "Voluntary Associations and Rural-Urban Migration." In Emily Martin Ahern and Hill Gates, eds., *The Anthropology of Taiwanese Society*, pp. 319–37. Stanford: Stanford University Press.

——. 1985. "Urbanization and the Culture Change on Taiwan." Paper presented at the International Conference on Anthropological Studies of the Taiwan Area, December 25–31, Taibei.

Index

Library of Congress Cataloging-in-Publication Data

Gates, Hill.
    Chinese working-class lives.

    (Anthropology of contemporary issues)
    Bibliography: p.
    Includes index.
    1. Taiwan—Social life and customs—1945–
2. Taiwan—Social conditions—1945–   I. Title.
II. Series.
DS799.812.G38   1987   951′.24905   87-47597
ISBN 0-8014-2056-3 (alk. paper)
ISBN 0-8014-9461-3 (pbk. : alk. paper)